THE BRAZILIAN CORPORATIVE STATE
AND WORKING-CLASS POLITICS

The Brazilian
Corporative State and
Working-Class Politics

KENNETH PAUL ERICKSON

UNIVERSITY OF CALIFORNIA PRESS

BERKELEY · LOS ANGELES · LONDON

University of California Press
Berkeley and Los Angeles, California

University of California Press, Ltd.
London, England

Copyright © 1977 by
The Regents of the University of California

ISBN 0-520-03162-8
Library of Congress Catalog Card Number: 75-40661
Printed in the United States of America

1 2 3 4 5 6 7 8 9 0

To my mother
and
the memory of my father

CONTENTS

LIST OF TABLES

ACKNOWLEDGEMENTS

In any research project, much of the investigation and writing must necessarily be done by the author alone. Nonetheless, it is the rarest of books which is not in some sense a collaborative enterprise, for many individuals and institutions provide the author with opportunities to develop, test, and improve his ideas. I would like to express here my debt to those who have helped make this a better book.

The theories and case studies presented herein have occupied much of my teaching and research time over the past decade. I happily acknowledge the contributions of my students at Hunter College, City University of New York, and, before that, at the State University of New York at Stony Brook. Their objections, questions, and quizzical looks helped me discover, sharpen, illustrate, or improve many of the ideas advanced here.

The following organizations sponsored forums or panels where I floated trial balloons of many of these ideas: American Political Science Association; Caucus for a New Political Science; Center for Inter-American Relations; Duquesne History Forum; Latin American Council of Yale University; Latin American Institute of Rutgers University; Latin American Studies Association; Pacific Coast Council on Latin American Studies; State University of Campinas (São Paulo State, Brazil); and the Columbia University Seminars on Brazil and on Latin America. Critiques and comments from fellow panelists and members of the audience have added much to the clarity of my argument and exposition.

H. Jon Rosenbaum and William G. Tyler gave me an early opportunity to present some of my ideas on corporatism, in their book, *Contemporary Brazil: Issues in Economic and Political Development* (New York: Praeger, 1972). The *Proceedings* of the Pacific Coast Council on Latin American Studies (1975) provided me with a forum in which to air some of the material on populism which appears here in Chapters Four and Five. And the *Occasional Papers* of the New York University Ibero-American Language and Area Center (1975) enabled me to test my material on political strikes.

I wish to thank the following scholars for their critical reading of all or part of the present or earlier versions of this study: Almino Afonso, Robert J. Alexander, Cândido Mendes de Almeida, Douglas A. Chalmers, Robert T. Daland, James F. Guyot, Michael M. Hall, Octávio Ianni, Herbert S. Klein, Nathaniel H. Leff, Patrick V. Peppe, Paulo Sérgio Pinheiro, Leôncio Martins Rodrigues, Thomas G. Sanders, Ronald M. Schneider, Amaury de Souza, Hobart A. Spalding, Jr., and Howard J. Wiarda.

The contributions of my occasional coauthors and fellow students of the Latin American working class, Patrick Peppe and Hobart Spalding, deserve further mention. Our joint work, which our friendship sustained through the trying pressures of deadlines and seemingly endless rewrites, has enabled us to share many insights and has led each of us to greater rigor and self-discipline in our research and writing. My work is surely the better for it.

Juan J. Linz' almost daily lunchtable discussions with his graduate students at Columbia University in the mid-1960's greatly deepened my understanding of authoritarian polities and ways to analyze them, a contribution certainly reflected in this book. James W. Wilkie made the valuable suggestion that I separate official rhetoric from actual labor policy by contrasting projected and real expenditures of the Ministry of Labor; this analysis appears in Chapter Four. In Rio de Janeiro, Othongaldi Rocha and Waltrudes Santos provided invaluable assistance in introducing me to the labor-court system and helping me penetrate the thicket of Brazilian labor law.

I owe much to the many Brazilian intellectuals, officials, workers, and other friends who gave very generously of their time to deepen my understanding of their political and social system and to increase my appreciation of their culture.

Several institutions provided material support which directly or indirectly aided my research on this project. The Metropolitan Area Graduate Summer Field Training Program in Latin America introduced me to Brazil in 1964, an experience which led to my interest in working-class politics there. Most of the research for this study was carried out in Brazil between June 1966 and September 1967, with support from the Foreign Area Fellowship Program. I gathered data on recent years during return trips to Brazil in July 1974 and May 1975; the second of these was provided by the State University of Campinas, which sponsored my participation in a conference there. I gratefully acknowledge and express my appreciation of all these sources of support.

With the study in its final stages, Alain Hénon and Susan Peters of the University of California Press provided patient and speedy assistance in preparing the way for publication. Marjorie Hughes edited the entire manuscript with such scrutiny that many hitherto undetected slips of the pen were eliminated. Carole A. Sanford generously provided additional valuable editorial criticism and suggestions.

Grateful thanks go to my mother, Ruth Erickson, and my father, Paul Erickson, for the support they gave me as I embarked upon my academic career. This book is in part a result of their efforts, and not only in the general sense that it is a product of their moral and material support. The manuscript even imposed directly upon their lives, for my mother gave up many weeks to type two of the early drafts. To my mother and the memory of my father, I dedicate this book.

Finally, I give special thanks for their numerous sacrifices to my wife, Mira Nikolić, and our daughter, Ingrid Maria. Over the past year they put up with an often absent husband and father who was out working on the book or, worse yet, was home and still working on the book! For the many evenings and weekends I stole from them, for their forgiveness for the times my clattering typewriter jarred their sleep, and for the joy of unwinding together when I took time away from the manuscript, I thank them.

Naturally, I assume sole responsibility for the material in this book. None of the above-named individuals and institutions bears any responsibility for the facts and judgments presented here.

K.P.E.

ABBREVIATIONS

Organizations

ARENA: Aliança Renovadora Nacional (National Renovation Alliance)

CEBRAP: Centro Brasileiro de Análise e Planejamento (Brazilian Center for Analysis and Planning)

CGT: Comando Geral dos Trabalhadores (General Labor Command)

CIFTSP: Centro das Indústrias de Fiação e Tecelagem de São Paulo (Spinning and Weaving Industries Center of São Paulo)

CLT: Consolidação das Leis do Trabalho (Consolidation of Labor Laws)

CNTC: Confederação Nacional dos Trabalhadores no Comércio (National Confederation of Commercial Workers)

CNTI: Confederação Nacional dos Trabalhadores na Indústria (National Confederation of Industrial Workers)

CPOS: Commissão Permanente de Organizações Sindicais (Permanent Committee of Trade-Union Organizations – CGT affiliate at state level in Guanabara)

CTB: Confederação dos Trabalhadores do Brasil (Confederation of Brazilian Workers)

DASP: Departamento Administrativo do Serviço Público (Administrative Department of the Public Service)

DIEESE: Departamento Intersindical de Estatística e Estudos Sócio-Econômicos (Interunion Department of Socioeconomic Studies and Statistics)

DNES: Departamento Nacional de Emprego e Salário (National Department of Employment and Wages)

DNPS: Departamento Nacional de Previdência Social (National Social Welfare Department)

FGTS: Fundo de Garantia do Tempo de Serviço (a fund to guarantee severance pay)

FMP: Frente de Mobilização Popular (Popular Mobilization Front)

FPN: Frente Parlamentar Nacionalista (Parliamentary Nationalist Front)

FSD: Forum Sindical de Debates (Trade-Union Discussion Forum – CGT affiliate in the city of Santos)

IAPB: Instituto de Aposentadoria e Pensões dos Bancários (Bank Workers' Social Security Institute)

IAPC: Instituto de Aposentadoria e Pensões dos Comerciários (Commercial Workers' Social Security Institute)

IAPETC: Instituto de Aposentadoria e Pensões dos Empregados em Transportes e Cargas (Transport Workers' Social Security Institute)

IAPFESP: Instituto de Aposentadoria e Pensões dos Ferroviários e Empregados em Serviços Públicos (Railroad and Public Utilities Workers' Social Security Institute)

IAPI: Instituto de Aposentadoria e Pensões dos Industriários (Industrial Workers' Social Security Institute)

IBGE: Instituto Brasileiro de Geografia e Estatística (Brazilian Institute of Geography and Statistics)

IMF: International Monetary Fund

INPS: Instituto Nacional de Previdência Social (National Social Welfare Institute)

IPASE: Instituto de Previdência e Assistência dos Servidores do Estado (State Employees' Welfare and Assistance Institute)

MDB: Movimento Democrático Brasileiro (Brazilian Democratic Movement)

MIA: Movimento Intersindical Anti-Arrocho (Interunion Movement Against the Wage Squeeze)

MSD: Movimento Sindical Democrático (Democratic Trade-Union Movement)

MTIC: Ministério do Trabalho, Indústria e Comércio (Ministry of Labor, Industry, and Commerce)

MTPS: Ministério do Trabalho e Previdência Social (Ministry of Labor and Social Welfare – after the Ministry of Industry and Commerce was split off from the Ministry of Labor in 1961)

MTR: Movimento Trabalhista Renovador (Labor Renovation Movement)

ORIT: Organización Regional Interamericana de Trabajadores (Inter-American Regional Labor Organization)

PAC: Pacto de Ação Conjunta (Pact for Joint Action – CGT affiliate at state level in São Paulo)

PSD: Partido Social Democrático (Social Democratic Party)

PTB: Partido Trabalhista Brasileiro (Brazilian Labor Party)

PUA: Pacto de Unidade e Ação (Pact for Unity and Action – CGT-affiliated coordinating body for rail, port, and maritime workers)

SAMDU: Serviço de Assistência Médica Domiciliar de Urgência (Emergency Home Medical Assistance Service)

SAPS: Serviço de Alimentação da Previdência Social (Social Welfare Food Service)

UDN: União Democrática Nacional (National Democratic Union)
UNE: União Nacional dos Estudantes (National Union of Students)
UST: União Sindical dos Trabalhadores (an unofficial umbrella organiza-
            tion of trade unions)

Newspapers

CM: *Correio da Manhã*

DC: *Diário Carioca*

DN: *Diário de Notícias*

HAR: *Hispanic American Report*

JB: *Jornal do Brasil*

JC: *Jornal do Commercio*

NR: *Novos Rumos*

OESP: *O Estado de São Paulo*

OG: *O Globo*

UH: *Última Hora*

GLOSSARY OF
PORTUGUESE TERMS

Dispositivo: refers to a source of power at the disposal of someone (generally the president)

Dispositivo militar: the (political) power base in the military

Dispositivo sindical: the (political) power base in the labor organizations

Estado Novo: Vargas' authoritarian, corporative regime between 1937 and 1945

Imposto sindical: trade-union tax

Inquérito sindical: the Labor Ministry's annual survey of trade unions

Interventor: an appointive executive officer who takes the place of a previously elected one; interventors governed the states during the authoritarian period between 1930 and 1945, and the minister of labor may appoint interventors to replace elected heads of sindicato organizations

Pelego: a pejorative term referring to trade-union leaders who are considered agents of the state or the employers, used particularly to describe the group of leaders who were edged out of important positions in the late 1950's and early 1960's by the radical nationalists; the term is taken from the word for the sheepskin horseblanket which makes it easier for the horse to bear the saddle and rider

Sindicato: trade union

PART I

Corporatism and Labor
in Brazil

Note: When the national capital moved from the city of Rio de Janeiro to Brasília in 1960, the former Federal District became the State of Guanabara. In 1975, Guanabara was merged into the neighboring State of Rio de Janeiro.

Chapter 1

INTRODUCTION

The Rediscovery of Political Corporatism

One of the most important enduring characteristics of the Brazilian political system is its corporative nature. The term "corporatism" derives from the Latin word for body, and we use it here to refer to a school of political thought or an ideology which sees the body politic as a kind of living organism not unlike the human body in its complexity, functional specialization, and hierarchical ordering of components. In the human body, the brain controls the hierarchy of organs and muscles and decides on actions which, in its view, will serve the interests and needs of the person as a whole. Similarly in a corporative state, the leader or leaders pursue policies designed so that their view of the general will prevails over particular interests. A corporative state, then, is one whose political culture, institutions, and processes reflect a hierarchical, organic view of society.

Pursuing the analogy of the body politic with the human body helps to illuminate the essence of corporatism. Each part of a body performs a specific, specialized function. Because some of these functions are more essential to life than others, one may rank the corresponding organs, limbs, or muscles in a hierarchy of importance. The brain, heart, and liver, for example, are more important than a finger or even an entire limb. So too in corporative thought, persons or organizations that perform functions deemed most important to

NOTE TO READER: Brazilian usage of proper names differs from that found in the United States. First names and even nicknames are frequently used in formal address where the English custom would restrict usage to the surname. The author has chosen to follow Brazilian practice by using the name or names which Brazilian scholars use when referring to the individuals who appear in this study. Thus Getúlio Vargas will be referred to as either Getúlio or Vargas; João Belchior Marques Goulart as Goulart or Jango; Almino Monteiro Álvares Afonso as Almino, but never as Afonso; and so on.

Several reforms have simplified Portuguese spelling and the usage of accent marks during the period covered by this study. The footnotes and bibliography follow the spelling of the original rather than modernize them, and hence there are some apparent inconsistencies.

society occupy the highest and most privileged positions. It is, for example, a revealing comment on the corporative essence of Brazilian social organization and political culture that plant owners rather than workers are termed *classes produtoras,* or producing classes.

Brazil established its modern corporative structures in the wake of the Revolution of 1930. The victorious politicians, led by Getúlio Vargas, deplored the class conflict which accompanied industrialization, so they immediately established political institutions designed to harmonize the interests of labor and capital. Vargas' decrees created symmetrical hierarchies of associations for employers and workers, assured institutionalized contact between the two at all levels, and established the state — the repository, according to corporative theory, of the nation's general will — as arbiter between them.

Corporatism differs sharply from liberal democracy in its view of citizens' roles in politics and society. Liberalism is highly individualistic and seeks to promote and protect the freedom of citizens as individuals. Corporatism's organic-state view, on the other hand, leads corporatist theorists and lawmakers to conceive of society as composed of groups differentiated and ranked according to their productive or economic role. Individuals therefore participate politically through state-approved, carefully regulated associations.

In corporative theory, and to a great extent in practice, administration supersedes politics, for conflicts are resolved through adjudication rather than through confrontations of economic or political power. Regarding the working class — the focus of this study — three basic sets of institutions sustain Brazil's corporative system: (1) the *sindicatos,*[1] or trade unions; (2) the labor courts; and (3) the social security system. Of greatest importance for us will be the relationships between state and union organizations and between union organizations and workers. These corporative institutions of social control have remained in Brazil since the 1930's. It should be pointed out, however, that between 1946 and 1964 the Brazilian political system was only semi-corporative. It combined the corporative structures with the representative institutions of liberal democracy. Indeed, a directly elected, bicameral legislature operated with a good deal of freedom, leading many contemporary observers — particularly those from the United States — to neglect the corporative elements and describe Brazil as a liberal democracy.

Most American scholars, steeped in the traditions of liberalism and liberal democracy, have described a "normal" or "healthy" path to development as one in which a nation's political structures and processes increasingly approximate those of the Anglo-Saxon democracies.[2] In the eyes of these writers, only one

1. The Portuguese word *sindicato* will be used frequently in the text because the sindicato is quite different in nature from the trade union of English usage. Thus the Brazilian term will serve to remind readers that they are dealing with a phenomenon which is far from an exact replica of Anglo-Saxon trade unions.
2. See, for example, the model which emerges in Gabriel A. Almond and G. Bingham Powell, *Comparative Politics: A Developmental Approach* (Boston: Little, Brown, 1966).

alternative exists to the liberal model: Marxism. Corporatism, the third major current in Western political thought and one with roots in such important thinkers as Aristotle and Saint Thomas Aquinas, has been almost completely ignored by American political scientists. Only recently have scholars been rediscovering it.[3] Most major American surveys of political thought, for example, completely ignore the sixteenth-century Iberian adaptation of Saint Thomas' thought and its continuing vitality and influence in today's Iberian and Latin American countries. To highlight this blind spot of American political science, Howard J. Wiarda, a scholar who has studied several corporatively organized nations, refers to corporatism as "the other great 'ism.' "

By the mid-nineteenth century, Wiarda notes, many European writers had begun to develop corporative theories or schemes to cope with the growing problems of capitalism, industrialization, urbanization, and the general breakup of the old social order. Modern corporatism, in other words, was not simply an anachronistic attempt to return to an idealized vision of medieval society. Rather, it accepted the inevitability of industrialization and modernization. It therefore sought to organize society and polity in a way that would preserve or reestablish the social order, harmony, and "natural" elite structure of simpler times. To this end, corporative thought restored to the state its important moral role as promoter of the general will and national interest, thus elevating it from the position of mere referee to which liberal thought had relegated it.[4]

One of the few American political scientists to argue that the state has interests separate from those groups which compose it is Samuel P. Huntington, who writes: "The public interest . . . is whatever strengthens governmental institutionalization of government organizations." Yet even in his case, the liberal bias of American political thought leads him to focus on institutionalizing political parties and prevents him from seeing the corporative model for strengthening and institutionalizing the polity. Quote is from Huntington's "Political Development and Political Decay," in Claude E. Welch, Jr. (ed.), *Political Modernization; A Reader in Comparative Political Change* (Belmont, Calif.: Wadsworth, 1967), p. 229.

3. Among the exceptions are: David Chaplin (ed.), *Peruvian Nationalism: A Corporatist Revolution* (New Brunswick, N.J.: Transaction Books, 1975); James M. Malloy (ed.), *Authoritarianism and Corporatism in Latin America* (Pittsburgh, Pa.: University of Pittsburgh Press, 1977); Patrick V. Peppe, "Corporatism and Dependent Capitalist Modernization: The Frei Government Experience," *Proceedings of the Pacific Coast Council on Latin American Studies,* IV (1975), 145-170; Frederick B. Pike and Thomas Stritch (eds.), *The New Corporatism: Social-Political Structures in the Iberian World* (Notre Dame, Ind.: University of Notre Dame Press, 1974); Susan Kaufman Purcell, *The Mexican Profit-Sharing Decision: Politics in an Authoritarian Regime* (Berkeley: University of California Press, 1976); Philippe C. Schmitter, *Interest Conflict and Political Change in Brazil* (Stanford, Calif.: Stanford University Press, 1971); Amaury de Souza, "The Nature of Corporative Representation: Leaders and Membership of Organized Labor in Brazil" (dissertation prospectus, Massachusetts Institute of Technology, Cambridge, Mass.: 1975); Alfred Stepan, *The State and Society: Peru in Comparative Perspective* (Princeton, N.J.: Princeton University Press, forthcoming); Martin Weinstein, *Uruguay: The Politics of Failure* (Westport, Conn.: Greenwood Press, 1975); Howard J. Wiarda, *Corporatism and Development: The Portuguese Experience* (Amherst: University of Massachusetts Press, 1977); and Howard J. Wiarda (ed.), *Politics and Social Change in Latin America: The Distinct Tradition* (Amherst: University of Massachusetts Press, 1974).

4. Wiarda, *Corporatism and Development,* ch. 3.

Two important institutions perpetuated the corporative legacy of the Iberian nations in their American offspring: legal systems based on Roman law, and the Roman Catholic Church. The Roman law tradition is intensely hostile to autonomous interest groups — whose pursuit of their own private ends, it is believed, necessarily must take place at the expense of the general or national interest. This legal tradition gives official recognition only to associations whose activities it duly specifies, circumscribes, and supervises.

The Catholic Church, itself an authoritarian, hierarchical institution, helped perpetuate the authoritarian, corporative tradition in several ways. The scholars who adapted Saint Thomas' thought in sixteenth-century Iberia were members of Catholic orders, and the Catholic Church was the established church of the state. Later, in the late nineteenth and early twentieth centuries, the Church's response to industrialization and class conflict played a major role in the revival of corporatism. Pope Leo XIII (1878-1903) took the first steps in developing a social conscience for the Church, but he did so in profoundly corporative and paternalistic terms. A Thomistic scholar who was largely responsible for reviving St. Thomas' thought in Catholic circles, he opposed the liberal concept that all people are created equal and defended instead an organic conception of society in which human equality was neither possible nor desirable: "But if all work together for the general welfare *and are content with their differences in dignity and responsibility,* the State will function smoothly and in accord with nature."[5] Developing this organic theme in one of the most famous of modern encyclicals, *Rerum Novarum* (1891), he stated:

> The great mistake in regard to the matter now under consideration is to take up with the notion that class is naturally hostile to class, and that the wealthy and the working men are intended by nature to live in mutual conflict. So irrational and so false is this view that the direct contrary is the truth. Just as the symmetry of the human frame is the result of the suitable arrangement of the different parts of the body, so in a State is it ordained by nature that these two classes should dwell in harmony and agreement....[6]

If the essence of corporative thought can be caustically summed up as, "a place for everybody, and everybody in his place," the place for workers is clearly a subordinate one.

In 1931 Pope Pius XI marked the fortieth anniversary of *Rerum Novarum* with a new encyclical, *Quadragesimo Anno* ("On Reconstructing the Social Order"). More explicitly corporative than its predecessor, it urged that class conflict be eliminated by creating guilds or associations "in which men may have their place not according to the position each has in the labor market but

5. Richard L. Camp, *The Papal Ideology of Social Reform: A Study in Historical Development, 1878-1967* (Leyden, Holland: E. J. Brill, 1969), pp. 30-31; emphasis added.

6. *Ibid.,* p. 81.

according to the respective social functions which each performs."[7] Following the first of these encyclicals and right through the period when Vargas' nation-builders were fashioning the corporative institutions which still regulate Brazilian political life, Catholic social organizations, intellectuals' associations, and workers' circles propagated corporative ideas in Brazil and other Catholic countries.[8] Corporatism was, by the 1930's, a concept for which Brazil was well prepared. Chapters Two and Three describe the corporative system which evolved between 1930 and 1945.

Populism and the Weakening of Corporative Controls

In 1945, Getúlio Vargas was overthrown by a civil-military movement, and, in 1946, a popularly elected Constituent Assembly drafted a constitution which established regular elections and guaranteed many of the freedoms generally associated with liberal democracy.[9] Nonetheless, the drafters of the Constitution of 1946 did not break totally with the corporative tradition, for they left intact a number of important principles and practices of corporative social control. These included the entire network of sindicato structures, buttressed by the labor laws elaborated during the Estado Novo. The lawmakers, coming principally from middle- and upper-class backgrounds, clearly did not wish to give the working class complete freedom to organize.

The political system from 1946 to 1964, therefore, incorporated two contradictory principles: liberalism and corporatism. Workers' organizations remained under strict state supervision, but now workers as individuals could vote for political officeholders. While workers were relegated to a subordinate place in Brazilian corporative practice, electoral politics offered a means for them to try to change the system itself or at least their status within it. Much of this book focuses on the tensions which developed between the liberal and corporative principles during the "populist" era of the 1950's and early 1960's. Populism, in Latin American usage, refers to political movements which have working-class or peasant followings and are led by middle- or upper-class

---

7. Cited in Weinstein, *Uruguay,* p. 18.

8. Wiarda, *Corporatism and Development,* ch. 3.

9. This section presents only briefly some of the main issues and processes of postwar Brazilian politics. Readers interested in detailed coverage should consult a history. The most complete volume in English on this period is Thomas E. Skidmore, *Politics in Brazil, 1930-1964; An Experiment in Democracy* (New York: Oxford, 1967). A brief but very insightful account in Portuguese is Paul Singer, "A política das classes dominantes," in Octávio Ianni et al. (eds.), *Política e revolução social no Brasil* (Rio de Janeiro: Civilização Brasileira, 1964), pp. 65-125. A chronology of the turbulent years leading to Goulart's overthrow is John W. F. Dulles, *Unrest in Brazil: Political-Military Crises, 1955-1964* (Austin: University of Texas Press, 1970). A detailed, thoroughly researched chronology of Brazilian labor in the postwar period is Timothy Fox Harding, "The Political History of Organized Labor in Brazil" (doctoral dissertation, Stanford University, 1973). A detailed treatment of Brazil from 1964 through 1970 is Ronald M. Schneider, *The Political System of Brazil: Emergence of a "Modernizing" Authoritarian Regime, 1964-1970* (New York: Columbia University Press, 1971).

politicians. Vargas, who appealed to the workers for support during his dictatorship from 1930 to 1945, was a populist, but his strict application of the corporative controls prevented workers' representatives from exercising any political initiative. As we shall see in a more detailed discussion of populism in Chapter Four, increasingly radical labor leaders, promising to deliver large numbers of workers' votes, began to win help from populist politicians as they struggled to increase their political leverage. Popular participation accelerated as divisions within the political elites deepened and populist politicians broadened their support by transferring political resources to representatives of the working masses. The loss of cohesion among the political elites meant there was no longer *one* clear government line which labor leaders had to follow. Union heads consequently began to act with increasing autonomy, using the power which they accumulated through their posts in the sindicatos and in para-government structures to win concessions from government leaders.

Let us conclude this chapter with an overview of the ways in which Brazilian labor leaders pyramided their political leverage in the years before 1964, thereby weakening the corporative controls. First, we must describe the decision-making context. In an insightful study, Brazilian sociologist Raymundo Faoro argues that, both historically and in recent times, the most important political decisions in Brazil have been made by an elite stratum of professional government administrators.[10] Certainly the Faoro thesis holds true in the important area of economic decision making, according to Nathaniel H. Leff's monograph on Brazilian development policy between 1947 and 1964. Leff analyzed protection policies for domestic industry, policies allocating resources between private industry and the public sector, and policies regulating direct foreign investment. He concluded that the most significant decisions were made by an elite stratum of administrators, whom he estimated to have numbered only forty in the early 1960's. In this period, these administrators structured issues and public opinion for policy action, they made important decisions without consulting elected representatives, and they often imposed policies injurious to the interests of such important socioeconomic groups as coffee growers and domestic indus- trialists. Brazil's president usually felt safe in delegating a large amount of power to these top-level civil servants, because they were not his political competitors for elective posts and because their success in economic expansion provided him with additional resources to distribute.[11]

The politically relevant values which make up Brazil's political culture have greatly facilitated the decision-making supremacy of the top civil servants. The organic-state concept upon which the corporative writers of the 1930's based their theories has retained great vitality, and this sustains what Leff describes as "the myth of the 'technical solution' in Brazilian politics."[12] It is generally

10. Raymundo Faoro, *Os donos do poder* (Porto Alegre: Globo, 1958), p. 262.
11. Nathaniel H. Leff, *Economic Policy-Making and Development in Brazil, 1947-1964* (New York: Wiley, 1968), pp. 32-34, 50, 73-75, 143-150.
12. *Ibid.,* p. 148.

accepted that society is organic and that its general will should prevail over the will(s) of the individual interests of which it is composed. Indeed, one study found the organic view of the state widely held not only by upper-level civil servants, but also by the representatives of the key sectoral groups whom those civil servants regulate – industrial, trade-union, and civic bodies.[13] And Leff notes that this view is even held by representatives of the Coffee Planters' Association of São Paulo, the Confederation of Industries, and large industrial groups and trade associations.[14] Given this political culture, government officials, who define the general interest by their own criteria, can easily mobilize public opinion against a group, whether industrialist or labor, which seeks to impose its specific goals against the general interest.

In this political system where top-level civil servants make the most important decisions, the acquiescence of those outside that elite – especially during relatively democratic periods – has been secured by distributing patronage-type benefits to key groups and individuals. This pattern is deeply rooted in Brazil's past, for the landed elites who dominated the political system for the century prior to the Revolution of 1930 employed middle-class persons in civil-service posts of low utility for the society but great utility for the ruling class: these posts coopted a stratum which might otherwise have threatened the regime.[15] Indeed, the famous Brazilian writer and political figure, Joaquim Nabuco, denounced this system in 1885:

> In this regime, everything is expected of the state which, as the sole active organization, sucks up and absorbs through tax and loan all available capital and distributes it among its clients, through public employment. Thus it bleeds the poor of their hard-earned savings and renders precarious the fortunes of the rich. In consequence, the civil service is the noble profession and the vocation of all.[16]

With the broadening of suffrage and the entry of social strata below the middle class into political participation, politicians sought to provide patronage benefits to ever more numerous groups. Leff's adaptation of the patronage model of American machine politics provides insight into the ways that groups have pursued their interests in Brazil:

> ... Congressmen and other politicians are elected and maintain themselves in office largely on the basis of the patronage they trade for the electoral support of individuals and groups within their district. In this pattern, politicians organize individual political "machines," which mobilize financial support, public relations, and voters. This support may be

13. Schmitter, *Interest Conflict* (n. 3 above), pp. 98-102.
14. Leff, *Economic Policy-Making,* pp. 54, 113-114.
15. Hélio Jaguaribe, *O nacionalismo na atualidade brasileira* (Rio de Janeiro: Instituto Superior de Estudos Brasileiros, 1958), pp. 41-42. Jaguaribe uses the term "cartorial state" to refer to this cooptive system based on public-sector jobs.
16. Joaquim Nabuco, *O abolicionismo* (São Paulo: Progresso, 1949). p. 158.

drawn from a variety of sources — individuals, cliques, family and business associates, local newspapers, individual firms, and previously organized political groupings such as clubs, trade associations, and trade unions. Some public-sector economic corporations have also been important sources of financial and voter support for politicians. In return, the politician provides political representation for his clients vis-à-vis the government, especially in matters of loans, imports, and tax treatments.[17]

Patronage politics made a wide variety of benefits available to all social classes and economic groups in Brazil. By selectively distributing loans, exemptions from customs duties, or import licenses to industrialists and businessmen, the nation's top economic policy makers were able to prevent economic sectors from unifying to demand sector-wide benefits from the state.[18] Such selective distribution of benefits was a relatively low-cost way for the policy makers to secure freedom for themselves in setting the main policy guidelines.

How did labor leaders and the working class fit into this patronage system? One of the principal activities of labor leaders in the relatively free years before 1964 (and to a lesser extent in the authoritarian system since then) was to seek favors or services from government agencies for themselves and their constituents. For example, one industrial union officer claimed that in the decade before 1964, he and his colleagues had obtained the following services or benefits for the workers of his medium-sized industrial city (about 100,000 inhabitants): construction by the Industrial Workers' Social Security Institute (IAPI) of a special medical service building and of workers' homes; establishment of an emergency clinic with doctor and ambulance 24 hours a day, through the federal government's Emergency Home Medical Assistance Service (SAMDU); establishment of subsidized, low-price food stores and a restaurant, through the Social Welfare Food Service (SAPS); creation of the first university-level technical course and the first public, state-supported secondary school in the city (the latter over the objection of local private secondary-school interests); establishment of a government office to inspect job safety and hygiene; and distribution of credits for workers to build their own homes.

Most of these items, it is clear, came from the government and not from employers. Labor leaders applied their leverage through connections with deputies, ministers, and administrators. In some cases they campaigned for office and became deputies themselves, enhancing their own ability to provide for their constituents. At the national level, the head of the Confederation of Industrial Workers (CNTI) even wielded sufficient influence to convince the Bank of Brazil

17. Leff, *Economic Policy-Making,* p. 118.

18. Anthony Leeds, "Brazilian Careers and Social Structure: A Case History and Model," in Dwight B. Heath and Richard N. Adams (eds.), *Contemporary Cultures and Societies of Latin America* (New York: Random House, 1965), pp. 387, 393-394. See also Juárez Rubens Brandão Lopes, "Some Basic Developments in Brazilian Politics and Society," in Eric N. Baklanoff (ed.), *New Perspectives of Brazil* (Nashville, Tenn.: Vanderbilt University Press, 1966), pp. 64-66.

to make a substantial loan to a factory owner who needed the money to pay arrears to his workers.[19]

This process not only provided labor leaders with the specific benefits they sought, but it also afforded them an opportunity to accumulate political power. They gained this power by manipulating the contradiction that exists between the rational, universalistic theory which structures and regulates Brazilian public administration and the particularistic, individualized reality of the patronage system.

The Brazilian state regulates almost all aspects of social life according to elaborate sets of rules, a practice that is well adapted to the prevalent Brazilian attitude toward interpersonal or intergroup relations: in situations of conflict or potential conflict, Brazilians generally seek to avoid personal, face-to-face negotiations and instead prefer to rely on impersonal rules to resolve problems. In practice, however, highly articulated, bureaucratic rules and organizations cannot be completely successful in imposing rigorous impartiality and predictability. As one major study of bureaucratic organization concludes, "new power relationships develop around the loopholes in the regulatory system. Groups fight for control of the ultimate strategic sources of uncertainties, and their fates in the group struggle depend on their ability to control these."[20]

In Brazil, the highly structured, minutely regulated labor code is a superb example of the quest for rationality. Labor leaders easily upset this legalistic pattern, however, by converting several sources of uncertainty into power. For example, Brazilian labor law eschews the strike and directs wage disputes through the bureaucratic organization of the labor courts. Prior to 1964, nevertheless, the anti-strike law proved nearly unenforceable, so the labor leaders used the strike or its threat to force Labor Ministry officials to bring pressure upon the employer or the labor court. When the judges were thus prodded to cut through red tape, the benefits of a new contract settlement reached the workers more speedily.

Scarcity of resources was an even more important factor undermining the rational operation of Brazilian bureaucratic organizations. Since the government had generally neglected to pay its share of social security operating costs, for example, service was woefully inadequate. Thus if a labor leader had contacts in the social security system which enabled him to obtain service for his constituents, he had control over a most important source of uncertainty. The 1960 social security law assured labor leaders a hand in distributing these services. The union then dispensed them as favors to their clienteles and subsequently demanded that those in their debt cast their vote for a specific candidate or participate in a strike or political demonstration. In this manner,

19. All the examples in these paragraphs are drawn from Andrea Rios Loyola, "Les ouvriers et le populisme: les attitudes ouvrières à Juiz de Fora" (doctoral dissertation, École Pratique des Hautes Études, Paris, 1973), pp. 67-69, 80.

20. Michel Crozier, *The Bureaucratic Phenomenon* (Chicago: University of Chicago Press, 1965), pp. 111, 213-236.

the pre-1964 labor leaders converted into political power the leverage obtained from the clash between particularistic reality and universalistic principles in Brazilian public administration.

This book examines the mechanisms which enhanced the power of the labor leaders before 1964, enabling them successfully to pressure the president on policy matters. Essentially, there were two processes at work: the process of cooptation into the administrative units of the corporative state, which is covered in Chapters Four and Five, and astute use of the political strike, which is analyzed in Chapter Six. Chapter Seven then documents the labor leaders' deployment of this growing power vis-à-vis the president in the early 1960's. These case studies also highlight some fundamental weaknesses which were overlooked by most contemporary observers, who attributed considerable autonomous power to the labor leaders.

The populist system described in these chapters was overthrown in 1964, a victim of socioeconomic processes accompanying Brazil's pattern of economic modernization. The economy had grown rapidly during the 1950's, so conflicts over resources were not sharp enough to lead to the exclusion of any participant group from the political arena.[21] In the early 1960's, however, at the time that labor leaders were increasing their political leverage, economic growth slowed and the struggle over resources intensified. Forces on the left, including most prominent labor leaders, demanded fundamental reform of the socioeconomic system, to renew economic growth and to make income distribution more egalitarian. This assertiveness coincided with a dramatic shift in the attitude of Brazil's upper and middle strata. These latter groups found, after a decade of heavy foreign investment, that they could obtain middle-sector jobs, investment credits, and modern technology from foreign sources. Formerly, they had cooperated with populist politicians, and thereby with labor, in order to get these benefits from the state. Now, therefore, they rejected populism and sought to exclude workers from political participation. In cooperation with the armed forces, and fully assured of support from the United States government, the latter groups triumphed in the coup of 1964.[22] Chapter Eight shows how the post-1964 government dismantled the populist system, tightened the corporative controls, and made the working class pay a very great price for Brazil's dramatic economic growth over the past decade. Chapter Nine then speculates on the future of the Brazilian political system.

21. Celso Furtado, "Political Obstacles to Economic Growth in Brazil," in Claudio Veliz (ed.), *Obstacles to Change in Latin America,* (New York: Oxford University Press, 1965), pp. 152-154. See also Charles W. Anderson, *Politics and Economic Change in Latin America* (Princeton, N.J.: Van Nostrand, 1967), pp. 104-114.

22. Kenneth Paul Erickson and Patrick V. Peppe, "Dependent Capitalist Development, U.S. Foreign Policy, and Repression of the Working Class in Chile and Brazil," *Latin American Perspectives,* III, no. 1 (Winter 1976), 19-44. See official documents on U.S. support for the coup, in *Washington Post,* Dec. 29, 1976, pp. A-1, A-16.

Chapter 2

THE FORMATION OF
THE CORPORATIVE STATE
IN BRAZIL

Brazil entered the modern era with the "Revolution of 1930." This civil-military movement overthrew a federal political system controlled by the landed elites of the most wealthy and powerful states and established in its place a centralized polity favorable to urban interests. The revolution's victors, led by Getúlio Vargas, constructed a network of corporative political institutions to cope with modern socioeconomic conflict, and these institutions have endured to this day.

Only under Vargas' rule after 1930 did Brazilian law first recognize the workers' right to organize. Such recognition contrasted sharply with the practice of the previous regime, whose politicians, police, courts, and owning classes had brutally repressed labor organizations and their demands as illegitimate threats to public order. The Vargas regime wove the working class into the national political formula under the tutelage and dominance of the state, and it set down the principal guidelines for the current pattern of labor relations and labor's participation in the national political process.

This chapter describes the development and major characteristics of the Brazilian corporative political system, in order to set the context for the discussion of labor law which follows in Chapter Three. Before turning to the thirties, however, we first briefly describe the context in which labor organizations operated in the Old Republic.

The Old Republic

Brazil during the Old Republic (1889-1930) was a rural society dominated by the political elites of the three most powerful states of the federation: São Paulo, Minas Gerais, and Rio Grande do Sul. All three were primarily agricultural, with coffee providing the economic mainstay of the first two and livestock that of the third.[1] Although Brazilian manufacturing expanded in the latter half of the nineteenth century, due to tariff protection and other forms of governmental intervention,[2] industry played a minor role in the Brazilian economy prior to the fall of the Empire in 1889. Census data show that the aggregation of workers into large industrial establishments began only in the twentieth century.[3] Of 13,336 industrial establishments listed in the 1920 census, only 240 had been founded before 1880.[4] And many of those firms were of the small handicraft or workshop variety which the modernized criteria of the 1940 census would not even have classified as industrial.[5]

Predictably in this basically rural society, large landholders dominated the political system and held social mobilization to a minimum. The major states, whose politicians dominated the national government, enjoyed considerable internal autonomy. Still, control of the federal government was important to these landowners in their endeavors to protect and develop their rural economies. For instance, they had the government stabilize international coffee prices by purchasing excess stocks; they won protective measures for domestic beef interests; and they secured advantageous location of social overhead capital such as transport facilities.[6]

The key political actors in this system were the president, the governors, and, at the local level, the *coroneis,* or landowners who held the honorific rank of colonel in the state militias. These political relationships were of a patron-client nature, i.e., at each level the patron exchanged his support and that of his clients for favors from those above him. He then distributed a part of those favors to his clients to maintain their support. Patronage in the form of government jobs was one of the principal items of exchange at the upper and intermediate levels of such a pyramid of exchanges. At the base of this pyramid lay the unequal reciprocity of the traditional patron-client relationship in the countryside.[7]

This political system proved incapable of incorporating the urban middle sectors and industrial workers. The expansion of the urban centers during the teens and twenties of this century, therefore, added the measure of instability which ultimately brought the Old Republic down. In its last years, the dominant elites found they could no longer ignore the urban groups, so they tried to

1. Joseph L. Love, *Rio Grande do Sul and Brazilian Regionalism, 1882-1930* (Stanford, Calif.: Stanford University Press, 1971), pp. 109-135.
2. Nathaniel H. Leff, "Long-term Brazilian Economic Development," *Journal of Economic History,* II (September 1969), 478-479.
3. Werner Baer, *Industrialization and Economic Development in Brazil* (Homewood, Ill.: Irwin, 1965), pp. 13-15, 268.
4. Gustaaf Frits Loeb, *Industrialization and Balanced Growth: With Special Reference to Brazil* (Groningen, Netherlands: n.p., 1957), p. 87, cited in Baer, p. 13.
5. Baer, pp. 18-19.
6. Love, *Rio Grande do Sul,* pp. 112-113.
7. On the patron-client relationship in general, see Michael Kenny, "Patterns of Patronage in Spain," *Anthropological Quarterly,* XXXIII (January 1960), 14-23; on coronelismo, see Victor Nunes Leal, *Coronelismo, enxada e voto: o município e o regime representativo no Brasil* (Rio de Janeiro: n.p., 1948).

exclude them from politics. An amendment to the São Paulo State Constitution in 1928, for example, changed the status of the mayoralty of its capital city from an elective post to one appointed by the governor. The new urban groups were thus prevented from gaining control of an important institutional base from which they could confront the rural oligarchies who controlled the state and national governments.[8]

Within the urban setting, factory owners forced labor into a defensive role. Employers generally reacted to workers' demands by (1) trying to weaken labor organizations at the workplace and (2) enlisting the support of the state in repressing strikes.[9] To weaken workers' associations, particularly during moments of conflict, employers frequently dealt with their spokesmen and even made concessions. Once the strike or threat had passed, however, they often fired the leaders and withdrew the concessions.[10] Owners and state authorities sought to decapitate labor organizations by firing, arresting, or deporting their leaders. The director-general of the Spinning and Weaving Industries Center of São Paulo, for example, publicly urged employers to provide him with the names of strike leaders whenever a strike seemed to be brewing: "The Center will immediately see to it that the workers pointed out will disappear for some time, until the atmosphere of agitation has passed."[11] The importance of this directive is underscored by the fact that in 1920 the textile industry accounted for 41.5 percent of the workers in industry in the state of São Paulo.[12]

Employers took advantage of the prevailing elite view of social and economic relations, as sanctioned in law, to bring state repression down upon organized labor. Based upon the individualistic tenets of liberalism, this view held that no intervening bodies should interfere with private contracts between individuals. Employers, claiming to contract separately with each of their workers, thus called upon the state for strict interpretation of the section of the penal code dealing with "crimes against the freedom of labor." The police and courts, in turn, construed strikes as collective phenomena which transgressed the individual's right to work.[13]

The notion that "the social question is a matter for the police" is commonly attributed to Washington Luiz Pereira de Souza, the last president under the Old

8. Paulo Nogueira Filho, *Idéias e lutas de um burguês progressista; o Partido Democrático e a Revolução de 1930* (São Paulo: Anhambi, 1958), I, pp. 305-306, 310-313.

9. Azis Simão, *Sindicato e estado* (São Paulo: Dominus, 1966), pp. 122-123. On working-class politics during this period, see also Bóris Fausto, *Trabalho urbano e conflito social, 1890-1920* (São Paulo: Difusão Européia do Livro, 1976).

10. Ample documentation appears in Simão, pp. 122-126, and in Sheldon Leslie Maram, "Anarchists, Immigrants, and the Brazilian Labor Movement, 1890-1920" (doctoral dissertation, University of California, Santa Barbara, 1972), pp. 19-47.

11. Centro das Indústrias de Fiação e Tecelagem de São Paulo (CIFTSP), *Circulares,* March 3, 1923, quoted in Warren Dean, *The Industrialization of São Paulo, 1880-1945* (Austin: University of Texas Press, 1969), p. 166.

12. Simão, *Sindicato e estado,* p. 47, using 1920 census data.

13. See Antônio Bento de Faria, *Annotações Theórico-Practicas ao Código Penal do Brasil,* 4th ed. (Rio de Janeiro: Jacintho Ribeiro dos Santos, 1929), I, pp. 362-366.

Republic. This certainly is the way the director-general of the Textile Industry Center looked at the matter, and he noted proudly "how a great cordiality reigns between the Center and the state police headquarters."[14] In many cases, labor organizers of foreign origin were deported under legislation aimed specifically at them.[15]

There were several types of workers' organizations in Brazil during the Old Republic. The most important types were the mutual-aid societies and the resistance leagues. The only workers' associations recognized in law were mutual-aid and cooperative societies — i.e., those which would not create conflict between workers and employers.[16] The Church, which also had an interest in perpetuating the status quo, founded and supported many of these bodies. [17] Although Catholic organizations began to articulate workers' demands after the São Paulo general strike of 1917, their emphasis on peaceful resolution of conflict prevented them from making use of the strike.

The resistance leagues constitute the other type of worker organization, and it is because of their activity that the period prior to 1930 in Brazilian unionism has been called the period of militant minorities; this term contrasts the early period with the system of bureaucratic unionism which followed the Revolution of 1930.[18] Resistance leagues controlled by syndicalists accepted the economic system and believed that the strike was the last resort, to be used after negotiation failed. Leagues dominated by anarchists and Communists, on the other hand, did not accept the socioeconomic system at all, and for them the partial strike was to prepare the workers for the ultimate general strike which would bring the collapse of the capitalist system.[19] Due to the numerical weakness of the work force, its lack of class consciousness, tactical errors by union leadership, and the repressive activities of the employers and the state, workers' organizations in this period did not enjoy a stable existence.

Unable to assimilate the urban elements and decaying from within, the Old Republic collapsed with the world economic system following the crash of 1929. Its major philosophical underpinnings, the individualistic tenets of liberalism, had merely served to safeguard the avariciousness of the rich and to frustrate labor organization and social justice prior to 1930. In reaction, Brazil's rulers in the following decade rejected liberal democracy and ultimately create a modified corporative state within which labor organizations were granted official recognition but submitted to strict state supervision.

14. CIFTSP, *Circulares,* March 10, 1922, quoted in Dean, *Industrialization,* p. 166.
15. See Decreto 1641 of January 1907; Maram, "Anarchists, Immigrants," pp. 45-47.
16. Simão, *Sindicato e estado,* pp. 160-165.
17. Margaret Patrice Todaro, "Pastors, Prophets, and Politicians: A Study of the Brazilian Catholic Church, 1916-1945" (doctoral dissertation, Columbia University, 1971), pp. 431-434, 441-445. See also Howard J. Wiarda, *The Brazilian Catholic Labor Movement: The Dilemmas of National Development* (Amherst: University of Massachusetts Labor Relations and Research Center, 1969), pp. 14-15.
18. Simão, pp. 228-229.
19. *Ibid.,* pp. 162-164.

The Corporative Framework of the Estado Novo

Although three distinct phases comprise the years from 1930 to 1945, the period forms a clear-cut authoritarian unit for the purposes of our analysis. Some might point out that the Constitution of 1934 established electoral democracy, but for most of its three-year duration President Vargas ruled by decree under its state-of-siege provisions, thus justifying its inclusion within the authoritarian framework here.

The type of political system which developed through the thirties and, in 1937, reached its logical conclusion in the Estado Novo was an authoritarian regime, as defined by Juan Linz:

> Authoritarian regimes are political systems with limited, not responsible, political pluralism; without elaborate and guiding ideology (but with distinctive mentalities); without intensive nor extensive political mobilization (except at some points in their development); and in which a leader (or occasionally a small group) exercises power within formally ill-defined limits but actually quite predictable ones.[20]

The authoritarian regime is distinct from the democratic type, which must supply "regular constitutional opportunities for peaceful competition for political power (and not just a share of it) to different groups without excluding any significant sector of the population by force," and from the totalitarian model, which obliterates the distinction between state and society and which is characterized by total domination and mobilization of the individual by the state. [21]

Linz, drawing from Theodor Geiger, notes that authoritarian regimes are the expression of distinctive mentalities rather than of such elaborate ideologies as characterize totalitarian regimes. Ideologies are well-defined systems of thought with a strong utopian element which are elaborated by intellectuals. Mentalities, on the other hand, are ways of thinking and feeling which are more emotional than rational and are closer to the present or the past than to the future. Mentalities provide noncodified ways of reacting to situations.[22]

The Estado Novo did have its social and political theorists; but in support of Linz' observations on the behavior of authoritarian states, their work is most helpful in conveying the mentality of the period and providing guidelines to understanding the behavior of the regime. Their work did not serve to lay down clear rules in terms of which all action must be justified, as ideology does for totalitarian regimes. We devote the next pages to the underlying corporative-state mentality which characterized the period in which the foundations of the

20. Juan Linz, "An Authoritarian Regime: Spain," in E. Allardt and Y. Littunen (eds.), *Cleavages, Ideologies, and Party Systems: Contributions to Comparative Political Sociology* (Helsinki: Westermarck Society, 1964), p. 297. Linz comments on post-1964 Brazil in "The Future of an Authoritarian Situation or the Institutionalization of an Authoritarian Regime: The Case of Brazil," in Alfred Stepan (ed.), *Authoritarian Brazil: Origins, Policies, and Future* (New Haven: Yale University Press, 1973), pp. 233-254.

21. Linz, "An Authoritarian Regime: Spain," pp. 294-296.

22. *Ibid.*, p. 301.

modern Brazilian state were laid, for it still constitutes the essense of the Brazilian political culture today.

Elitism and paternalism dominated the thought of the Estado Novo's founders. One of the greatest intellectual influences during this period was an adviser to Vargas on labor and corporative affairs, Francisco José de Oliveira Vianna, who made no bones about his elitism[23] as he outlined the nation-building task of the elites in the Estado Novo: "Insofar as possible, we must provide, through the conscious action of individuals and of the state, what our historical evolution has not yet given us: structure, organization, and a collective consciousness." [24] Since sources of opinion and political participation had not developed and independently coalesced into interest groups as had happened in the Anglo-Saxon countries, he argued, it was the duty of the state to organize such groups, and it could best accomplish this through the corporative framework.[25] Although the rhetoric might evoke a totalitarian or "mobilization" system, Vargas' administrators in fact restricted political mobilization by the state to those sectors which advancing industrialization had already released from traditional controls. The Labor Ministry, for example, carefully supervised and controlled mobilization of the workers, and it prevented peasant mobilization.[26]

The elitist nation-builders of the 1930's, seeing themselves as tutors to the new generation of Brazilians, assigned two functions to education. First, in terms of political socialization, the school system should provide civic training, thereby enabling an increasingly well-informed citizenry to participate in national affairs through the corporative institutions. Second, by increasing the population's technical skills, the educational system would increase national productivity. This new wealth would then fund the state's paternalistic functions, for these writers called upon the state to guarantee to its citizens the right to education, creative activity and employment, social security, and a reasonable standard of living under healthy conditions.[27]

Prevailing political attitudes in Brazil in the thirties manifested severe disillusionment with liberal democracy. Brazilian political thought, even under the Old Republic, included a major component which dismissed liberal democracy as a foreign import which ill suited Brazil's social, economic, and political heritage and reality. The major exponent of this position, Alberto Tôrres, achieved limited impact at the time his principal political and sociological essays appeared

23. Francisco José de Oliveira Vianna, *Problemas de organização e problemas de direção (o povo e o govêrno)* (Rio de Janeiro: José Olympio, 1952), p. 170; and *O idealismo da Constituição,* 2nd ed. (São Paulo: Ed. Nacional, 1939), p. 87. For a summary of Oliveira Vianna's thought, see Eli Diniz Cerqueira and Maria Regina Soares de Lima, "O Modêlo Político de Oliveira Vianna," *Revista Brasileira de Estudos Políticos,* no. 30 (January 1971), 85-109.

24. Vianna, *O idealismo,* pp. xiv-xv.

25. See *ibid.,* pp. 179-248.

26. On the mobilization system, see David E. Apter, *The Politics of Modernization* (Chicago: University of Chicago, 1965), pp. 357-390.

27. Francisco Campos, *O estado nacional; sua estructura, seu conteudo ideologico* (Rio de Janeiro: José Olympio, 1940), p. 55.

(1907-1916), but he significantly influenced the next generation and thus contributed to the tide of nationalist, anti-liberal literature that appeared after 1930.[28] Indeed, his greatest student and advocate was none other than Oliveira Vianna, one of the major architects of the Brazilian corporative state.

The lessons of past and present eroded liberalism's hold on Brazilian political thinkers and actors. Although the contemporary Italian, Portuguese, and German experiences inspired some of them, strong domestic roots fed their anti-liberalism. Throughout most of the nineteenth century, the Brazilian monarchy (1822-1889) afforded no practice in the workings of liberal democracy, and the liberal constitution of the Old Republic which followed seemed to give sanction to monumental political corruption and injustice. Finally, political immobilism under the hybrid liberal-corporative constitution from 1934 to 1937 further bolstered Brazilian anti-liberalism.

The founders of the Estado Novo believed that the liberal state could not function in modern industrial society and that the only way to prevent its degeneration into a Communist regime was to establish a corporative state. Francisco Campos, Vargas' minister of justice and author of the Constitution of 1937, stated that the advent of the masses into modern politics posed problems of such magnitude that the liberal states were forced to remove the most important issues from the realm of legitimate discussion. The logical consequence of this dialectical process, he argued, was the use of repression against those who disagreed and, finally, "the transformation of the liberal democratic regime into a totalitarian or integral state."[29]

Campos pointed out that the principal activity of modern society was economic. While political disputes in the past had concerned "purely political" issues such as suffrage, government controls over the economy had increased so much in modern times that the objective of political competition had become the conquest of the national economic forces. This implied that the liberal state framework would be unable to prevent the degeneration of labor relations into the class struggle.[30]

The solution to this problem lay in the establishment of a new type of political system which would prevent the use of the state apparatus as a weapon in partisan politics and class conflict. Campos claimed that the authoritarian corporatism of the Estado Novo provided such a framework, enabling the state to serve the entire nation rather than just one class or group.[31]

Brazil's corporative theorists believed the essential function of modern society to be economic, and they naturally expected the main social and political

28. On Alberto Tôrres, see Barbosa Lima Sobrinho, *Presença de Alberto Tôrres* (Rio de Janeiro: Civilização Brasileira, 1968), pp. 305-520; on anti-liberal literature in the thirties, see Hélgio Henrique C. Trinidade, "Plínio Salgado e a Revolução de 30: antecendentes da A. I. B.," *Revista Brasileira de Estudos Políticos,* no. 38 (January 1974), 9-33.

29. Campos, *O estado nacional,* p. 23.

30. *Ibid.,* pp. 39-40.

31. Antônio José de Azevedo Amaral, *O estado autoritário e a realidade nacional* (Rio de Janeiro: José Olympio, 1938), p. 257.

divisions to run along economic lines as well. A range of corporative organizations, structured hierarchically from the local "sindicato" to the national "confederation" and embodying each of the main sectors of economic activity, was to include and represent the entire population:

> The principle upon which the corporate State is based is that of the representation of society through the basic organizations of its economic and professional groups. In accordance with this theory, the expression of the many elements which make up the national will shall originate in the sindicatos and converge in the State. These expressions can be considered the authentic representative forces in the State.[32]

According to its professed doctrine, the Estado Novo was merely to watch over and superintend the activities of these various groups; and, by so doing, it would look after the interests of the entire nation. There is an interesting parallel between this function of the state and the *poder moderador*, or "moderating power," of the Brazilian monarchy a century earlier. In both cases one of the specific functions of the state was to prevent a single party, group, or sector from abusing the power of government or taking unfair advantage of the others.[33] In protecting the interests of society as a whole, the absolute supremacy of the state was not to be challenged, as Estado Novo publicist Azevedo Amaral made abundantly clear:

> Docile submission to the authority of the State is not repugnant and cannot be repugnant to normal individuals, for they intuitively understand that in order for a people to transform itself into a nation, it must organize itself into a hierarchical structure. The solidity and efficient functioning of this structure requires the action of an authority capable of coordinating and orienting the elements which are juxtaposed in society.[34]

The Estado Novo's defenders were quick to claim that the Brazilian authoritarian state was democratic in nature because of its superintending or moderating function. They juxtaposed this mediatory role with that of the totalitarian corporative states such as Italy, where they claimed that the meaning of corporativism had been perverted, so the sindicato "is merely a bureaucratic tentacle through which the State exercises its arbitrary power upon the many sectors of the nation, which are oppressed and suffocated in the web of totalitarian organizations."[35] These claims of the regime's propagandists reflected the early flush of enthusiasm over the new political system which they

32. *Ibid.,* p. 183.
33. On the *poder moderador,* see João Camillo de Oliveira Tôrres, *A democracia coroada* (Rio de Janeiro: José Olympio, 1957), pp. 137-172. Alberto Tôrres' proposed constitutional revisions had included a *"poder coordinador"* which would perform this function, and he also proposed corporative political representation; Lima Sobrinho, *Presença,* pp. 36-364.
34. Amaral, *O estado autoritário,* p. 171.
35. *Ibid.,* p. 183.

wished to legitimize. In reality, the Estado Novo was hardly more democratic than fascist Italy.

The Brazilian experience under the Estado Novo lends support to Linz' observation that under authoritarian regimes pluralism is limited and political participation is circumscribed to those areas which do not challenge the government. "Rather than enthusiasm or support, the regime often expects – even from officeholders and civil servants – passive acceptance, or at least that they refrain from public anti-government activity."[36] The Estado Novo did not find itself compelled to shape all the minds of the nation in one mold. Intellectual activity was permitted as long as "it would remain on the philosophic plane or in the field of historical research and its arguments would be directed to the intelligence and would not be of the type to excite dangerous social passions." However, a pamphleteer who might try to mobilize the people politically would be "controlled by the state."[37] Such selective controls included concentration camps, as documented by imprisoned author Graciliano Ramos in his *Memórias do cárcere.*[38]

Noting the limited pluralism of the authoritarian regime, Linz observes that "the cooptation of leaders is a constant process by which different sectors or institutions become participants in the system."[39] In trying to reduce political activity to a minimum, Vargas refrained from forming an official party and thereby ensured a limited degree of pluralism. Moreover, the government allowed many groups access to the administrative apparatus of the state, the most notable being the military, church, business, and labor.

To demonstrate Vargas' successful cooptation of the military sector, we need only note the critical role of military officers in the Revolution of 1930, in the civil war when São Paulo seceded in 1932, and in the coup of 1937. Indeed, Vargas' tenure in office remained secure as long as he had military support. When he lost it, he was overthrown in 1945. The liberal Constitution of 1891 had separated church and state, but Cardinal Leme's astute political maneuvering in the 1930's regained for the Catholic Church a position of influence in the councils of state as well as in public schools, hospitals, and charitable activities. Bruneau, in his study of the Brazilian Church, observed: "[Vargas] used the symbols and beliefs of Catholicism to give his rule legitimacy. . . . Vargas' daughter explained to me that her father placed the backing of the Church on an equal basis with that of the military."[40]

Vargas imposed the Estado Novo in 1937 when he finally recognized that the pre-1929 world trading system could not be resurrected and that Brazil's

36. Linz, "An Authoritarian Regime: Spain" (n. 20 above), p. 304.
37. Amaral, *O estado autoritário,* p. 298.
38. Graciliano Ramos, *Memórias do cárcere* 4 vol., (Rio de Janeiro: José Olympio, 1954).
39. Linz, "Spain," pp. 300-301.
40. Thomas Charles Bruneau, *The Political Transformation of the Brazilian Catholic Church* (London: Cambridge University Press, 1974), pp. 38-43; quote, pp. 39-40.

long-run economic and political stability depended upon sustained domestic industrialization. He thus moved to include the industrialists within his political formula. Warren Dean recorded the cooptation of the São Paulo industrialists, noting that "The trade associations had been transformed into technical and consultative organs that had, with rare exceptions, collaborated in writing the decrees that affected them."[41] The cooptation of labor leaders in the new corporative structures assured them some influence on decisions affecting workers, once Getúlio had weeded out union heads who manifested tendencies toward autonomy; he eliminated the last of these leaders after the attempted coup by the National Liberation Alliance in 1935.[42] The likelihood of a resurgence of labor opposition diminished in the early forties, because even the Communist labor leaders collaborated with Vargas after he had joined the Allies and the Soviet Union in the war. The body of this book illustrates the cooptive pattern and the nature of the relationship between government and union head.

Immediately prior to the establishment of the Estado Novo, an experiment with functional representation in the Constituent Assembly and in the legislature during the short-lived constitutional period from 1934 to 1937 set the precedent of corporative pluralism. The original drafting committee appointed by Provisional President Vargas in 1932 opposed the inclusion of class deputies in the Chamber, but he managed to win the point by including them in the decree which called the Constituent Assembly.[43] In that body 214 representatives were elected directly by the people and another 40 by class or professional organizations: employees (18), employers (17), liberal professions (3), and civil servants (2). Once Vargas had embodied the principle of functional representation in the Constituent Assembly, the constituents naturally assured the perpetuation of their offices in the document which they themselves drew up. They designed it to fit the corporative sindicato structure, and of the 300 deputies, 50 were directly elected by occupational organizations. A breakdown (Table 1) shows the rising importance of industry in the national economy.

Because the revolutionary government had already enacted much more social legislation than the Old Republic, it was logical that the workers' representatives would support it.[44] Moreover, the government possessed leverage over both employers' and workers' sindicatos through the Ministry of Labor, so the class deputies became its useful allies within the legislature as well as within the class organizations.

However, while Vargas obtained functional representation in the legislature, his opposition, which included a significant Catholic element opposed to the

41. Dean, *The Industrialization of São Paulo* (n. 11 above), pp. 207-233; quote, p. 227.
42. Everardo Dias, *História das lutas sociais no Brasil* (São Paulo: Edaglit, 1962), pp. 193, 196.
43. Afonso Arinos de Melo Franco, *Curso de direito constitucional: formação constitucional do Brasil*, II (Rio de Janeiro: Forense, 1960), p. 187; and Decreto 22,653 of April 20, 1933.
44. See listing of social legislation, 1891-1940, in Simão, *Sindicato e estado* (n. 9 above), pp. 89-98.

TABLE 1

Class Deputies Under the Constitution of 1934

Category	Employers	Employees
Agriculture and livestock	7	7
Industry	7	7
Commerce	4	4
Transportation	3	3
Liberal professions	4	–
Public functionaries	–	4
Total	25	25

Source: Brazil, MTIC, *Boletim do MTIC,* no. 6 (February 1935), 365-368.

secularizing tendencies of the first years of his provisional government, won the constitutional guarantee of plural trade unionism and union autonomy.[45] This combination of union pluralism *and* functional representation provided more autonomy for labor leadership and operated to loosen the strict tutelage of the state over the sindicatos. After the Estado Novo had been imposed, Labor Minister Marcondes Filho delivered an attack on union pluralism which serves equally well to demonstrate the inherent weaknesses of a trade-union movement which is imposed from the top down; it suggests that trade-union pluralism was in fact allowing the sindicatos to slip from Vargas' control before the coup of 1937:

> This plural unionism with freedom to organize for all those with their occupational papers in order was transformed into a political instrument. In order to elect class deputies, over 2000 sindicatos were founded under the law of 1934. The establishment of a sindicato was permitted with one-third of the employees in a given occupation in their respective localities. Each administrative district could have one or two sindicatos in the same occupation. In some localities, 50 persons founded a sindicato. What happened afterward? The most eloquent took it upon themselves to obtain the working papers for their associates, created the sindicatos, had themselves elected officers, and came to the capitals for the party meetings. Totally without funds, the sindicatos themselves remained mere fictions.[46]

In the pattern of authoritarian regimes, political mobilization in the period

45. Alceu Amoroso Lima, *Indicações políticas: da revolução à Constituição* (Rio de Janeiro: Civilização Brasileira, 1936), p. 139.
46. Brazil, Comissão Técnica de Orientação Sindical, *Curso de orientação sindical* (Rio de Janeiro, 1944), pp. 55-56. Marcondes' total includes sindicatos for employers and liberal professionals, as well as workers' sindicatos.

from 1930 to 1945 was not particularly intensive, with the brief exception of the three years under the Constitution of 1934. After 1930, the government depended upon a grand coalition of urban middle sectors, industrialists, and, most important, nearly all regional factions of Brazil's landed oligarchy. Vargas held the coalition in precarious balance through concessions, force, and the promise to resolve the domestic economic crisis caused by the collapse of the world trading system. An economically militant or politically independent working class would have upset that balance.[47]

The electoral rolls and trade-union registration data provide indices for judging the degree of political mobilization in Brazil during this period. Taking first the electoral data (presented in Table 2), we see that less than 6 percent of the population figured on the voter rolls during the Old Republic, and registration totals for the election to the Constituent Assembly in 1933 show that the early years of the provisional government did not change that pattern. However, the political competition guaranteed by the Constitution of 1934 brought pluralist mobilization, and the electorate nearly doubled by the legislative elections of that year. Such rapid political mobilization threatened Vargas' grip on the political system, leading him in 1937 to annul the Constitution of 1934 and strengthen his formal controls.

TABLE 2

Voters Registered in Selected Election Years
in Brazil, 1908-1966

Years	Registered voters (in millions)	Population (in millions)	Registered voters (as percent of population)
1908	1.0	21.3	4.8%
1912	1.3	23.2	5.6
1933	1.5	35.7	4.1
1934	2.7	36.4	7.3
1945	7.3	46.2	15.9
1947	7.7	48.4	15.9
1950	11.4	52.0	22.0
1954	15.1	57.1	26.5
1955	15.2	58.5	26.1
1958	13.8	62.7	22.0
1960	15.5	71.0	21.9
1962	18.6	75.3	24.7
1966	21.9	84.7	25.9

Source: Brazil, IBGE, *Anuário Estatístico do Brasil*, 1937, 1966.

47. Robert Rowland, "Classe operária e estado de compromisso," *Estudos Cebrap,* no. 8 (April 1974), 5-40.

Once the brief period under the Constitution of 1934 had passed, limitations and controls over mobilization became more evident. The coup of 1937 occurred precisely to prevent the elections of 1938 from taking place, and depoliticization was furthered by the express absence of any political party, official or unofficial. Francisco Campos even frankly admitted that he considered the unimplemented constitutional provision for elections to be "mere window dressing."[48] When Vargas fell in 1945, mobilization again rose sharply, as the table reveals.

The labor system served as an instrument for controlling mobilization in this authoritarian system. Although all three basic labor laws of the period embody the underlying abhorrence of class conflict and the desire to achieve class cooperation through corporative institutions, they typify each of the three phases of the Revolution of 1930 with respect to political and social mobilization. The first, in 1931, reflected the early flush of the revolution and encouraged mobilization in the government-directed sindicatos. It imposed the corporative structure upon labor organizations, permitted only one union per category, and restricted to sindicato members the right to bring cases to the labor courts. By early 1934, the pressure for unionization increased when the government promulgated a degree providing mandatory annual vacations exclusively for sindicato members.

In mid-1934, labor law was brought into conformity with the new Constitution. It now permitted plural unionism and eliminated the provisions restricting its benefits to union members. Government-directed mobilization declined, but pluralistic mobilization increased, as Minister Marcondes Filho's comment made clear. Finally, the decree law of 1939 brought labor organization into conformity with the directives and realities of the Estado Novo by again restricting sindicatos to one per category in each geographic zone. This law, whose essential provisions remain in effect to this day, recognized government control over the sindicatos.

An analysis of the pattern of recognition of sindicatos (Table 3) shows that this succession of basic labor laws served to hinder the mobilization of the working class. The low number recognized in 1931, 1935, and 1940 indicates that recognition proceeded very slowly after each new law, probably because new bureaucratic procedures were being defined. The net effect of this succession of laws was to throw sindicato leaders off balance and disrupt the efficiency of their organizations. Furthermore, the law of 1939 dissolved all sindicatos and required them to register anew, cutting an even sharper hiatus in the pattern of social mobilization within the labor framework. As can be seen in the figures, the new registration process took several years.

José Albertino Rodrigues claims that from 1930 to 1934 nearly half of the registered sindicatos were in Rio or São Paulo, because the red tape was easier to

48. Karl Lowenstein, *Brazil Under Vargas* (New York: MacMillan, 1942), p. 360.

TABLE 3

Workers' Sindicatos Recognized by
the Ministry of Labor,
1931-1945

Year	Recognition	Total in existence
1931	39	32
1932	116	115
1933	259	256
1934	208	367
1935	21	440
1936	106	682
1937	139	916
1938	145	955
1939	–	1208
1940	8	8
1941	–	396
1942	–	644
1943	–	759
1944	–	816
1945	–	873

Source: For recognition conferred, Brazil, IBGE, *Anuário Estatístico do Brasil*, 1937-1940, 1959; for total recognized sindicatos in existence, José Albertino Rodrigues, *Sindicato e desenvolvimento no Brasil* (Sao Pãulo: Difusão Européia do Livro, 1968), p. 124.

Note: Dash indicates figure not available (throughout tables).

cut there than in less urbanized areas.[49] This suggests that it was easier for the Vargas government to control the sindicatos in urban areas where the administrative agencies of the Ministry of Labor were most extensive. Labor Minister Marcondes Filho's comment suggests that parties and other groups were better able to organize in the countryside, where the new Ministry had not yet established strong administrative underpinning.

Official mobilization through the corporative sindicatos picked up in the early 1940's, but the legal prohibition of multiple unions in each category and the government's desire to retain a firm hand kept the total number below the high point reached under the 1934 law. Labor Ministry budgets and expenditures, analyzed in detail in Chapter Four, reveal a significant rise in the government's attention to the working class in the early forties. Proposed and actual expenditures for Labor Ministry programs and social welfare shot up in these years. Brazilian troops were fighting against fascism in Europe, and many

49. José Albertino Rodrigues, *Sindicato e desenvolvimento no Brasil* (São Paulo: Difusão Européia do Livro, 1968), p. 127.

Brazilians expected that once the war was over, electoral democracy would inevitably replace authoritarian government at home. Vargas began preparing for this by increasing spending on workers' programs, thus cultivating the electoral potential of the working class.

Authoritarian regimes are characteristically run by one leader or a small group. In the case of the Estado Novo, Vargas was the central leader around whom political life revolved. A contemporary analysis pointed out that Vargas was a sound administrator who appointed competent cabinet members. He frequently met with them on an individual basis, though plenary cabinet meetings were rare.[50] Such a style of consultation prevented coordinated opposition to the leader, while it allowed him firmly to control the policies of the nation. That the behavior of the government did follow some ill-defined but predictable limits is also attested to in the same study:

> But even the most hardened opponents of the regime have to admit that such violations of the rule of law as have occurred are neither numerous nor do they affect a large number of individuals. They are the incidentals of any authoritarian government, but they are not sufficient in quantity and quality to stamp the regime as a whole as arbitrary.[51]

Finally, the bureaucratic pattern of authority which developed from 1930 to 1945 in Brazil is an example of the dominance of administrators over politicians. Max Weber predicted that the tension between these two groups would be one of the central issues of modern political history.[52] In *Os donos do poder*, Raymundo Faoro applies a Weberian analysis to Brazilian history and concludes that a bureaucratic or administrative elite dominates that nation's political system:

> In addition to being differentiated functionally, the administrative elite is differentiated socially and acts as a community, having at its disposal a monopoly over the political domain. The bureaucratic status group is the arbiter of the nation and its classes, regulating the economy and functioning as proprietor of its sovereignty. The other social strata, classes, and status groups are dependent upon it as they lack their own symbolic values. Unable to organize themselves on their own, they exist "simply as administrative imitation and practice."[53]

For Faoro, the new bureaucratic elite of the Estado Novo included the top military officers as well as upper-level civil servants who controlled the most important economic agencies and banks. In the field of economic development, research by Nathaniel H. Leff supports Faoro's generalizations.[54]

50. Lowenstein, p. 79.
51. *Ibid.,* pp. 327-328.
52. Reinhard Bendix, *Max Weber: An Intellectual Portrait* (Garden City, N.Y.: Doubleday, 1962), pp. 439-440.
53. Raymundo Faoro, *Os donos do poder* (ch. 1 above, n. 10), p. 262.
54. Leff, *Economic Policy-Making* (ch. 1 above, n. 11), pp. 4, 147-148.

Although political power has had a pendular movement in Brazil, the dominant pattern has been the one Faoro describes, of centralization and of domination of administrators over politicians. Brazil has spent twice as much time under centralized administrative rule (104 years: 1821-31, 1841-89, 1930-76) as under decentralized rule which favored the state politicians (50 years: 1831-41, 1890-1930).

The imperatives of economic development and the modern tendency toward centralization in all nations suggest that the pattern for centralized authority re-established by the Revolution of 1930 will never again be challenged in Brazil. Within this political system, which is characterized by bureaucratic domination, the pattern of labor activity in the political process has also been largely bureaucratic. The following chapter, therefore, discusses the legal and administrative framework of Brazil's corporative labor system.

Chapter 3

THE STRUCTURAL AND LEGAL FOUNDATIONS OF BRAZILIAN LABOR ORGANIZATION

The corporative institution builders of the Estado Novo, seeking to secure state control over the social strata generated by industrialization, minutely regulated the economic, social, and political activities of workers' organizations. This chapter discusses the provisions of Brazilian labor law which have had the greatest impact upon the behavior of labor leaders and their unions. Even though the state has not enforced these provisions with equal rigor at all times, selective enforcement at critical moments has assured continued state domination.

This chapter first examines the political forces which gave rise to the present system of labor law. It then covers the rules which subjected labor organizations to state control from the 1930's through 1964 and which, with some modifications, still serve the same purpose. With the legal and institutional context thus set, Chapters Four through Seven describe the dynamics of working-class politics in the period prior to the military takeover in 1964. Chapter Eight then describes the changes in law and practice which the military governments since then have used to bring the working class once more under strict state control. Indeed, recent modifications of Brazil's labor law in no way do violence to the original intent of Vargas' corporative advisors, for they strengthen the position of the state. In essence, these new rules merely adjust the Estado Novo labor system in order to make it work more effectively for the nation's ruling class.

Political Foundations of the Corporative Labor Law

The Revolution of 1930 immediately placed the corporative imprint upon activities by both workers' and employers' organizations. The labor law of 1931 required such organizations to register with the just-created Ministry of Labor, Industry, and Commerce (MTIC). Brazil's first labor minister, Lindolfo Collor, expressed his hope that the new law would do away with class conflict and give the nation "a new social countenance, oriented toward class collaboration."[1] Provisional President Vargas reiterated this corporative view to the Constituent Assembly in 1933 when he attacked "the false impression that sindicatos are organizations for class struggle," noting that " . . .they are in fact for defense and for the collaboration of labor and capital with the government."[2]

Oliveira Vianna, a legal adviser with the Ministry of Labor and one of Brazil's most influential corporatist writers, signaled the three central principles which oriented the nation's trade-union policy after 1930: (1) separation of two concepts which had generally been assumed to be inseparable — labor organization and socialism — thereby leaving Brazilian labor unionism "professional, corporative, and Christian"; (2) rigorous separation of labor unions from political parties; and (3) careful structuring of the sindicatos so as to make them instruments of social integration in the nation-building process. This latter point meant building social solidarity through conscious emphasis on the integrative, educational, and socializing aspects of the sindicatos.[3]

The body of social legislation which emerged in Brazil in the 1930's is voluminous, and scholars do not yet agree on the process which produced it. Evaristo de Moraes Filho claims that union militants in the decades before 1930 provided the ideas, goals, organizational forms, and in some cases the personnel with which the Ministry drew up the new laws.[4] On the other hand, Estado Novo administrators such as Labor Minister Marcondes Filho argue that the social legislation had been a purely paternalistic gesture by Vargas, the "father of the poor":

> In other nations, workers first joined together in order to win, subsequently, rights and prerogatives. The trade union was the cause. In Brazil, rights and prerogatives preceded their joining together. The sindicato is the consequence.[5]

Both arguments have a basis in fact. Oliveira Vianna himself stated that, in practice, existing customary relations between employers and employees in the port and maritime sector served as the basis for the public law governing labor relations which the Ministry drew up in the thirties. In keeping with the corporative ideal, Ministry jurists and technicians brought together representa-

1. From Collor's speech, Dec. 26, 1930, in Paulo Nogueira Filho, *Idéias e lutas* (ch. 2 above, n. 8), II, p. 751.

2. Vargas' speech to the Constituent Assembly in November 1933, cited in Omar Gonçalves da Motta, *O syndicato e a realidade brasileira* (Curitiba: n.p., 1936), p. 32.

3. Francisco José de Oliveira Vianna, *Direito do trabalho e democracia social* (Rio de Janeiro: José Olympio, 1951), pp. 79-84.

4. Evaristo de Moraes Filho, *O problema do sindicato único no Brasil* (Rio de Janeiro: A Noite, 1952), p. 190.

5. Brazil, CTOS, *Curso de orientação sindical* (ch. 2 above, n. 46), p. 46.

tives of both sides, and they elaborated drafts of laws which were "more a systematization of previously existing law than the real creation of new law."[6] However, he was referring to sectors with four centuries of experience in Brazil, sectors whose workers were among the most highly articulate and organized. They figure, moreover, among those favored sectors which had carved out their niches in the cartorial state described by Jaguaribe.[7] Oliveira Vianna notes, however, that in urban commercial and industrial activities such a body of customary practices had not yet evolved.[8] Therefore, while Vargas' social legislation did not just appear out of the blue, It must be recognized that for the new sectors which were then gaining importance and which are now the most significant in the Brazilian economy, such legislation in fact entered into quite virgin territory. Its impact in those sectors, therefore, was significant and served to perpetuate the paternalistic tradition in Brazil.

Legal and Structural Foundations of the Labor System

This section briefly describes the organizational framework which Vargas established through decree laws during the Estado Novo. This body of labor legislation, which has changed little since the 1930's, establishes the basic structural outlines for labor organizations and tightly regulates their political and economic activity. Although the letter of the law has not always been enforced in practice, the importance of these controls cannot be underestimated, because those in power have employed them whenever it suited their purposes. During the Estado Novo, under the Dutra administration (1946-50), and again since 1964, the state has used this corporative framework to impose its will upon the trade-union movement, thus curtailing labor's autonomous action.

Three major institutions channel and regulate state-labor relations in Brazil: the sindicatos, the social security system, and the labor-court system. The sindicatos are to represent the interests of the workers, provide them with certain social services, and collaborate with the government. The social security system is supposed to provide modern social welfare services for all workers. And the system of labor courts adjudicates disputes between employers and employees.

The following discussion is based upon the Consolidation of Labor Laws (CLT), which Getúlio Vargas promulgated on May 1, 1943. The CLT represents the compilation, coordination, and systematization of the body of relevant

6. Francisco José de Oliveira Vianna, *Instituições políticas brasileiras,* 2nd ed. (Rio de Janeiro: José Olympio, 1955), I, p. 32.

7. See Hélio Jaguaribe, *O nacionalismo* (ch. 1 above, n. 15), pp. 41-42; also Jaguaribe's *Desenvolvimento econômico e desenvolvimento político* (Rio de Janeiro: Fundo de Cultura, 1962), p. 190.

8. Oliveira Vianna, *Instituições,* I, p. 31.

social legislation written since the Revolution of 1930.[9] Embodied in it is the corporative spirit of the three principal laws (of 1931, 1934, and 1939) which regulated labor organization during the thirties. The reestablishment of a liberal democratic government with the Constitution of 1946 did not alter the corporative nature of the labor system, for the Constituent Assembly soundly defeated a proposed amendment to free the sindicatos from state tutelage or interference.[10] Indeed, even the literature of the major anti-Vargas party of the time, the União Democrática Nacional, never explicitly treated the incompatibility of the Constitution's liberal democratic and statist corporative principles. In elections, UDN candidates paid no more than mere lip service to labor's demands for trade-union autonomy. On the other end of the political spectrum, the Communist Party also accepted the corporative system and worked within it. Rather than seeking to replace this system with a network of autonomous unions, the Communists merely sought to reform some aspects of it while continuing to benefit from such provisions as the trade-union tax, to be covered below.[11] Vargas' labor law therefore remained almost untouched through 1964, after which the military government made only minor modifications to reinforce the state controls.

The CLT provides for three hierarchical levels of union organization: the sindicato, which generally covers one or more *municípios* (roughly comparable to a U.S. county or township); the federation, usually at the state level; and the confederation at the national level. The sindicato deals mainly with workplace grievances, economic demands, and welfare services, while the federations and confederations, whose leaders usually enjoy institutionalized contact with ministry officials, act mainly in the political and administrative field. As the CLT is of corporative inspiration, there is a symmetry of structures for both employees and employers, and similar organization is also provided for the liberal professions. Table 4 shows the evolution of membership in workers' sindicatos from 1953 through 1973.

Federations are composed of at least five sindicatos in the same branch of the economy and generally in the same state, although there are exceptions such as air transport and maritime workers, who have national federations. At least three

9. In terms of jurisprudence, the Consolidation is a step short of being a labor code but is more systematic than loose fragmented legislation. Arnaldo Lopes Sussekind, Délio Maranhão, and José de Segadas Viana, *Instituições de Direito do Trabalho,* 4th ed. (São Paulo: Freitas Bastos, 1967), I, p. 58.

10. Maria Hermínia Tavares de Almeida, "O sindicato no Brasil: novos problemas, velhas estruturas," *Debate e Crítica,* no. 6 (June 1975), 49.

11. On the UDN, see, for example, Major-Brigadeiro Eduardo Gomes, *Campanha de libertação* (São Paulo: Martins, 1946); Herbert V. Levy, *O Brasil e os novos tempos; considerações sôbre o problema de reestruturação política, econômica e social do Brasil* (São Paulo: Martins, 1946); Virgílio A. de Mello Franco, *A campanha da U.D.N. (1944-45)* (Rio de Janeiro: Zélio Valverde, 1946), and *Sob o signo de resistência* (Rio de Janeiro: Zélio Valverde, 1947). On the Communist Party, see Francisco C. Weffort, "Sindicatos e política" (thesis presented for the *livre docência,* University of São Paulo, 1972), pp. II.27-II.35 and passim; also Weffort's "Origens do sindicalismo populista no Brasil: a conjuntura do após-guerra," *Estudos Cebrap,* no. 4 (April 1973), 65-105.

TABLE 4

Workers' Sindicato Membership, by Sector of the Economy, 1953-1973

Year	Total	Industry	Commerce	River, maritime, and air transport	Land transport	Communications and advertising	Banking and insurance	Education and culture
1953	807,442	452,143	132,887	66,542	100,607	18,236	30,170	6,857
1954	862,992	477,332	137,188	81,623	97,255	21,009	39,285	9,300
1955	961,931	571,969	139,100	69,576	108,049	20,340	48,823	9,074
1956	940,024	560,446	127,752	68,999	106,967	19,882	44,270	11,708
1957	1,055,390	612,001	168,808	83,876	102,831	23,272	52,898	11,704
1958	1,120,193	654,923	176,230	86,348	108,380	26,194	55,318	12,800
1959	1,108,602	641,906	176,719	87,790	100,575	26,875	61,457	13,280
1960	1,217,655	692,184	203,469	89,135	122,466	25,476	67,670	17,255
1961	1,203,570	639,903	207,742	97,713	132,589	36,715	71,092	17,816
1962	1,394,761	823,210	203,121	104,565	131,441	24,352	93,459	14,613
1963	1,448,151	855,617	205,627	107,928	122,854	32,921	101,995	21,209
1964	—	—	—	—	—	—	—	—
1965	1,602,021	954,309	223,195	86,188	148,688	46,947	108,456	34,238
1966	1,628,202	962,329	249,971	82,422	142,821	43,910	118,472	28,277
1967	1,740,377	1,052,583	270,538	73,771	153,476	48,061	98,830	43,118
1968	1,873,898	1,113,580	283,919	82,096	155,626	57,455	134,863	46,359
1969	1,952,752	1,145,825	322,262	86,711	161,520	55,520	133,732	47,180
1970	2,132,086	1,239,363	364,590	93,042	180,295	58,937	142,010	53,849
1971	2,317,775	1,354,437	409,635	92,813	191,944	63,049	148,823	57,074
1972	2,488,208	1,453,524	438,139	102,655	208,783	66,634	156,806	61,667
1973	2,730,055	1,595,580	498,257	105,237	222,393	72,448	159,256	66,884

Source: Brazil, IBGE, *Anuário Estatístico do Brasil*, 1955 through 1975. The data are from the Labor Ministry's annual survey of trade unions, the *inquérito sindical*.

Note: The membership figures are those from the sindicatos which returned the Labor Ministry's annual questionnaire. From 23 to 34 percent failed to respond during the years between 1953 and 1965, so the figures above may understate actual membership in that proportion. Nonresponses gradually declined after 1966, so by 1973 only 4 percent did not return the questionnaire.

federations are necessary to constitute a confederation. The terms "sindicato," "federation," and "confederation" may be used only by labor organizations officially recognized by the Ministry of Labor. Unrecognized or ad hoc workers' organizations cannot legally use them or obtain the benefits conferred by recognition.

In addition to regulating workers' organizations, the CLT also established the labor-court system to resolve conflicts between employers and employees according to the criteria and norms of social and labor legislation (art. 643). We mentioned earlier that Brazilians generally seek to channel problems through the offices of the administrative state in order to avoid direct, face-to-face conflict. These labor courts, whose professional judges share the bench with employer and employee delegates, institutionalize this political-culture trait. The principles of the labor-court system clearly reflect the organic view of the state, which holds that the general will of a society is discernible and must prevail over special interests:

> In the absence of legal or contractual provisions, administrative authorities and the Labor Courts will base their decisions, depending on the case, on jurisprudence, analogy, equity, or other principles and general rules of law — principally labor law — and also in accordance with usage and customs and comparative law, but *always in such a manner that no class or personal interests prevail over the public interest.* (Art. 8, emphasis added.)

The final structural mainstay of the labor system in Brazil is the social security system, which is referred to only briefly in the CLT and is organized in a separate body of law. Its planners intended it to maintain social harmony through distributive social justice, but it has not lived up to its promise. The costs of its benefits were to be covered by equal contributions from workers, employers, and the national government. As the following chapter will show, the government has paid only a fraction of its statutory contribution, and many employers failed to pay theirs before 1964, so service was inadequate. The government usually did not enforce penalties against these employers before 1964, and even when it did, the penalty was less than the amount saved in the inflationary interim through the depreciation of the currency. Hence it was in the employers' interest to cheat. The military government amended the law in 1966 to penalize employers more severely for noncompliance, but rising inflation in the mid-1970's is mitigating the effect of such penalties. New legislation also created instruments for the government gradually to pay off its whopping debt to the system.[12] Only the workers have been unable to evade their social security contributions, since these take the form of payroll deductions.

The social security system, therefore, though actuarily sound in its conception, could not possibly deliver all of the services due its beneficiaries. The

12. Marcelo Pimentel, Hélio C. Ribeiro, and Moacyr Pessoa, *A previdência social interpretada* (Rio de Janeiro: Forense, 1969), pp. 320-323, 365-368. This book annotates each article of the social security law.

workers, who alone among the contributors had met their financial obligations, thus received shamefully inadquate health care and retirement benefits. James Malloy's recent study of the social security system, moreover, finds it has not served to redistribute income down the social pyramid. Rather, thoughout its 40-year history, it has reinforced the prevailing unequal pattern of income distribution.[13]

Several major changes in the social security system's organizational structure have significantly affected the political role of organized labor. Prior to the overthrow of Goulart, the system included a number of institutes organized along sectoral lines roughly parallel to those of the sindicato system, i.e., separate institutes for workers in industry, commerce, banking, maritime trades, etc. Until 1960, these institutes and agencies were administered by state-appointed technicians and experts. The Social Security Act of 1960 changed this by establishing tripartite administrative and judicial councils in all of the principal organizations: labor, management, and the government now had equal votes on these boards. The administrative councils chose their officers from among their own members, so labor leaders achieved control of numerous social security institutes. In 1966, the military government unified most of these institutes into a single centralized body and replaced its tripartite administrative council with a government-appointed president. The subdivision of the social security system into a series of separate institutes during the liberal-democratic period from 1946 to 1964 furthered government domination of the working class. Malloy's study of the system concludes: "The highly particularistic approach of the government encouraged a group-specific orientation among working groups which divided them, fostered intergroup competition, and undermined any basis of class solidarity."[14]

Between 1960 and 1964, the period which supplies the case studies for the next four chapters, the social security system provided several important types of patronage which union officers converted to political power. In the first place, labor leaders on the institutes' governing councils gained great influence in their personnel practices and policies. As these bodies employed about one-seventh of all federal civil servants, this patronage carried considerable weight. Secondly, the chronic shortfall in revenues required social security employees to discriminate among clients, distributing or withholding service according to their own criteria rather than purely technical rules. They simply could not attend to all of the contributors who rightfully deserved their services. Workers desiring attention from hospitals, housing boards, or other agencies therefore sought the assistance of labor leaders with contacts or influence in the social security apparatus. In other words, as political criteria had come to govern appointments

13. James M. Malloy, "The Evolution of Social Security Policy in Brazil: Policy Making and Income Distribution," paper presented at the 1975 Annual Meeting of the American Political Science Association, San Francisco, pp. 27-29.

14. James M. Malloy, "Social Security Policy and the Working Class in Twentieth-Century Brazil," *Journal of Inter-American Studies and World Affairs,* in press.

within the system after the social security law of 1960, so political criteria came to determine who would receive benefits. This, as we will see in Chapter Five, greatly increased the political leverage of well-placed labor leaders.

The CLT, in addition to structuring the labor system and establishing institutional controls for ministerial dominance, also lays down the norms of daily industrial relations. Little research exists on the effectiveness of these laws. However, one survey of 153 populist voters in São Paulo in the early 1960's indicates that workers viewed these laws with skepticism. Only 30 percent agreed with a statement that Brazilian labor law protects the worker and is against the employer. On the other hand, 90 percent of the respondents agreed that its provisions should be extended to rural workers, indicating that they considered the existing legislation better than none at all.[15] These findings suggest that the labor laws have led the workers to subscribe to the organic view of society, for they see the state as an appropriate intermediary and patron in labor relations, even though they are not satisfied with its performance.

Since the CLT regulates industrial relations, a principal activity of the sindicatos has been to signal infractions of the law to the authorities. In the freer climate before 1964, the struggle for new norms or for a change in them often took the form of political action. Strikes were sometimes used to focus public opinion on problems where prompt administrative or political action was desired. This pattern of industrial relations, in which workers seek to resolve problems through political action which indirectly reaches the employers via agencies of the state, is typical in countries with Latin-Catholic political cultures.[16]

Government Controls on Workers' Organizations

The legal philosophy and political culture which inform the CLT differ radically from those in the Anglo-Saxon, common-law countries. This cultural heritage profoundly affects the role of organized groups, as one writer, whose observations on Hispanic America apply equally well to Brazil, succinctly observes:

> On the part of the State, the legal regime is one intensely hostile to the *autonomous* existence of intermediary bodies. The origins lie deep in the Roman Law, in the Roman "concession" theory, of which it has been said, "groups existed only in the legal contemplation of the sovereign." In this tradition, the State does not take cognizance of a group; it *creates* the group by endowing it with juridical personality. Therefore, in systems like those of Spanish America, in which the State's recognition and patronage

15. Francisco C. Weffort, "Raízes Sociais do Populismo em São Paulo," *Revista Civilização Brasileira*, I, no. 2 (May 1965), 45-46, 51-52. This was not a survey of workers per se, but four-fifths of the respondents were employed by others rather than self-employed, thus permitting its use here.

16. On France, for example, see Michel Crozier, *The Bureaucratic Phenomenon* (ch. 1 above, n. 20), pp. 245-247; on Peru, see James L. Payne, *Labor and Politics in Peru: The System of Political Bargaining* (New Haven, Conn.: Yale University Press, 1965), pp. 12-18.

are all-important for privilege, places, and institutional legitimacy, the unrecognized group drifts in an uncomfortable, harassed limbo.[17]

In this spirit, Brazilian labor legislation provides for official recognition by the Ministry of Labor, carefully circumscribes the legitmate activities of workers' and employers' organizations, and creates mechanisms for government intervention in union elections, finances, and internal affairs.

The labor law of 1939, which was based largely upon the Carta del Lavoro of the Italian fascist state, provides the legal basis for government control over the sindicatos. The CLT differed from the Italian model in that it reflected the preference of the Estado Novo for indirect controls rather than the direct incorporation of the sindicatos into the state structure.[18]

Although they were not officially organs of the state, the sindicatos in fact enjoyed little autonomy in the Estado Novo, since the government kept a tight rein on the working class. The government's task was made easier because it had brought most unions under control during the 1930's and, once Hitler's armies invaded Russia in 1941, even Communist union heads collaborated fully with Vargas.[19]

The corporative role of the sindicatos in the national political, economic, and social systems is clearly spelled out in the CLT. Note especially section "a":

Art. 514. The duties of the sindicatos are:
a. to collaborate with the public authorities in the development of social
   solidarity;
b. to maintain legal aid services for their members;
c. to promote conciliation in labor disputes.

Paragraph one: Employees' sindicatos will also have the duty of:
a. promoting the establishment of consumers' credit cooperatives;
b. establishing and maintaining primary and vocational schools.

Furthermore, the statutes of the sindicato must contain the "assurance that the association will act as an organ of collaboration with the public authorities and other associations with a view to furthering social solidarity and to the subordination of economic or professional interests to the national interest" (art. 518). Since partisan political activity is considered inimical to national harmony, a decree-law banned partisan political activity within the sindicatos when political parties were again permitted to exist at the end of the Estado Novo.[20]

17. Ronald C. Newton, "On 'Functional Groups,' 'Fragmentation,' and 'Pluralism' in Spanish American Political Society," in Wiarda (ed.), *Politics and Social Change* (ch. 1 above, n. 3), pp. 141-142 (emphasis in original). The citation within the quote is to Robert A. Nisbet, *Community and Power* (New York: Oxford University Press, 1962), p. 113.

18. Francisco José de Oliveira Vianna, *Problemas de direito sindical* (Rio de Janeiro: Editôra Max Limonad, 1943), pp. 32-33.

19. Jover Telles, *O movimento sindical no Brasil* (Rio de Janeiro: Vitória, 1962), pp. 38-39; Robert J. Alexander, *Communism in Latin America* (New Brunswick, N.J.: Rutgers, 1957), p. 114.

20. Decreto-lei 9502 of July 22, 1946.

One of the principal means for increasing state control over the sindicatos lies in the *imposto sindical* or trade-union tax (arts. 578–610). Equivalent to one day's pay per year, it is collected in March from all organizable workers, regardless of their actual membership in a sindicato. Labor Ministry records show that between 1954 and 1964, 60 percent of sindicato revenues came from the trade-union tax, thus giving the state considerable leverage over the unions.[21]

Before 1965, receipts from the imposto sindical were distributed in the following manner:

Sindicato	54%
Federation	15
Confederation	5
Fundo Social Sindical	20
Bank of Brazil	6
	100%

The Bank of Brazil deducts 6 percent for handling charges on the account.[22] The Fundo Social Sindical was supposed to attend to the general interests of Brazilian union organization and to provide social assistance for workers who were not in sindicatos, but many observers considered it simply a patronage slush fund. In 1965, the government abolished the Fundo, and a National Department of Employment and Wages, to be discussed in Chapter Eight, absorbed its share. The bank transfers the remainder to the respective sindicatos, which in turn pass on the stipulated proportion to the appropriate federation and confederation. If a sindicato fails to comply, the bank automatically freezes its account. Since the law bars all but a few types of strikes, the bank also automatically freezes striking unions' accounts to prevent their use as strike funds.

Representation of the interests of a specific economic category or profession is only one function of the sindicatos. They are primarily organs for collaboration with the state and for providing the types of social services generally associated with old-time mutual-aid societies and with the modern welfare state. The state controls their pursestrings and requires them to be conduits for social services. Indeed, the law restricts the use of imposto sindical revenues to the

21. Brazil, IBGE, *Anuário Estatístico do Brasil,* 1956 through 1966 (Rio de Janeiro), using data from the Labor Ministry's annual survey of trade unions, the *inquérito sindical.* Although Decree-law 27 of Nov. 14, 1966 changed the name of the trade-union tax to "trade-union contribution," most Brazilians still refer to it by its original name. Therefore, this book also uses the former name.

22. Brazilian jurists dispute whether the imposto sindical is really a tax or, rather, just an enforced contribution, and this is reflected even in the CLT, where it is referred to as both. See Mozart Víctor Russomano, *Comentários à Consolidação das Leis do Trabalho* (Rio de Janeiro: José Konfino, 1955), II, p. 876; Teotônio Monteiro de Barros Filho, "O impôsto sindical," *Legislação do Trabalho* (São Paulo), February 1951, p. 39; "Impôsto sindical e assistência social," *Boletim do DIEESE,* I, no. 11 (March 1961), 7.

following specifically delineated activities: placement services; primary and vocational schools; libraries; maternity, medical, dental, and legal assistance; credit and consumers' cooperatives; holiday camps and sporting activities; and payment for jobs created by the above activities (art. 592).

Table 5 presents the sums spent on social assistance by the sindicatos between 1953 and 1963. To make cruzeiro figures more comparable, we have divided each year's total by the percentage of sindicatos responding to the annual Ministry survey and by the cost-of-living increase. The general trend upward in column *g* reflects increasing social-assistance activity as the Brazilian economy absorbed increasing numbers of workers and more sindicatos were founded. In most years from 1958 to 1965, Labor Ministry data show that sindicatos operated between 170 and 200 schools, about 40 percent of them at the primary level, and they enrolled roughly 10,000 students. Table 6 shows that the number of sindicato schools and their enrollment began rising sharply in 1966, so that by 1972, 472 schools registered nearly 36,000 students. This rise reflects renewed government emphasis on the unions' social-service rather than representative functions. Library data appear in Table 7. The rapid rise in library holdings in the early sixties may be an indicator of increasing dynamism and politicization of the sindicatos. Following the coup, the military seized many of the sindicatos' books, accounting for the sharp reduction in holdings between 1963 and 1965.[23]

The predominantly social-service orientation of Brazilian labor unions diverts workers' attention from economic activities which might contribute to militant class consciousness. A survey of the 30 textile-workers' sindicatos in the state of São Paulo in 1960 reveals workers' attitudes toward the various union activities. Officers of 15 of the sindicatos stated that new members join principally because of their social-service programs, and five more felt that their recreational opportunities, such as picnics, dances, and movies, were the chief drawing-cards for new members. Of the eight responses which could be related directly to furthering economic interests of the working class, only two specifically stated that members join because they feel the sindicato can raise their income.[24] Other surveys consistently indicate that workers perceive the sindicatos as dispensaries of social-welfare benefits.[25]

One might assume that in any country the most industrialized areas would have the highest indices of union membership. However, since we find that in Brazil the economic function of the sindicatos is not valued as highly as the social function, one might hypothesize the opposite: that membership would be higher in the smaller cities than in the larger ones. In the smaller cities, the

23. Brazil, IBGE, *Anuário Estatístico do Brasil,* 1955 through 1968, *inquérito sindical* data.

24. "A organização sindical dos trabalhadores textís no Estado de São Paulo," *Boletim do DIEESE,* I, no. 9 (January 1961), 16-17.

25. Leôncio Martins Rodrigues, *Industrialização e atitudes operárias: estudo de um grupo de trabalhadores* (São Paulo: Brasiliense, 1970), p. 109; Andrea Rios Loyola, "Les ouvriers et le populisme" (ch. 1 above, n. 19), p. 275.

TABLE 5

Sindicato Expenditures on Social Assistance, 1953-1963
(1000 cruzeiros)

Year	(a) Total	(b) Workers' sindicatos	(c) Employers' sindicatos	(d) Liberal professionals, sindicatos	(e) Percent worker sindicatos responding	(f) Cost-of-living increase	(g) Index (b) / (e) (f) 1954 = 100
1953	84,608	68,132	15,623	852	—	22.00%	100
1954	123,118	102,763	19,329	1,025	72.0%	23.77	117
1955	138,457	120,117	17,662	678	66.4	20.53	152
1956	171,785	140,580	30,697	508	69.7	16.48	248
1957	295,809	204,061	90,358	1,390	77.1	14.62	382
1958	316,747	258,017	56,843	1,887	71.3	39.09	178
1959	394,044	313,365	77,088	3,591	69.5	29.30	280
1960	502,146	390,781	94,119	17,246	73.3	33.41	341
1961	597,172	496,154	85,550	15,468	67.2	51.63	385
1962	1,012,026	864,609	136,953	10,464	67.2	70.47	512
1963	1,864,286	1,611,304	242,389	11,593	68.9		

Source: Columns *a, b, c, d, e* are from Brazil, IBGE, *Anuário Estatístico do Brasil*, 1955 through 1965 (Rio de Janeiro: IBGE, 1956-1966), *inquérito sindical* data. Column *f* is from cost-of-living data on Guanabara state, in *Conjuntura Econômica*.

Column *g* divides the expenditures of the workers' sindicatos by the percentage of sindicatos responding to the survey each year and by the increase in the cost of living, to make the data comparable, demonstrating the increase in social-assistance activity of the sindicatos. These results are expressed as an index with 1954 set at 100.

TABLE 6

Number of Schools Maintained by Workers' Sindicatos,
and Their Enrollment, 1955-1973

Year	*Number of schools*		*Number of students*	
	Total	*Primary schools*	*Total*	*Primary schools*
1955	176	101	9,694	5,913
1956	203	140	7,401	3,848
1957	144	70	8,308	4,385
1958	182	81	9,248	4,945
1959	170	77	10,447	5,309
1960	449	172	24,022	10,858
1961	195	95	10,704	5,431
1962	182	86	13,037	6,063
1963	116	50	9,340	4,419
1964	178	67	9,827	3,300
1965	148	58	10,289	3,967
1966	184	79	14,808	5,939
1967	271	92	22,987	7,739
1968	328	119	28,447	10,706
1969	350	129	29,888	11,231
1970	342	119	32,749	11,418
1971	361	116	28,801	11,034
1972	472	144	35,835	12,411
1973	421	154	35,121	11,931

Source: Brazil, IBGE, *Anuário Estatístico do Brasil,* 1957 through 1975 (Rio de Janeiro: IBGE, 1957-1976), *inquérito sindical data.*

sindicatos' social functions would be highlighted because there are fewer competing centers of social activity. Data covering a broad range of workers are hard to come by; but in the textile-union survey, the 16 sindicatos in cities under 40,000 inhabitants (1960 census) reported an average membership of 69 percent of the workers eligible, while the 13 sindicatos in cities over 40,000 averaged only 48 percent; and the largest sindicato, that in the capital city of São Paulo, averaged only 16 percent, even though its 14,000 members constituted one-quarter of all the union members in the state.[26] This provides an interesting hypothesis on the Brazilian political culture, but one would need more representative data before generalizing about all regions and economic sectors of Brazil.

Official recognition enables sindicatos to undertake basic activities which are denied to unrecognized labor organizations. Brazilian law entitles legally recognized sindicatos to represent the interests of the category or of its members before the administrative and judicial authorities, to negotiate collective labor

26. Percentages in "A organização sindical dos trabalhadores textís," p. 4 annex; population recorded in demographic census material in Brazil, IBGE, *Anuário Estatístico do Brasil, 1963,* pp. 30-31.

TABLE 7
Holdings and Circulation of Workers'
Sindicato Libraries, 1953-1973

Year	Volumes held	Annual circulation
1953	116,600	53,900
1954	125,900	75,100
1955	131,500	112,400
1956	126,200	78,500
1957	139,500	85,100
1958	148,000	74,100
1959	149,600	90,900
1960	167,700	99,600
1961	131,200	65,400
1962	252,500	94,400
1963	238,600	83,000
1964	156,612	99,129
1965	121,400	88,300
1966	177,600	88,300
1967	180,943	90,978
1968	212,666	88,783
1969	198,005	82,915
1970	208,854	85,504
1971	208,491	91,884
1972	240,299	130,509
1973	242,136	116,293

Source: Brazil, IBGE, *Anuário Estatístico
do Brasil,* 1955 through 1975, *inquérito
sindical* data.

contracts, to collaborate with the state in the study and solution of problems related to the category, and to impose dues upon their members (art. 513). Although dues are nominal, many members fall into arrears. This limits somewhat the importance of dues, though they nevertheless provided about 40 percent of sindicato revenues between 1954 and 1964.

To gain Ministry recognition (arts. 515–521), the sindicato should include at least one-third of the workers in its territory, although the Ministry is empowered to waive this rule. In reality, many sindicatos do not come close to this figure, so the Ministry generally requires that they include 10 percent of the workers in their sector.[27] This has not changed since 1964; of the 35 sindicatos surveyed in greater São Paulo in 1972, for example, only 20 enrolled one-third of the workers in their categories.[28] Civil servants and employees of state

27. This base figure was customarily accepted and was formally established in a ministry regulation, Portaria 648 of August 10, 1964.
28. Kenneth Scott Mericle, "Conflict Regulation in the Brazilian Industrial Relations System" (doctoral dissertation, University of Wisconsin, 1974), p. 70.

companies do not have the right to form sindicatos, and rural workers gained the right to organize only after 1963.[29]

For sindicatos, the territory is usually a município; but in exceptional circumstances it may cover a subdivision of a município, two or more municípios, a state or several states, or the entire nation. Within their territorial base, unions may install branch offices to give better attention to their members. These offices generally distribute social services and hear members' grievances about their jobs and employers. Some sindicatos have factory delegates; their identity, however, is often kept secret so they can report to the sindicato on infractions of the labor law without fear of reprisals by their employers.[30] Since 1968, legally unrecognized and often rather informal "factory committees" have appeared in certain plants, particularly in the modern sector; Chapter Eight discusses them.

Data on the internal organization of sindicatos are very scarce, but the replies of the textile-workers' sindicatos in São Paulo again provide an indicator. Of 26 responding, only 7 had factory committees or local branch offices; most of these figured among the 9 which had factory delegates.[31] São Paulo has a higher degree of union activity than other states, so the national average should be appreciably lower. Indeed, of 178 responding delegates out of 197 at a national conference of metalworkers' union leaders, only 42 had union representation in the factory where they worked, and 25 of those came from São Paulo. Thus, 60 percent of the group which had factory representation came from São Paulo, although the Paulistas comprised only 41 percent of the delegates at the conference.[32]

Only in the large cities and in the most dynamic fields does one find branch offices. The shop steward, in the American sense, is almost never seen in Brazil, largely because the CLT does not endow the factory-delegate post with meaningful protection and power. The grassroots movement toward factory committees, however, has recently demanded legal recognition for plant-level posts like the shop steward's. Thus far at least, the major function of the few branch offices has been to dispense social services and assistance at more convenient locations, an activity which does little to strengthen the associational life of the workers through active participation in the organization of their class. Indeed, the workers remain mere recipients of services in much the same way that their rural counterparts receive "largesse" through the patron-client relationship.

For recognition, the Consolidation requires that an association of workers or employers present statutes providing for acceptable election procedures, administration of its property, and rules for its dissolution. If two associations in the same area apply for recognition, the Ministry is to select the most active. Criteria

29. Lei 4214 of March 2, 1963.
30. José Albertino Rodrigues, *Sindicato e desenvolvimento* (ch. 2 above, n. 49), p. 148.
31. "A organização sindical dos trabalhadores textís," pp. 7-8.
32. "Características sócio-econômicas dos delegados ao III Congresso Nacional dos Metalúrgicos," *Boletim do DIEESE,* II, no. 4 (August 1961), 3-4.

for determining the most active are the number of members, the social services offered, and the value of its property.

The Ministry's power of recognition and the legal tradition which supports it have created great difficulties for those who seek to organize the Brazilian working class against the desires of the government, because the law divides rather than unites workers' organizations. The organization chart of official labor bodies is a truncated pyramid, providing for separate confederations for the seven principal sectors of the economy while making no mention of a central labor organization which would preside over these seven and speak in the name of the entire working class. Therefore, the Confederação dos Trabalhadores do Brasil (CTB), founded by radical labor leaders in the immediate postwar period, the Comando Geral dos Trabalhadores (CGT), organized by left-wing militants in 1962, and other ad hoc bodies stirred much debate in political and legal circles, because they constituted steps toward the organizational unification of the Brazilian working class. Their supporters claimed that they were extralegal but not illegal. Although such status deprived them of the benefits which the CLT conferred upon the official bodies, it did not prevent them from functioning as voluntary civil associations.[33] Conservative spokesmen, on the other hand, argued that because the CLT made no provision for a central labor confederation, such ad hoc bodies were illegal and should be closed by the government.[34] In 1947, these groups prevailed and the government closed the CTB at the same time that it outlawed the Communist Party. After the coup of 1964, the government suppressed the CGT and affiliated state and local umbrella organizations.

In addition to the power of recognition, the Ministry also has the power to intervene directly in the internal affairs of a labor organization by appointing a delegate or junta to administer it. The right of intervention may occur only in the case of internal discord or other circumstances which prevent its normal operation, and the interventors may remain only as long as necessary to restore it to normal operation. In reality, it has not been difficult for the government to find a pretext to intervene in unions it considers troublesome, because internal squabbling and errors on the books — intentional or accidental — almost always exist. Political considerations have motivated most interventions, as in the purges of labor leadership in 1947 following the proscription of the Communist Party and in 1964 following the military coup. Next in importance as a cause for intervention is improper handling of union funds.[35] Table 8 presents intervention data.

The Ministry also exerts strong controls over the electoral process within the workers' organizations. Among the conditions necessary for voting rights are a minimum age of 18 years, participation in the same branch of the economy for

33. See Minister of Labor Almino Afonso's comment when he revoked the ministerial regulation which prohibited such central confederations, in *JB,* April 23, 1963, p. 9; April 4, p. 4; *OESP,* April 2, p. 8.
34. See *OESP,* April 18, 1963, p. 17, for an excellent example of this argument.
35. Russomano, *Comentários* (n. 22 above), II, p. 842.

two years and in the union for at least six months, and membership on the union's active list, which usually means being up-to-date in one's dues. Barred from election to administrative or representative posts within the sindicato are those guilty of embezzlement or activities injurious to union assets, those whose accounts of a previous administration were not approved in general assembly, and those with "duly proven bad conduct." Prior to 1952, a provision prohibited the candidacy of those who "professed ideologies incompatible with the institutions or interests of the Nations."[36]

In August 1946, workers' sindicatos' rules were brought into conformity with those of employers' and liberal professions' sindicatos by prohibiting the reelection of all but one-third of the members of their governing bodies. For the latter, immediate reelection was permitted only once.[37] Finally, the national legislature eliminated the reelection restriction in 1955.[38] Such a prohibition was designed to fulfill a nation-building function by enabling greater numbers to participate actively in social organizations while at the same time preventing control of the sindicatos by an oligarchy. It was circumvented in practice, however, because those ineligible on one governing body switched to another council within the sindicato and ran again. The same cliques, therefore, often controlled their sindicato for long periods, despite the formal prohibition. On the other hand, even occasional strict enforcement considerably increased ministerial advantage over the sindicatos by removing experienced and seasoned leaders.

These controls over the leadership of the labor organizations enabled the government to maintain relatively docile individuals at the helm of the most important federations and confederations until the late 1950's. These leaders, who were satisfied to enjoy the perquisites of their position without fighting aggressively for their class, were dubbed *pelegos*, after the sheepskin horseblanket which makes it easier for the horse to bear the burden of the rider. In this analogy, the horse represents the working class, and the rider the state and employers.

In keeping with the corporative ideal, a number of the CLT's provisions are designed to promote social cohesion by strengthening the sindicatos and encouraging unionization. Employers will be penalized if they create obstacles to unionization or to their employees' exercise of administrative posts within the sindicato (art. 543). Employers must also deduct union dues from wages if the union gives them a list of its members (art. 545), but most unions, fearing employer reprisals against their members, keep such lists secret. "Union members shall receive preference, other considerations being equal, in admission to the employ of enterprises operating public utilities or those which maintain contracts with government authorities" (art. 544). The symmetry of the corporative system is maintained by similar preferential treatment for firms belonging

36. Art. 530, a; revoked by Lei 1667 of September 1952.
37. Decreto-lei 9675 of Aug. 29, 1946.
38. Lei 2693 of Dec. 23, 1955.

TABLE 8

Ministerial Intervention in the Corporative System, 1938-1970

Year	Sindicatos			Federations		Confederations	
	Workers	Employers	Liberal professionals	Workers	Employers	Workers	Employers
1938	0	0	0	0	0		
1939	0	0	0	0	0		
1940	0	0	0	0	0		
1941	0	0	0	0	0		
1942	0	0	0	0	0		
1943	0	0	0	0	0		
1944	0	0	0	0	0		
1945	0	0	0	0	0		
1946	6	0	0	1	0	0	0
1947	144	0	0	1	0	0	0
1948	63	5	0	3	1	0	0
1949	2	0	0	0	0	0	0
1950	4	0	0	0	0	0	0
1951	1	1	0	0	0	0	0
1952	0	0	0	0	0	0	0
1953	3	0	0	1	0	0	0
1954	3	0	0	0	0	0	0
1955	2	2	0	1	0	0	0
1956	1	0	1	0	0	0	0
1957	12	1	0	0	1	0	0

TABLE 8 (Continued)

Year	Sindicatos			Federations		Confederations	
	Workers	Employers	Liberal professionals	Workers	Employers	Workers	Employers
1958	13	1	1	0	0	0	0
1959	2	0	0	0	0	0	0
1960	1	1	1	0	0	0	0
1961	—	—	—	—	—	—	—
1962	—	—	—	—	—	—	—
1963	—	—	—	—	—	—	—
1964	(409 sindicatos)		(80 sindicatos and federations)	(43 federations)		4	1
1965			(7 sindicatos and federations)			0	0
1966			(24 sindicatos and federations)			0	0
1967			(29 sindicatos and federations)			0	0
1968			(26 sindicatos and federations)			0	0
1969			(18 sindicatos and federations)			0	0
1970						0	0

Source: 1938-1960 compiled from the listing of the ministerial regulations (*portarias*) in Brazil, MTIC, *Boletim do Ministério do Trabalho, Indústria e Comércio*, Vols. 5 through 10 (1955-1960). The format of the *Boletim* changed after 1961 and the portarias were only selectively listed. Data for 1964 are from speech by Minister of Labor Arnaldo Lopes Sussekind, as reported by Joaquin F. Otero, representative in Brazil of International Transport Federation, in letter to Pieter de Vries, International Transport Federation General Secretary, July 31, 1964. The 1964 data on sindicatos and federations were not broken down further. Data for 1965-1970 are from Argelina Maria Cheibub Figueiredo, "Política Governamental e Funções Sindicais," (master's thesis, University of São Paulo, 1975), pp. 44-50; data for 1965 calculated by subtracting the above 1964 figures from Figueiredo's 1964-1965 total. Data on workers' confederations for 1964 are from United States Department of Labor, Bureau of Labor Statistics, *Labor Law and Practice in Brazil* (BLS Report no. 309; Washington, D.C.: GPO, 1967), pp. 76-77.

to employers' unions in bids for contracts from state offices or companies (art. 546). Union membership is necessary to obtain other sinecures and benefits, such as "the exercise of any representative function of an economic or occupational category on any official organ for collective deliberation as well as for the right to tax exemptions and reductions, except where non-economic activities are concerned" (art. 547).

The Estado Novo marked a rise in Brazilian nationalism, and this was reflected in the law which required that two-thirds of all workers in each firm be Brazilian, with exceptions to be approved by the President of the Republic (art. 354). To protect the corporative, nationalist system from foreign interference, the law prohibited affiliation with international labor organizations. However, after the overthrow of the Estado Novo, such affiliation was permitted with the permission of the Congress, and it was further facilitated in 1956 by a law requiring only the approval of the president.[39]

Conclusion

The corporative institutions which Vargas formalized during the Estado Novo have endured intact through three constitutional periods and four decades. The dynamics of populist politics, to be illustrated in the next four chapters, led Brazil's ruling politicians first to vacillate in their enforcement of the regulations described above and, by the early 1960's, to relax them considerably. The CLT nonetheless remained on the books and, after 1964, enabled the military-conservative coalition to impose its version of the public interest upon the working class.

These first chapters have shown that the organic view of society prevails in Brazil and has exerted a profound influence upon the institutional structure of the state and, most particularly, upon labor organization. Renewed emphasis on corporatism's control functions after 1964, reinforced by repression, suggests that this heritage will remain an important factor in Brazilian politics well into the future. With this description of the formal aspects of the Brazilian corporative system to set the context, the following sections of this book discuss and illustrate labor's political role in Brazil.

39. Decreto-lei 9502 of July 23, 1946, and Lei 2802 of June 18, 1956.

PART II

The Ministry of Labor
in the Corporative State

Chapter 4

THE MINISTRY OF LABOR
IN BRAZILIAN POLITICS

Precisely because it deals directly with social sectors seeking fuller participation in Brazil's social, economic, and political life, the Ministry of Labor is one of the institutions most illustrative of change in political style and content during periods of rapid modernization. Command of the Ministry carries considerable political power in Brazil, because it influences large numbers of people through the sindicato system and it controls vast patronage resources.

This chapter isolates the basic political styles which have characterized ministerial politics. First, it analyzes the politics and career patterns of the labor ministers from 1930 to 1976. Then, in order to evaluate the performance of the Ministry against the promises of official rhetoric, it scrutinizes the financial transactions of the Ministry as recorded in the national budgets and accounts. The following chapter will present a case study of the brief but illustrative six months during which Almino Afonso held the portfolio in 1963. That period offers insight into the links between patronage politics and the Ministry's role in political mobilization. It is especially significant because Almino attempted, against the wishes of President Goulart, to change the nature of the Brazilian political system.

The two major styles which this study illuminates are the classical populist, or paternalistic-administrative, and the radical populist. Populism, as the term is used in Latin America, refers to a type of nationalist political movement which appears when incipient industrialization brings on rapid social change. Populist movements espouse apparently anti-establishment policies and enjoy mass support among the lower classes, but they are organized and led by politicians from the ruling class. These movements occur when internal struggles within the ruling class lead at least one of the rival factions to bid for the support of the masses by promising them material benefits. In serving the class aims of their leaders, however, these movements channel the political participation of the urban masses and the peasantry into activities which do not challenge the existing social structure.

Both styles highlighted below are forms of populism, for both are efforts by one faction of the nation's ruling class to strengthen its political position by building working-class (and later, peasant) support.[1] In classical populism, politicians grant workers benefits such as legal recognition for labor organizations, minimum wage increases, and social legislation – but all the while they keep tight control so the workers themselves do not gain any real political power. This political style is deeply rooted in the paternalism of traditional Brazilian rural culture and in the practice of governmental predominance over political, social, and economic spheres.[2] João Café Filho, the vice-president who succeeded to the presidency on Vargas' death, illustrates this paternalism in his description of audiences with ordinary citizens:

> In a sense, the President and even the Vice-President of the Republic perform a paternal function in the feelings of the people; the President is the head of a great family to whose protection one may run. Whatever the President and Vice-President might do and say will be accompanied with gratitude and confidence.[3]

Radical populism arises when the political elites permit the lower classes a greater margin of maneuver. As E. E. Schattschneider observed of American politics, the outcome of any conflict can be altered if the antagonists extend participation to individuals or groups who were not originally parties to it. In a conflict with narrow scope, the loser will generally attempt to shift the balance of forces by broadening its scope to include new allies. He notes that electoral democracy is the greatest single instrument for the socialization of conflict.[4] The Constitution of 1946 instituted electoral democracy, albeit limited by literacy and other requirements, and thus permitted the extension of conflict.

This expansion of suffrage allowed a radical populist type of movement to begin to supplant the paternalistic-administrative one. Radical populist movements, because they seek a social base in the lower class and because their rhetoric emphasizes economic nationalism, state enterprise, and equitable distribution of goods and services, are sometimes confuséd with socialist ones. This is a fundamental misunderstanding for several reasons. Unlike socialist movements, populist ones fail to address themselves to two important aspects of production. In the first place, populist movements fail to confront squarely the

1. For a comparison of the characteristics of Latin American populism with those of European and U.S. populist movements, see Kenneth Paul Erickson, "Populism and Political Control of the Working Class in Brazil," *Proceedings of the Pacific Coast Council on Latin American Studies,* IV (1975), 119-125.

2. Raymundo Faoro, *Os donos do poder* (ch. 1 above, n. 10), p. 262.

3. João Café Filho, *Do sindicato ao Catete* (Rio de Janeiro: José Olympio, 1966), I, pp. 275-297; quote p. 282.

4. E. E. Schattschneider, *The Semi-Sovereign People* (New York: Holt, Rinehart and Winston, 1960), pp. 2-4, 16, 40.

issue of the social relations of production — particularly the role of the worker as producer. Because they lack a comprehensive worker-based ideology, they see workers merely as consumers and thus focus solely on distributing goods and services to them. Secondly, their exclusive focus on distribution leads them to neglect the saving and investment necessary to create the goods and services. Such fundamental economic shortsightedness ultimately causes the economic and, hence, the political collapse of populist movements which do attain power. Populist leaders can avoid such a collapse if they develop and implement an ideology which addresses these two questions.

In a perceptive discussion of populism, Brazilian economist Celso Furtado observes that the benefits conferred upon the lower classes by populist politicians at first tend to numb class consciousness, because the recipients have not actively sought them through their own autonomous organizations. Furtado adds that if labor or peasant leaders take advantage of the grants or benefits accorded them in this struggle among political elites — particularly benefits that increase their organizational resources or autonomy — they may be able to accumulate power which can then be used to pressure politicians for ever-increasing concessions. By obtaining measures which allow them to institutionalize autonomous organizations, the working class and the peasantry can establish an independent power base which would allow them to participate effectively in what Furtado hoped would be a pluralist democracy.[5] Schatt-schneider made a similar observation in his study of American democratic politics: "So great is the change in the nature of any conflict likely to be as a consequence of widening involvement of people in it that the original participants are apt to lose control of the conflict altogether."[6] Indeed, our study finds that control slipped from the hands of the political elites who had dominated the political system since 1930, as labor leaders and more radical politicians turned the populist game to their advantage. Conservative forces, frightened by this turn of events, therefore overthrew President Goulart and established an authoritarian regime in 1964.

This description of populism and its capacity to evolve away from elite domination provides a framework for analyzing the Ministry under the liberal democratic Constitution of 1946. It becomes apparent that the six months which Goulart spent in the Labor Ministery in 1953 and 1954 can be characterized as an early stage of radical populism when apparent concessions or benefits to the workers still served primarily to advance the careers of politicians in the established political elite. This generally held true through the transitional period of the fifties.

A participatory form of populism began to emerge, however, when a more

---

5. Celso Furtado, *Dialética do desenvolvimento* (Rio de Janeiro: Fundo de Cultura, 1964), pp. 83-85. Robert E. Ward made a similar observation when discussing the expansion of participation in Japan, in "Political Modernization and Political Culture in Japan," in Welch (ed.), *Political Modernization* (ch. 1 above, n. 2), pp. 101-102.

6. Schattschneider, p. 3.

able leadership replaced the old *pelegos* at the command of the most important labor organizations in the early 1960's. During the early stages of populism, the pelegos had been content to treat the benefits of populism as purely personal profit. They had not sought to convert them into autonomous power or real material benefits for their constituents. The new leaders, in contrast, consciously set out to use populist benefits, particularly those of an organizational nature, to increase their power within the political system as a whole. Their success marks the later stage of radical populism, which increasingly mobilized the working class and, in an incipient form, the peasantry.

As Furtado points out, however, the positive benefits of populism can be wiped out if the rising groups make a false move before they achieve effective power, based firmly upon autonomous organizations.[7] This caveat, written before Goulart's overthrow, was prophetic of the military intervention and the return to the administrative tradition.

By analyzing the Ministry in terms of the paternalistic-administrative versus radical populist dichotomy, its history may be divided into six periods summarized in Table 9. The first, a classical populist phase, runs from 1930 to 1953. Its general characteristics include ministerial paternalism through social welfare and strict government control of the sindicatos to prevent their political or economic autonomy.

TABLE 9

Predominant Patterns in the Relationship Between Political Elites and the Working Class, 1930-1977, as Derived from Labor Ministers' Policies and Career Patterns

Years	Pattern
1930-1953	Classical populist (paternalistic-administrative)
1953-1954	Radical populist
1954-1955	Classical populist (paternalistic-administrative)
1956-1962	Mixed, with paternalistic-administrative dominant
1962-1964	Radical populist
1964-1977	Paternalistic-administrative

The next period, a radical populist one, opens with Goulart's appointment to the Ministry in July 1953 and terminates with Vargas' suicide in August 1954. The third phase, that of the Café Filho and succeeding interim governments, is merely a restoration of the administrative tradition of the Estado Novo.

The fourth period, which runs from the Kubitschek presidency until 1962, constitutes a transition combining features of both of the preceding types. The Labor Ministry used its controls to maintain docile leaders at the highest posts in the sindicato framework, and labor did not yet possess an organizational base for

7. Furtado, p. 86.

pressuring the government to accord it more political importance. Vice-President Goulart, however, aimed his major appeals at the working class, and he increased labor's freedom at the lower levels.

This transition finally culminated in the fifth period, where the radical populist characteristics clearly predominate over the paternalistic-administrative ones. Dating from the general strikes of 1962, and particularly after Goulart gained full presidential power in the plebiscite of January 1963, the populism of this period allowed labor leaders considerably more participation in the political process.

After 1964, the economic planners who formulated policy in the Castello Branco administration perceived workers merely as factors in production. Ministerial policies, therefore, reverted to the paternalistic-administrative pattern, emphasizing governmental control and only secondarily focusing on the paternalistic aspects. In effect, populist politics have been dead in Brazil since 1964, because strict authoritarian controls have eliminated any need for the ruling faction to secure its position by making coalitions with the lower class. These controls have also prevented the opposition from organizing.

The Ministers and the Politics of the Ministry

To describe the evolution of ministerial politics from administrative paternalism to radical populism, this section examines the career patterns of the officially designated ministers of labor and of interim ministers who held the post for at least six months. Table 10 summarizes relevant data about them.

Although this chapter deals specifically with the ministers, we should bear in mind that it is the president who appoints them. Thus, when a new minister reflects a basic change in political style, primary responsibility is the president's. First, who were the labor ministers? Background data for the 33 labor ministers between 1930 and 1976 reveal a very high level of education, which suggests they came from middle- or upper-class families; at least 27 of them (educational data were unavailable for one) had a university education, and 3 more were trained in the military academy. Only 2 – a highly successful businessman, and an Army general who rose from the ranks – did not go beyond secondary school. Very few Brazilians – well under 2 percent – reached the university prior to 1960, and nearly all of those who did came from middle or upper socioeconomic strata.[8]

A significant contrast in age occurs between the radical populist ministers, who averaged 37 years on assuming the post, and those of other periods, who

8. The number of students enrolled in Brazilian higher education was exceedingly small during the period under study, and nearly all of these students came from upper- or middle-class families. Of the 18- to 21-year-old population in Brazil in 1930, 1940, 1950, and 1960, respectively, the percentage enrolled in higher education was: .63, .58, 1.07, and 1.74 percent. From Robert J. Havighurst and J. Roberto Moreira, *Society and Education in Brazil* (Pittsburgh, Pa.: University of Pittsburgh Press, 1965), p. 187.

TABLE 10

The Ministers of Labor, 1930-1977

Name	Dates in office	Months in office	State of birth	Date of birth	Age on taking office	Careers	School of highest education
1. Lindolfo Boekel Collor	11/26/30 to 4/4/32	17	Rio Grande do Sul	1891	40	Politician (fed. dep.) and journalist	Faculty of Social and Political Science, Rio de Janeiro
2. Joaquim Pedro Salgado Filho	4/6/32 to 7/23/34	27	Rio Grande do Sul	1888	43	Lawyer; politician (fed. dep.) civil servant; police chief; police commissioner	Faculty of Law, Rio de Janeiro
3. Agamemnon Sérgio de Godoy Magalhães	7/23/34 to 11/25/37	40	Pernambuco	1893	41	Lawyer; politician (state and fed. dep., state gov.); civil servant; public prosecutor; interventor	Faculty of Law, Recife
4. Waldemar Cromwell do Rêgo Falcão	11/25/37 to 6/13/41	43	Ceará	1895	42	Lawyer; politician (fed. dep. and sen.); civil servant; police commissioner	Faculty of Law, Ceará
5. Alexandre Marcondes Filho	11/29/41 to 10/29/45	46	São Paulo	1892	49	Lawyer; politician (fed. dep.); civil servant; journalist; public prosecutor	Faculty of Law, São Paulo
6. Roberto Carneiro de Mendonça	10/30/45 to 1/31/46	3	Federal District (Guanabara)	1894	51	Military officer; civil servant; inventor	Realengo Military Academy
7. Otacilio Negrão de Lima	1/31/46 to 10/16/46	8	Minas Gerais	1897	48	Engineer; civil servant; mayor; large landholder; journalist	Faculty of Engineering, Belo Horizonte

TABLE 10 (Continued)

	Name	Dates in office	Months in office	State of birth	Date of birth	Age on taking office	Careers	School of highest education
8.	Morvan Dias de Figueiredo	10/25/46 to 9/28/48	23	Pernambuco	1890	56	Businessman	Ginásio Mineiro (High School)
9.	Honório Fernandes Monteiro	10/20/48 to 6/29/50	20	São Paulo	1894	54	Lawyer; professor; director of law school	Faculty of Law, São Paulo
10.	Marcial Dias Pequeno	6/29/50 to 1/31/51	7	Ceará	1908	42	Journalist; civil servant	—(biodata suggest he had higher education)
11.	Danton Coelho	1/31/51 to 9/5/51	7	Rio Grande do Sul	1906	44	Lawyer; politician (fed. dep.); civil servant; police chief	Faculty of Law, Porto Alegre
12.	José de Segadas Viana	9/5/51 to 6/15/53	21	Federal District (Guanabara)	1906	45	Lawyer; civil servant; public prosecutor	Faculty of Law, Rio de Janeiro
13.	João Belchior Marques Goulart	6/15/53 to 2/22/54	8	Rio Grande do Sul	1918	35	Lawyer; politician (state and fed. dep.); cattle rancher	Faculty of Law, Porto Alegre
14.	Hugo de Araújo Faria	2/22/54 to 8/24/54	6	Federal District (Guanabara)	1915	38	Lawyer; civil servant	Faculty of Law, Bahia
15.	Napoleão de Alencastro Guimarães	8/24/54 to 11/11/55	15	Rio Grande do Sul	1899	55	Military officer; politician (alderman, fed. sen.); appointive public servant; journalist	Realengo Military Academy
16.	Nelson Backer Omegna	11/11/55 to 1/31/56	2	Rio de Janeiro	1903	52	Politician (alderman and fed. dep.); teacher; journalist	Faculties of Theology and Philosophy, São Paulo

TABLE 10 (Continued)

Name	Dates in office	Months in office	State of birth	Date of birth	Age on taking office	Careers	School of highest education
17. José Parsifal Barroso	1/31/56 to 6/30/58	29	Ceará	1913	42	Lawyer; politician (fed. dep. and sen.); teacher; civil servant; journalist	Faculty of Philosophy, Ceara
18. Fernando Carneiro da Cunha Nóbrega	7/16/58 to 4/17/60	21	Paraíba	1904	53	Lawyer; politician (state and fed. dep.); civil servant	Faculty of Law, Recife
19. João Batista Ramos	4/17/60 to 11/7/60	7	São Paulo	—	—	Politician (fed. dep.); physician; civil servant	Faculty of Medicine, Rio de Janeiro
20. Alírio de Sales Coelho	11/7/60 to 1/31/61	2	Minas Gerais	1904	56	Lawyer; civil servant	Faculty of Law, Minas Gerais
21. Francisco Carlos de Castro Neves	1/31/61 to 8/28/61	7	São Paulo	1914	46	Lawyer; politician (state dep.); journalist	Faculty of Law, São Paulo
22. André Franco Montoro	9/8/61 to 7/12/62	10	São Paulo	1914	47	Lawyer; politician (alderman, state and fed. dep.)	Faculty of Law, São Paulo
23. Hermes Lima	7/12/62 to 9/14/62	2	Bahia	1902	59	Lawyer; politician (fed. dep.); professor	Free Faculty of Law, Salvador (Bahia)
24. João Pinheiro Neto	9/17/62 to 12/4/62	3	Minas Gerais	1928	33	Lawyer; civil servant; journalist	Faculty of Law, Minas Gerais
25. Benjamín Eurico Cruz	12/4/62 to 1/23/63	1	Federal District (Guanabara)	1915	47	Lawyer; civil servant	National Law Faculty

TABLE 10 (Continued)

	Name	Dates in office	Months in office	State of birth	Date of birth	Age on taking office	Careers	School of Highest education
26.	Almino Monteiro Álvares Afonso	1/23/63 to 6/17/63	6	Amazonas	1929	33	Lawyer; politician (fed. dep.)	Faculty of Law, São Paulo
27.	Amaury de Oliveira e Silva	6/17/63 to 4/4/64	10	Paraná	1925	38	Lawyer; politician (alderman, state dep., fed. sen.); civil servant	Faculty of Law, Curitiba
28.	Arnaldo Lopes Sussekind	4/4/64 to 12/3/65	20	Federal District (Guanabara)	1917	46	Lawyer; civil servant	National Law Faculty
29.	Walter Peracchi Barcellos	12/3/65 to 7/15/66	7	Rio Grande do Sul	1907	58	Military officer; politician (state and fed. dep.)	(Rose through ranks in Army)
30.	Luiz Gonzaga do Nascimento e Silva	7/28/66 to 3/15/67	8	Minas Gerais	1915	51	Lawyer; civil servant; professor	National Law Faculty
31.	Jarbas Gonçalves Passarinho	3/15/67 to 10/30/69	31	Acre	1920	47	Military officer; politician (fed. sen.); governor	Realengo Military Academy

TABLE 10 (Continued)

Name	Dates in office	Months in office	State of birth	Date of birth	Age on taking office	Careers	School of highest education
32. Júlio Carvalho Barata	10/30/69 to 3/15/74	53	Amazonas	1905	64	Lawyer; Superior Labor Court judge; professor	Faculty of Law, Rio de Janeiro; Doctorate in Classics and Philosophy from University of Guanabara; Superior War College
33. Arnaldo da Costa Prieto	3/15/74 to 2/77	*	Rio Grande do Sul	1930	44	Politician (alderman, fed. dep., state labor and housing secretary)	Engineering School of Federal University, Rio Grande do Sul; post-grad. in Economics Faculty, same

Sources: This table was assembled from data from the files of the official government news agency (Agência Nacional) and from the following sources: Brazil, MTIC, *Documentário fóto-biográfico dos ex-ministros que ocuparam a pasta do Trabalho, Indústria e Comércio* (Rio de Janeiro: MTIC, 1955); British Chamber of Commerce of São Paulo and Southern Brazil, *Personalidades no Brasil–Men of Affairs in Brazil* (São Paulo: 1933); Antônio Maria Cardozo Cortes, *Homens e Instituições no Rio* (Rio de Janeiro: IBGE, 1957); Luiz Correia de Melo, *Dicionário de autores paulistas* (São Paulo: Irmãos Andrioli, 1954); *Quem é quem no Brasil: biografias contemporâneas* (São Paulo: Sociedade Brasileira de Expansão Comercial, 1948); Trajano Pires da Nóbrega, *A família Nóbrega* (São Paulo: Instituto Genealógico Brasileiro, 1956).

*Costa Prieto was still labor minister when this book went to press.

averaged 49 years. This distinction suggests that the younger ministers, less socialized by time and experience into acceptance of the status quo and less firmly integrated into the power bases of the establishment than older men, were more disposed to offer concessions to the lower class.

The Ministry's essential function during the paternalistic-administrative periods, of course, was *to control* the working class. The career patterns of the 12 ministers prior to the first break with the paternalistic-administrative pattern graphically illustrate this point, for 7 of them had previously served in one or more of the following capacities: police chief, police commissioner, public prosecutor, or *interventor* (chief executive of states appointed by President Vargas during the authoritarian period, 1930–1945). These 7 men occupied the Ministry for 187 of the 262 months between 1930 and 1953.

Examining the political generations that have occupied the Ministry of Labor, we note the striking fact that the same generation held the Ministry for its first twenty years of operation. All 10 ministers between 1930 and 1950 were born between 1888 and 1897. They took over the Ministry in their early forties and relinquished it in their fifties. This continuity from the Estado Novo right through the Dutra administration is significant, for it provides additional evidence in support of the argument in Chapter Three — i.e., that the end of the Estado Novo and the establishment of a liberal democratic constitution did not alter the functioning of the corporative framework in any meaningful way. In fact, Dutra's ministers intensified ministerial control, intervening in many sindicatos, as Table 8 shows, and they prohibited sindicato elections during his presidency.

The shift to radical populism occurred midway through Vargas' constitutional presidency. Getúlio's rhetoric to labor had radical populist overtones as early as the campaign of 1950. By his own admission, he promised more than he knew how to fulfill while on the hustings.[9] Biographical and budgetary data, however, show that in terms of actual performance, the practice of the Labor Ministry did not diverge radically from the Estado Novo norms of administrative paternalism until 1953. Although Vargas' two ministers in 1951-52 were a decade younger than their predecessors, both had pursued careers within the control apparatus of the Estado Novo. Danton Coelho served in several capacities, including chief of police for the state of São Paulo, and Segadas Viana was a Labor Ministry official who had co-authored the Consolidation of Labor Laws. Thus, they did not represent a break from the pattern.

The first interruption of the paternalistic-administrative tradition occurred in 1953, when Vargas appointed 35-year-old João Goulart to the Ministry. Goulart's radical populist style became apparent when he aided a maritime strike opposed by Minister Segadas Viana in June 1953.[10] This occurred at a time when he was residing in the presidential palace,[11] making clear Getúlio's

9. Café Filho, *Do sindicato,* I, p. 194.
10. *DC,* June 14, 1953, p. 12; *CM,* June 16, p. 1.
11. *CM,* June 16, 1953, p. 1.

position in the clash. Segadas, therefore, submitted his resignation, and the president appointed Goulart.[12]

Why did Vargas change his political style? The increasingly serious economic difficulties of the early fifties rendered it impossible for the government to sustain its paternalistic operations; as Table 13 reveals, there was an extremely sharp drop in the governmental contribution to the social security and assistance programs beginning in 1953. This cutback coincides with the sudden decline in the annual increase of real aggregate economic output to 3.2 percent, fully 3 percent below the annual average over the preceding five years.[13] Thus, Vargas evidently decided to shift his appeal for working-class support from the services of administrative paternalism to the demagogy of radical populism. This proved economically beneficial to the government, because by raising the minimum wage and permitting or encouraging strikes, Goulart helped Vargas shift the financial burden to the private sector.

Goulart applied his control of the Ministry to the task of strengthening his own political base. He courted sympathy by decrying financial mismanagement in the Ministry and by urging workers to report violations of the labor law to the Ministry so administrative or judicial action could be taken.[14] He intervened in the Federation of Maritime Workers to replace the unpopular president who had opposed the strike and who was considered a corrupt pelego,[15] and he shrewdly used his patronage power to multiply his supporters. For example, he changed the composition of the local minimum-wage commissions so they would dutifully approve the 100-percent minimum-wage increase of 1954 in their districts.[16]

The proposal to double the minimum wage gained many supporters among the masses, but the opposition which it aroused in the military brought Goulart's ouster in February 1954. The nation's financial problems had put the squeeze on the military budget as well, and a group of colonels sent a memorandum to the minister of war to protest the deterioration of military installations and declining remuneration of the officer corps relative to comparable civilian posts. They denounced Goulart's intention to double the minimum wage, claiming that in the big cities it would approach that of warrant officers and senior noncommissioned officers.[17]

12. The differences between the styles of the two were highlighted by their speeches at Goulart's inauguration; the texts are given in Brazil, MTIC, *Boletim do Ministério do Trabalho, Indústria e Comércio,* new series, III (July-September 1953), 23-28.

13. Data from Getúlio Vargas Foundation in Nathaniel H. Leff, *Economic Policy-Making* (ch. 1 above, n. 11), p. 89.

14. *DC,* July 5, 1953, p. 1; Oct. 13, pp. 2 and 12.

15. *CM,* June 23, 1953, p. 12; *DC,* July 19, p. 4; Aug. 20, pp. 1 and 2; Aug. 21, p. 12.

16. Confidential interview. Ministerial regulations (*portarias*) show that Goulart changed the composition of 21 of the 22 Minimum Wage Commissions in Brazil during his six-month ministry. *Boletim do MTIC,* new series, III (July-September 1953), 91-92; III (October-December 1953), 201-202; and IV (January-March 1954), 231-232.

17. Text of memorandum in Oliveiros S. Ferreira, *As fôrças armadas e o desafio da revolução* (Rio de Janeiro: Edições GRD, 1964), pp. 122-129. The colonels' calculation of military pay does not take into account the many fringe benefits which officers receive.

The radical populist policies did not terminate with Goulart's ouster, for Vargas chose to continue them. Hugo de Araújo Faria, head of Goulart's ministerial cabinet and also in his thirties, was appointed to the post, where he remained until Vargas' suicide in August. Faria, a close aide of Goulart's, perpetuated his predecessor's influence in the Ministry, keeping Goulart's chief labor adviser, Gilberto Crockatt de Sá, as head of the National Labor Department. And although the colonels obtained Goulart's removal, they failed to stave off the minimum wage hike, for Vargas decreed it on Labor Day, May 1.[18]

With the Café Filho interregnum, the generation of the Estado Novo returned to the Ministry. Café unsuccessfully tried to enlist Estado Novo Labor Minister Alexandre Marcondes Filho for the post, then settled on Vargas' friend Napoleão de Alencastro Guimarães.[19] A retired Army officer, Guimarães was well trained and socialized for emphasizing the control aspects of the administrative tradition. His official biographical sketch in the Ministry notes that he concentrated primarily on promoting and furthering the interests of commerce and industry.[20] He maintained tight control over the sindicatos and withheld paternalistic benefits. Table 13 shows that during 1955 the government did not even release one-quarter of the funds allocated for social welfare.

Succeeding this brief return to the administrative practices of the Estado Novo, a transition period from 1956 to 1962 includes elements from both classical and radical populist patterns. In preparing the alliance which won the 1955 elections, Kubitschek's PSD conceded the office of labor minister to the PTB, the party of vice-presidential candidate Goulart. During this period, therefore, Goulart renewed his influence within the Ministry, laying the foundations for the radical populist period which would follow.

Tension between classical populism's control function and radical populism's tendency to expand conflict characterized the Kubitschek period. Juscelino's first two ministers enforced the rules outlined in Chapter Three in order to limit political participation by the working class. José Parsifal Barroso vowed to take any measure necessary to prevent extremists from gaining control of the sindicatos, including the nullification of elections won by Communists.[21] After Barroso left the post to seek the governorship of Ceará, Fernando Nóbrega followed similar policies. Kubitschek had placed Nóbrega in the Ministry at Jango's behest, but by the end of 1959 many PTB officials were seeking his ouster, because they felt he had allowed himself to be used by Kubitschek to repress working-class demands.[22] Immediately before his removal from the post in April, he issued a decree which prolonged the mandates of the directorates of

18. Vargas' defense of the hike is presented in Afonso César, *Política, cifrão e sangue* (Rio de Janeiro: Andes, 1955), p. 159.

19. Café Filho, *Do sindicato*, II, pp. 370-371.

20. Brazil, MTIC, Serviço de Documentação, *Documentário fóto-biográfico dos ex-ministros que ocuparam a pasta do Trabalho, Indústria e Comércio (Edição comemorativa do XXV aniversário do MTIC)* (Rio de Janeiro, 1955).

21. *CM,* Feb. 3, 1956.

22. *OESP,* Dec. 29, 1959, p. 3; Jan. 5, 1960, p. 4.

all labor organizations until early 1962. This clearly constituted an attempt to slow the advancing autonomy which Goulart's support for radical populism was affording labor.[23]

Nóbrega's successor, João Batista Ramos, favored the radical populist tendency and revoked the ministerial decree. Radical and classical populist tendencies eventually came into open conflict when Kubitschek tried to repress a rail and maritime strike in November 1960. Batista Ramos opposed this measure, attacked the president, and resigned.[24] Juscelino then demonstrated his firm adherence to the administrative tradition by replacing Batista Ramos with Alírio de Sales Coelho, a Labor Ministry career official for over two decades. Sales Coelho attempted to crush the strike, but to no avail, as we will see in Chapter Six.

The most important single event of these transitional years, for our study of Ministry politics and for the political power of labor leaders, was Congressional passage of the 1960 social security law.[25] This law assured labor leaders one-third of the seats on the governing councils of all social security agencies, thus providing them with a major lever to increase their political influence. Chairmanship of the councils now rotated among the three participant groups: labor, government, and employers. Prior to 1960, labor had no delegate on the executive bodies, and the chairman had always been a Ministry official or an appointed expert in social legislation.

This new law, therefore, gave labor leaders a firm foothold in patronage, a major currency in Brazilian politics. The social security agencies employed nearly 100,000 of Brazil's 700,000 federal civil servants and disposed of a budget larger than that of any state except São Paulo.[26] The autonomy of these councils offered protection against control from above, and their political use of the power of appointment, even in defiance of the president and labor minister, has been documented in a case study of patronage.[27]

From Goulart's occupancy of the Ministry in the fifties through the transitional phase, there had been little danger that ultimate control of the labor movement would slip from the hands of the political establishment. The passage

23. *CM,* April 21, 1960, p. 7; the decree is Portaria 55, annulled by Portaria 67, published in Brazil, *Diário Oficial,* April 13 and May 7, 1960, respectively.

24. *JB,* Nov. 8, 1960, p. 7; Nov. 12, p. 3; *OESP,* Nov. 8, p. 56; Nov. 10, p. 60.

25. Lei No. 3807 of Aug. 27, 1960, regulated by Decreto 48,959-A of Sept. 19, 1960. Subsequent modifications, particularly those after 1964, are complied in Ronaldo Waldemiro Groehs, *A lei orgânica da previdência social,* 4th ed. rev. (Porto Alegre: Sulina, 1967).

26. Brazil, DASP and IBGE, Serviço Nacional de Recensamento, *Censo dos Servidores Públicos Civis Federais, 31 de maio de 1966, resultados preliminares* (Rio de Janeiro: IBGE, mimeo.), p. 2. These results are from a census of civil service employees rather than civil service records, and they reveal that many more jobs existed in the civil service than had been recorded. Compare with the total of 346,548 recorded on DASP records for 1962, in Brazil, IBGE, *Anuário Estatístico do Brasil, 1965,* pp. 462, 470.

27. Carlos Veríssimo do Amaral, "As controvertidas nomeações para a Previdência Social em 1963: estudo de um caso," in Carlos Veríssimo do Amaral and Kleber Tatinge do Nascimento (eds.), *Política e Administração de Pessoal* (Rio de Janeiro: Fundação Getúlio Vargas, 1966), pp. 24-33.

of the social security law, however, increased its likelihood. Although the government still possessed certain controls, labor leaders began to demonstrate their autonomy vis-à-vis establishment politicians like João Goulart, now president. Chapters Six and Seven will show that top labor leaders ignored Goulart's personal plea to cancel a major general strike in July 1962, that they forced policy concessions from him in another general strike two months later, and that they consistently planned demonstrations and strikes between 1962 and 1964 with an eye toward increasing their leverage within the political system. In 1963, Labor Minister Almino Afonso sought to further increase that autonomy against the wishes of the chief executive.

During the transitional period, populist politicians passed laws or interpreted rules so that labor leaders could free themselves from some of the government controls. In the matter of internal autonomy for labor organizations, the sindicatos gained increasing freedom in choosing their officers, particularly after Congress eliminated the loyalty oath in 1952. The Ministry sought to keep tighter rein on the federations and confederations, but by the early sixties they too began to elect militant directorates which challenged the government position on important issues. Goulart took advantage of this trend to strengthen his support in labor. In one of the clearest examples of this, he used the presidential office to assist the nationalist left to win control of the powerful National Confederation of Industrial Workers (CNTI) in 1961.

Only after the enactment of the social security law of 1960 did union leaders significantly increase their political power. Once they combined control over the sindicatos with political power rooted in patronage, they had set the stage for a significant challenge to the restrictive corporative controls. Goulart assisted them by shifting to a radical populist political style in late 1962. The first months of his presidency had hardly distinguished him from his predecessors. A serious economic slowdown, in which real economic output for 1963 grew by only 1.6 percent, as opposed to an annual average of 6.7 percent over the preceding five-year period, began exacerbating divisions within the ruling class. The president thus sought to strengthen his position by appealing to the workers. The successful general strikes of 1962 (covered in Chapter Six) convinced him that both labor and military forces supported him, so he prepared the transition to the new radical populist period. Hermes Lima, the last minister of the transitional phase, was a Socialist of long standing who promised organized labor greater participation in policy making. When he became prime minister in September 1962, a new generation of labor ministers succeeded him. The three officially designated ministers prior to the coup were all in their thirties, with two of them only 33 on inauguration.

From mid-1962 until Goulart's overthrow in 1964, and particularly during the ministry of Almino Afonso, this populist period witnessed rapidly increasing participation by the labor left in the national debate over basic reform of Brazil's political, social, and economic structures. Political demands accompanied the strikes analyzed in Chapter Six, as left-wing nationalists with a firm base in labor attempted to split the armed forces in order to bring military support to the drive for reform.

The final period is one of restoration. As was argued in Chapter Three, political leaders since 1964 have been attempting to perfect the control apparatus of the Estado Novo. The ministers are again in their forties, fifties, or sixties; and Arnaldo Lopes Sussekind, whom Castello Branco selected to manage the brusque return to the administrative tradition, had co-authored the Consolidation of Labor Laws and had been an aide in the Labor Ministry cabinet during the Estado Novo. Júlio Barata, the oldest and the one with the longest tenure ever in the Labor Ministry (over four years), had spent most of his career applying the provisions of the CLT as judge and, ultimately, president of the Supreme Labor Court. Two of the others were well prepared to demand discipline and respect, since they had been professional army officers.

Let us close this section by describing the training and career patterns of the labor ministers. Given the desire of Brazilian governments to use the complex labor law to their advantage, we might expect a high proportion of lawyers among the ministers. Indeed, 22 of the 33 had legal training, and lawyers held the post for 390 months of the total of 556 months from November 1930 through February 1977. Lawyers appear far more prevalent among appointive labor ministers than among elected representatives, though data on the latter are scarce. For example, a survey of 52 of the 55 deputies in the Guanabara assembly counted only 8 lawyers as against 9 physicians.[28] Ministers with military training number 4 among the 33. Also included are 2 men with social science or liberal arts training, a doctor, an engineer, and 2 for whom the biodata reported no higher education. The two most recent ministers, a lawyer and an engineer, also held graduate degrees in social science or liberal arts. Table 11 summarizes the occupations of the men, listing, where possible, a first, second, and third activity in order of importance. The most important occupation of 17 of the 33 ministers was in professional politics, while this appeared second for another 3; these 20 held the post for a total of 359 months.

Although the 4 Army officers totaled 54 months in the Ministry, they served only during periods of military intervention — i.e., in the interregna after both removals of Vargas and again after 1964. These military men had not been alien to politics, however, for Alencastro Guimarães and Peracchi Barcellos enjoyed elective careers after retiring from the military, and Jarbas Passarinho was elected senator several months prior to his appointment to the Ministry. Carneiro de Mendonça had governed two states as interventor in the thirties. Civil service employment provided the primary occupation for 9 ministers, including the engineer, and it was the second occupation for 9 more and third for another 3. The fact that lawyers and politicians in Brazil dabble in journalism

28 Nilda Águeda Martínez Pita and José Maria de Arruda, "Composição sociológica da Assembléia Legislativa do Estado da Guanabara," *Revista de Direito Público e Ciência Política,* IX (July 1966), 128.

TABLE 11
Career Patterns of the Labor Ministers

Career	Most important	Second in importance	Third in importance
Professional politician (elective)	17	3	–
Public functionary	9	9	3
Military officer	4	–	–
Journalist	1	4	2
Professor, teacher	1	5	–
Businessman	1	–	–
Landowner, rancher	–	1	1
Engineer	–	1	–
Physician	–	1	–

and teaching is witnessed in the incidence of these vocations in the second and third columns.

Ministry Finances and Ministry Performance

Analysis of the Ministry budgets and the national accounts helps cut through official rhetoric to lay bare governmental practices and performance. The budget (*orçamento*) is the financial expression of the government program and is voted in December for the coming fiscal year, which coincides with the calendar year in Brazil.

The national acc unts (*balanços*), on the other hand, are the balance sheets of receipts and expenditures drawn up after the year's books are closed. By comparing the two in Table 12, we may see whether the government made good on the policy and programmatic promises of the budget. The table immediately reveals that the Labor Ministry consistently received less than the proportion which the budget allocated for it. Only once (1944) did it receive as much as budgeted.

The budget also helps us assess the political importance which the national executive attributed to the working class. A high labor budget suggests that the president and his staff ascribed considerable importance to the working class. Analysis of the budgets of the Vargas years from 1930 to 1938 shows that proposed expenditures did not match the symbolic and institutional commitment to labor embodied in the creation of the Ministry in 1930. Its allocations average 1 percent of the total government budget prior to 1937, when they rise to about 1.8 percent. The jump to 3.9 percent in 1940 and the 3.8 percent average from then until the overthrow of the Estado Novo therefore reflect Vargas' increasing awareness of the political importance of the working class.

Comparing these figures with the actual expenditures recorded in the national accounts, we see a lag of several years before the changed perception embodied in the 1939 budget actually effected a change in performance. Expenditures did not surpass 1 percent of total government outlays until 1941, with the exception of 1.5 percent in 1939. In 1942, however, expenditures actually shot over 3 percent, falling back to 1.5 percent in 1943 and then rising to their alltime high of 5 percent in 1944. The average for the last four years of the Estado Novo was 3.2 percent. This run of figures through the Estado Novo supports Hélio Jaguaribe's hypothesis on the shift Vargas made in the social composition of his base of support.

In Jaguaribe's analysis, the growing pre-industrial, "cartorial" middle sectors in the cities sparked and sustained the Revolution of 1930. These urban sectors made their livelihood in positions of low social utility in the state bureaucracy, and they opposed the depression-induced austerities which were reducing public employment. In 1930, therefore, they captured control of the state from the rural oligarchy in order to protect their jobs and income.

Jaguaribe claims that when Vargas established the Estado Novo in 1937, he acted at the urging of members of this middle class who feared they would lose control of the governmental apparatus to the rural oligarchy in the approaching elections. The landowners dominated the vast rural population, which could have swamped the relatively small urban vote. Vargas subsequently perceived the impossibility of supporting a state solely on the basis of unproductive civil service posts, so he began to shift his major base of support away from the pre-industrial middle class and toward the industrial bourgeoisie and the urban working class. He saw he could secure the backing of both of these through a policy of industrialization, and Jaguaribe claims Vargas definitively committed himself to this policy in 1943.[29]

Table 12 provides evidence that Vargas perceived the working class as an effective potential counterbalance to the old middle class by 1939, for in that year he increased the Ministry budget and expenditures considerably. A two-year slump follows the increase in actual expenditures in 1939, supporting the contention that Vargas' commitment to labor was only partial until 1942. Table 13 shows that in that year the government parted ways with past practice by paying almost all of its mandated contributions to the social security and welfare systems. This table reveals the percentage of the Ministry's budgetary allocations for transfers and services which the Treasury actually disbursed. Because nearly all of the transfer funds went to the social security and welfare programs, their disposition is an indicator of government commitment to the welfare of the working class and the poor. These transfers comprise the major

29. Hélio Jaguaribe, "The Dynamics of Brazilian Nationalism," in Veliz (ed.), *Obstacles to Change* (ch. 1 above, no. 21), pp. 170-171; and his "Political Strategies of National Development in Brazil," in Irving Louis Horowitz, Josué de Castro, and John Gerassi (eds.), *Latin American Radicalism* (New York: Random House, 1969), pp. 401-402.

TABLE 12

Ministry of Labor Budgets and Annual Expenditures, as a
Percentage of Total National Budget and Expenditures, 1934-1968

Year	Budget allocation (orçamento)	Period average: budget	Actual expenditures (balanço)	Period average: expenditures
1934	1.1%		1.0%	
1935	0.7	1934-39:	0.5	
1936	0.7	1.2%	0.4	
1937	1.7		0.9	
1938	1.8		1.0	1934-41: 0.9%
1939	2.8		1.5	
1940	3.9		0.9	
1941	3.7	1939-45: 3.8%	1.0	
1942	3.8		3.2	
1943	3.6		1.5	1942-45:
1944	4.8		5.0	3.2%
1945	3.9		3.2	
1946	3.8		1.4	
1947	3.2	1946-50:	1.8	1946-50:
1948	3.1	3.4%	2.3	2.1%
1949	3.8		3.2	
1950	3.4		2.1	
1951	3.2		2.4	1951-54: 1.9%
1952	2.6	1951-54:	2.3	
1953	3.1	2.9%	1.5	1951-52: 2.4%
1954	2.6		1.4	1953-54: 1.4%
1955	3.7		1.4	
1956	3.2		0.7	
1957	2.2	1956-60:	1.0	1956-60:
1958	1.9	2.3%	1.4	1.2%
1959	2.0		1.5	
1960	2.4		1.2	
1961	3.6	1961-64:	2.6	
1962	6.2	4.3%	2.0	
1963	3.6		—	
1964	3.8		1.8	

TABLE 12 (Continued)

Year	Budget allocation (orçamento)	Period average: budget	Actual expenditures (balanço)	Period average: expenditures
1965	2.3	1965-68:	0.4	
1966	1.3	1.4%	—	
1967	1.1		—	
1968	1.0		—	

Sources: The budget figures were taken from the budget law (*orçamento*) passed by Congress or decreed by the president, as transcribed in the *Diário Oficial* at the time of passage. The expenditures are found in the national accounts (*Balanços Gerais da União*), which are drawn up by the Contadoria Geral da República in the Ministry of Finance several years after the close of each fiscal year. Only sums which were actually *paid* in each year were considered expenditures, because most transfers encumbered but not liquidated by the end of the fiscal year were never paid. Period averages were computed from annual averages before the latter were rounded to one decimal place, which accounts for some apparent minor discrepancies.

part of the Ministry budget, and, when total Ministry expenditures appear low, it usually means the government withheld a large portion of the transfers.[30]

During the last four years of the Estado Novo, the government actually released 65.5 percent of the transfers, the highest average of any government before or since. This attempt to win the support of the working class through efficient service from the administrative state coincides with Getúlio's effort to win electoral support by integrating the working class into the Brazilian Labor Party (PTB), a creation of his Labor Ministry officials. They founded the party in anticipation of the return to electoral democracy which would surely follow the end of the war. Although Vargas focused primary attention on industrialists and labor in this period, he was a shrewd politician and did not turn his back on the cartorial middle class; he created a party for the beneficiaries of civil service jobs as well, the Social Democratic Party (PSD), and for many years it was the largest of Brazil's many parties.

In the Dutra presidency, budgetary promises to the working class remained at the same high level as Vargas' from 1939, but performance fell off sharply. The annual average expenditure for the Ministry was held to 2.1 percent.

When Vargas returned as constitutional president, his budgetary allocations were somewhat lower than in the early forties while actual expenditures were much lower, averaging 2.4 percent for his first two years and 1.4 percent for 1953 and 1954. The drop in the second half of his presidency, a period of severe economic difficulties for the nation, is all the more striking when one juxtaposes it with the radical promises to workers during that period.

Vargas responded to the mounting economic problems, which included spiral-

30. The "serviços e encargos" allocation includes social security institutes, the Brazilian Social Assistance League, the Fundação da Casa Popular, and the Fundo Social Sindical.

ing inflation and a foreign exchange crisis, by cutting back on the government's administrative paternalism. Table 13 shows that during his first two years as elected president, the Ministry released the very high average of 78.7 percent of the transfer allocations, demonstrating that he was again relying on the paternalistic element in the administrative tradition. However, transfers to social welfare drop to less than half that figure in the last two years of his presidency. This is evidence that the currency exchanged for labor support in Getúlio's last two years did not come from the national treasury. Rather, a new toleration of strikes and the minimum-wage decree of 1954 shifted the costs to the private sector, while the government provided workers with the symbolic benefits of populist rhetoric.

Financially conservative caretaker governments followed Vargas' overthrow, and expenditures on the Ministry of Labor in late 1954 and 1955 fell to the lowest level since 1941. Moreover, the Ministry released less than a quarter of the transfers for social welfare. Despite the high Ministry budget allocation that year, therefore, labor and the poor bore the brunt of Finance Minister Eugênio Gudin's inflation control program.

More striking is the decline in both budgets and expenditures during the economically expansive Kubitschek years. The five-year average budget of 2.3 percent and average expenditure of 1.2 percent were the lowest since the thirties. These figures suggest that Kubitschek willingly sacrificed administrative attention to labor in favor of his economic development program. His Labor Day speeches not only highlighted the benefits which labor would derive from economic expansion, but they also made the unfulfilled promise to maintain welfare and social security services.[31] Table 13 reveals that, on the contrary, his government released less than half of the allocations for these programs.

Developmentalism's success in slowly lifting the real wage curve (Tables 16 and 24) distracted attention from the fact that the working class was being shortchanged in an administrative sense. These reductions suggest that Kubitschek attributed far less importance to labor than did his predecessors. The figures also indicate that labor leaders did not have the power and channels of access to impose changes in the budget until after the social security law passed in 1960. Immediately afterward, in 1961 and 1962, the Ministry's proportion of the national budget rose sharply, and graphic evidence of the leverage obtained by labor leaders appears in the successful attempt by Dante Pelacani, an officer in the CNTI and CGT and director-general of the Social Security Department of the Ministry, to augment the allocation for his department in the congressional budgetary hearings in late 1963. He sought and obtained a threefold increase, raising his budget from 20 to 61 billion cruzeiros for the following fiscal year.[32]

31. Juscelino Kubitschek de Oliveira, *Discursos proferidos no primeiro ano do mandato presidencial, 1956* (Rio de Janeiro: Departamento de Imprensa Nacional), pp. 94-95; *Discursos proferidos no terceiro ano do mandato presidencial, 1958*, pp. 209-210.
32. *JC,* Dec. 23, 1963, p. 8.

TABLE 13

Percentage of Budget Allocation Earmarked for
Social Security and Social Assistance Which
Was Actually Released for Use,
1937-1964

Year	Transfers released	Average release by period
1937	27.2%	
1938	32.7	1937-41:
1939	67.9	26.4%
1940	6.7	
1941	6.5	
1942	98.0	
1943	6.9	1942-45:
1944	74.4	65.5%
1945	82.6	
1946	29.2	
1947	47.0	1946-50:
1948	63.8	55.2%
1949	83.4	
1950	52.7	
1951	74.1	1951-54: 57.7%
1952	83.2	
1953	33.4	1951-52: 78.7%
1954	40.0	1953-54: 36.6%
1955	24.0	
1956	24.0	
1957	10.2	
1958	63.2	1956-60:
1959	82.7	45.1%
1960	45.4	
1961	92.3	
1962	31.5	1962-63:
1963	62.0	46.7%
1964	43.3	

Source: Brazil, Contadoria Geral da República, *Balanços Gerais da União*, 1937-1964.

In a more general way, the increase in the Ministry budget in 1961, followed by
the very sharp rise in 1962, also reflected this power.

   Although Goulart's 1962 budget is higher than Jânio Quadros', actual performance turned out better under Jânio. This in part reflects a difference in the
type of political clientele to which they appealed. Quadros, like Goulart, sought

to establish a political clientele in labor, but his strategy — emphasizing efficient administrative performance — differed from Jango's because their followers differed in socioeconomic status and value structure. If we combine the 1960 election returns with an insightful survey analysis of the followers of São Paulo's two major populist postwar governors, Adhemar de Barros and Jânio Quadros, we can distinguish between Goulart's and Quadros' clienteles. Jânio's supporters were much more completely integrated into the capitalist industrial system than the followers of Adhemar de Barros, who were predominantly of petit-bourgeois, pre-industrial socioeconomic status. The Janistas expressed a higher degree of confidence in themselves and in the future than did the Adhemaristas, and to a far greater extent they felt they could advance economically through the fruits of their own labor if rational rather than traditional criteria were used to judge them.[33]

Data from the 1960 election for president and vice-president (which, in Brazil, were voted on separately rather than in a "package," as in the United States) suggest that Goulart's followers were similar to Adhemar's. In São Paulo State, Goulart's vice-presidential vote paralleled very closely Adhemar's totals in the presidential column, even though they were running on separate tickets. They lost almost every industrial area to Quadros and his UDN running mate, Milton Campos, while their sources of strength lay mostly in small towns.[34] Therefore, we conclude that Goulart's supporters were less likely to expect or demand that the welfare apparatus provide efficient service according to impersonal criteria.

Quadros, on the other hand, could best satisfy his electors and build a working-class clientele by distributing social security and welfare benefits according to rational criteria. In Jânio's truncated presidency, the Ministry spent 2.6 percent of the national budget, the highest figure since 1949, and his government released 92.3 percent of the transfer allocations for social assistance, a figure higher than that of any other year except 1942. Since Table 14 shows that Quadros actually cut back on personnel costs, the increase in Ministry spending went almost solely to sustaining a high level of administrative paternalism.

Goulart's rhetoric might lead the observer to believe that his presidency exerted every effort to expand material benefits for the working class, as attested by the record budget allocation of 6.2 percent. In actual practice, however, expenditures for the Ministry fell off somewhat in comparison with Quadros' presidency. Although political symbols such as the budgets and official rhetoric favored the working class, the government did not keep its promise to improve administrative services. And, unlike the earlier populist period, this one did not compensate workers by raising real wages.

When the military reimposed strict administrative controls in 1964, average

33. Weffort, "Raízes sociais" (ch. 3 above, n. 15), pp. 58-59.
34. Brazil, Tribunal Superior Eleitoral, *Dados estatísticos: eleições federais, estaduais, realizadas no Brasil em 1960* (Rio de Janeiro: Departamento de Imprensa Nacional, 1963), pp. 74-85.

budget and spending for the Ministry dropped to levels similar only to those of the dictatorship up to 1939. These data show that arbitrary governments in Brazil, which rely heavily on the Ministry's control apparatus and actively reduce the scope of political participation, also tend to neglect the paternalistic component in the administrative tradition. They do not even see a need to cater to the working class in the rhetoric of budgetary allocations. In the apparent exception of the Estado Novo between 1942 and 1945, Vargas highlighted paternalistic outputs only after he planned to broaden the scope of political conflict, for which he needed worker support.

These financial records also reveal the participation of the Ministry in patronage employment. In the absence of regular reports on the number of Ministry employees, the personnel expenditures in Table 14 provide an indicator of the extent to which the government used the Ministry to maintain a political clientele. It is impossible to know for certain the proportion of personnel increases which are devoted to salary hikes as opposed to additional staff, but periods of rapid rise suggest that there was an increase in salary and probably also some increase in the number of employees. Sharp declines in personnel outlay must represent a cut in staff, for it is safe to assume that under inflationary conditions salaries would not be reduced.

Rapid rises in personnel expenditures correlate with two factors: radical populist periods and the approach of federal elections. Let us compare the personnel costs shown in Table 14 with the social-welfare expenditures in Table 13. In the radical populist years, the government transferred even less of its statutory obligations to the social-welfare apparatus than in other years, yet personnel costs increased dramatically. Although Brazil's chronic inflation required regular salary hikes, the jumps in personnel expenditures during radical populist periods went well beyond the norm for other years. For the four radical populist years, personnel increases averaged 73.3 percent annually — more than twice the annual average of 34.4 percent for the other 15 years between 1946 and 1964. When we contrast the decline in overall Ministry expenditures with the rise in personnel outlays, therefore, we conclude that the initiators of radical populism consciously opted to protect their own political careers at the workers' expense. They reduced services for the working class as a whole and then directed some of the money saved, in the form of patronage, to labor leaders, politicians, and bureaucrats — key individuals in the corporative structures whom they expected to *control* the working class.

Only one of the four radical populist ministers — Almino Afonso — seriously tried to maintain state services for workers. A socialist by conviction, he aimed to convert distributive populism into socialism by emphasizing the organization of production and the need to develop labor union strength. If the president had backed him, his program might have corrected one of the most serious deficiencies of populism and given it a longer lease on life.

Turning to the second factor, the data show that personnel expenditures rise sharply in election years or the year immediately prior to an election, with the

TABLE 14

Personnel Expenditures for the Ministry of
Labor and Their Annual Increases,
1937-1964

Year	Expenditure (in million cruzeiros)	Annual increase (as percentage)
1937	16.4	—
1938	17.3	5.8%
1939	19.4	11.7
1940	19.6	1.3
1941	23.8	21.6
1942	27.5	15.3
1943	29.0	5.4
1944	40.3	39.0
1945	46.4	15.2
1946	86.2	85.8
1947	86.0	-2.0
1948	77.6	-9.8
1949	93.5	20.5
1950	94.3	8.3
1951	117.2	12.4
1952	124.9	6.5
1953	218.7	75.2
1954	247.9	13.3
1955	330.6	33.3
1956	229.5	-30.6
1957	618.1	169.4
1958	695.3	12.5
1959	713.7	2.6
1960	1,119.5	56.9
1961	734.9	-34.4
1962	1,522.4	107.2
1963	3,161.1	107.6
1964	6,280.2	98.7

Source: Brazil, Contadoria Geral da República,
Balanços Gerais da União, 1937-1964.

exception of 1950. Table 15 highlights these rises and compares them with the
increase in the cost of living. The low ratio in the last column for 1955 reflects
the emphasis on inflation control by the caretaker governments. It is probably
low in 1960 because Kubitschek had become concerned with Goulart's political

TABLE 15

Increases in Ministry Expenditure on Personnel and Cost-of-Living
Increases, in Election Years and Two-Year Periods
Prior to Elections, 1945-1962

| Election year | Increase in personnel expenditures | | Increase in cost of living | | $\frac{b}{d}$ |
	$\frac{a}{\text{Election year}}$	$\frac{b}{\text{Two-years}}$	$\frac{c}{\text{Election year}}$	$\frac{d}{\text{Two-years}}$	
1945	15.2%	54.2%	17.7%	–	–
1950	8.3	28.8	9.8	15.0%	1.92
1954	13.3	88.5	22.0	36.9	2.40
1955	33.3	46.7	23.8	45.8	1.02
1958	12.5	181.9	14.6	31.1	5.85
1960	56.9	59.5	29.3	68.4	0.87
1962	107.2	107.2*	51.6	85.0	1.26

Sources: a and *b* calculated from Brazil, Contadoria Geral da República, *Balanços Gerais da União*; *c* and *d* computed from Fundacão Getúlio Vargas cost-of-living data for the state of Guanabara, in *Conjuntura Econômica*.

*This does not include the 1961 figure, which was negative 34.35 percent.

ambitions by late 1958 and sought to minimize the patronage dealt out by his vice-president.[35] Ministry and social security agencies would be the principal subjects of such personnel controls. Furthermore, the fact that Kubitschek had made the alltime record jump in personnel expenditures – 169.4 percent – in 1957 may have lessened the need for another rise. It is interesting that the party in power was turned out of office in 1955 and 1960, the years of the two lowest ratios.

Rollbacks of the personnel expenditure were few, with the sharpest occurring when Jânio Quadros applied his famous broom to the civil service in 1961. Another took place in 1956. Both cuts occurred in the wake of electoral victories of the "outs" over the "ins," for Kubitschek represented the return of the Vargas forces after slightly over a year of interim anti-Vargas regimes, and Quadros belonged to the anti-Vargas current. The immediately succeeding years of 1957 and 1962, however, both witnessed rapid increases in the ministerial personnel expenditures. One study concludes that Kubitschek and Quadros acted like their predecessors in paying lip service to the merit system in the civil service while following patronage criteria in making many appointments. They differed from previous presidents only in that they declared wholesale annulments of nontenured patronage appointments as a prelude to employing their own followers.[36]

35. Lawrence S. Graham, *Civil Service Reform in Brazil* (Austin: University of Texas Press, 1968), p. 150. Graham notes that Kubitschek made many social security appointments in the last months of 1960, but these came too late to make a big impact on the 1960 balance sheet. Quadros subsequently annulled many of these appointments.
36. *Ibid.,* pp. 147-148, 151-153.

Conclusion

Several generalizations emerge from this analysis of Labor Ministry accounts. In the first place, with one exception, the Ministry constantly spent sums inferior to the amount budgeted, thus shortchanging programs for the working class. Table 13 showed that the programs most often sacrificed were social security and other social-assistance operations.

Since in most fiscal years national expenditures exceeded the amount budgeted, the working class obviously was being sacrificed to other interests. An examination of the budget and national accounts data for the three military ministries reveals that, between 1959 and 1967, the armed forces almost always spent more than the amounts allocated in the budget, so they do better than labor. However, in nearly every case the increase was so small that their percentage shares of the national accounts were in fact smaller than their percentages of the budget.

Who, then, was the principal beneficiary of these increases? During every fiscal year, the budget was supplemented by extraordinary credits, and by far the largest portion of these went to the Ministry of Finance.[37] Therefore, the economic planners and administrators, whose importance Leff highlights, have captured the lion's share of these reallocations, presumably for economic development projects.[38]

The data show that in periods of arbitrary rule, when the government restricts the scope of political conflict so as to exclude the workers, it likewise restricts material benefits available for the working class. In other words, when the government denies political participation to the working class, the denial of economic participation follows. The existence of electoral democracy, on the other hand, does not seem to guarantee improved material benefits for the working class, and the approach of an election does not consistently and directly affect the most important material benefits for the working class as a body — those of the social security and welfare apparatus. In only three of the seven federal election years did the Ministry release over 50 percent of its allocation for social services. Rather than make resources available for the working class and poor as a whole, then, politicians in power consistently directed these monies to people in the corporative structures whom they expected to control the working-class vote. Table 14 demonstrated that fluctuations in the personnel budget clearly correlate with elections.

Finally, the financial data showed that in the radical populist periods of 1953-54 and 1963-64, governments neglected the paternalistic-administrative apparatus, despite promises of increased attention to the working class. In material terms, the working class did benefit from the first radical populist period. By contrast, workers received no gains in the early sixties, for in that period of economic stagnation the private sector was unable to handle increases

37. *Anuário Estatístico do Brasil,* 1959 through 1968, in "Finanças públicas" section.
38. Leff, *Economic Policy-Making* (ch. 1 above, n. 11), pp. 143-153.

of the necessary magnitude. Real wages therefore declined (see Tables 16 and 24). Thus the most important promises of the populist rhetoric went unfulfilled.

For workers trying to increase their political and economic power, populism surely was not equivalent to autonomous class strength. Politicians, not workers, initiated the radical populist periods in which labor's political participation expanded. Moreover, these politicians made overtures to labor not principally to increase workers' real power or material wellbeing, but rather to shift their own base of political support when shrinking economic resources threatened ruling-class unity and, with it, their governing coalitions.

Despite President Goulart's apparent intention to keep labor under government control, however, major labor leaders began to accumulate substantial political influence and leverage through their important positions in the social security apparatus and through their astute manipulation of strikes. Turning this leverage to advantage, they enlisted presidential support in their vain efforts to raise their falling real wages and, more importantly, to press for a campaign for basic reform of Brazil's socioeconomic structures.

The power of the labor movement was being accumulated at the level of union leadership and, as Chapter Six will show, sindicato leaders had not yet institutionalized lines of command and organizational power down to the rank-and-file. Indeed, most union heads paid scant attention to improving their organizational apparatus and attracting new members. By collaborating with the corporative institutions of the state, these labor leaders gained opportunities for personal enrichment, social ascent, and political prominence. These cooptive opportunities simply blinded them to the fact that only the workers could supply them with a strong and autonomous power base.

It is common for observers, in explaining the rank-and-file's low level of organization, to point to the largely traditional value structure of many workers and the fact that they were usually better off materially than their relatives in rural areas. While this obstacle to militant unionization did indeed exist, one Brazilian scholar argues persuasively that few labor leaders or other professed friends of workers actually dedicated themselves to organizing the masses. Even the Communist Party, ignoring the precepts of Marxist-Leninist ideology, made no efforts to win union autonomy from the state. Indeed, rather than challenging the corporative system, Communist Party policy helped infuse vitality into it during the critical transition from the Estado Novo to the democratic system in the mid-1940's, as well as during much of the subsequent period up through 1964.[39] The corporative system, by diverting labor leaders from the pursuit of autonomous power, had thus achieved the goal of its founders.

In this context, even efforts to mobilize and organize the rank-and-file have come from within the system. Minister of Labor Almino Afonso attempted to foster such mobilization until President Goulart, heeding the appeals of the more traditional PTB politicians, ousted him. The following chapter studies Almino's effort.

39. Weffort, "Origens do sindicalismo populista" and "Sindicatos e política" (ch. 3 above, n. 11).

Chapter 5

THE LABOR MINISTRY UNDER
ALMINO AFONSO: A CASE STUDY
IN POLITICAL CHANGE

Almino Monteiro Álvares Afonso served as João Goulart's labor minister for six months in 1963, and his brief tenure in office offers a wealth of insights into the functioning of the Brazilian political system and the role of labor within it. As the preceding chapter pointed out, there were two radical populist periods under the Constitution of 1946, and Almino came to the Ministry during the second of these.

In the first period, established political figures such as João Goulart mobilized workers to strengthen their own (the politicians') political position. These populist politicians offered their followers short-run material benefits but carefully circumscribed their political activity. The second populist period, on which this chapter focuses, contrasts with the first because certain social forces – the most prominent being labor – began to use the organizational gains made during the intervening transitional phase to demand genuine participation in the political process. This case study shows how labor leaders took advantage of their control of patronage in the social security apparatus to increase their political leverage, and the following chapter demonstrates how they used strikes for the same purpose.

By 1963, radical labor leaders had taken control of an increasing number of workers' organizations, including the largest confederation of all, the CNTI. They had founded and strengthened many extralegal interunion bodies such as the CGT, and they had led the two major political strikes in 1962. Thus far, however, they had not frontally challenged the rules of the political game. In this context, Almino's ministry is of great political significance because, by placing the patronage of the Ministry in the hands of the nationalist left, he helped radical labor leaders pyramid their growing political power. This, at last, constituted an effort to alter the political system in a fundamental way. Such a change in power relationships posed a threat to the president and was one of the principal reasons Goulart ejected Almino from the cabinet in June. Indeed, after only a few months in office, the minister had already met with such success in strengthening his radical, nationalist clientele that he was able to frustrate for two months the president's desire to sack him.

Almino's brief tenure in the Ministry divides into two phases. In the first he attempted to foster social justice simply by enforcing Brazil's social legislation. To this end, he took steps to clean up the social security system and force debtors and the federal government to cough up their share, he urged labor leaders to participate in the inspection and enforcement of the labor law, and he encouraged union membership drives.

In his final phase, he renewed his pre-ministerial insistence upon the basic reforms. His initial administrative experience had led him to conclude that he could not achieve meaningful reform until the basic power relationships in Brazil were altered, because the nation's political and social system denied sufficient resources and leverage to administrators who desired reform. The following section documents Almino's relationship with President Goulart through these two periods in order to demonstrate the extent to which the Ministry of Labor may influence national policy.

The subsequent section sheds some light on the operation and functions of patronage, which is one of the traditional mechanisms for political system maintenance in Brazil. Moreover, since Almino used patronage not for traditional ends but rather to change the political system, this case study will also illuminate some aspects of political change in Brazil during a period of rapid political mobilization.

The Ministry's Impact on
National Politics in a Populist Period

Open political conflict diminished markedly during the last few months of the parliamentary regime. In October 1962, the moderates of the Goulart line had emerged victorious in the congressional elections. The president's function as conciliator of class interests, therefore, had stood him in good stead in both party and nation as the PTB delegation gained strength in the Chamber.

However, radical nationalists throughout the nation had begun organizing to press for adoption of the basic reforms. After the successful general strikes of July and September 1962, groups calling for the structural reforms manifested an increasing awareness of the value of organizational support. Congressmen, students, peasants, workers, military men, women's organizations, and even some industrialists formed ad hoc groups to back the reform campaign.

The parliamentary group affiliated with the radical nationalists and the reform campaign was the Frente Parlamentar Nacionalista (FPN); and within it, the PTB's left wing, known as the "Grupo Compacto," provided its most dynamic element. The *compactos* were led by PTB floor leader Almino Afonso and Deputy Leonel Brizola, who had won his seat in Guanabara in October with the largest total vote in history.

When the return to the presidential system in January 1963 brought an increase in the level of political activity, Goulart's conciliatory style came into direct confrontation with the radical nationalists and their campaign for the reforms. That clash even divided the government as the year progressed, for Labor Minister Almino Afonso came to openly oppose the government's economic policy despite his membership in the cabinet. An economic slowdown, combined with soaring inflation, pervaded this period. The austerity program of the Three-Year Plan, which Goulart had initiated in an attempt to qualify for International Monetary Fund aid, further intensified the economic pinch upon most Brazilians. The labor left had immediately rejected the plan, as it imposed painful belt-tightening upon the working class and the less well-off.

Goulart's opponents initially believed he had appointed Almino as labor minister to maintain a high level of labor agitation against the plan. Subsequent events suggest, however, that Almino was selected because he enjoyed enough confidence on the left to be able to keep a tight rein on labor while the president applied the Three-Year Plan's conventional economic solutions to the crisis.

A series of misunderstandings during his first week in the Ministry led many observers to believe that Almino had abandoned his radical commitments. In his swearing-in address, for example, Almino expressed his hope that labor and capital could collaborate in developing the nation economically, so that all Brazilians would enjoy a higher standard of living. Because he entered office when the maritime transport workers had been on strike for a month and workers in such key sectors as electric power, telephones, and tramways were threatening walkouts, he also urged labor to extend him a credit of confidence by postponing decisions until he could familiarize himself with their problems. Communist Party chief Luiz Carlos Prestes flatly rejected this call for restraint, apparently mistaking it for a demand that workers henceforth renounce their right to strike. Wide journalistic coverage of Prestes' reaction then led many to misinterpret Almino's intentions.

In truth, the young minister promised labor that he had no intention of freezing wages or repressing strikes, but he underscored his belief that wage demands would not solve the problems of the working class as long as the economy was ailing. He therefore asked workers to view their class interests from the perspective of the national interest. Operating within the financial constraints of the moment, he first chose to serve the workers by eliminating corruption and improving efficiency in the ministerial and social security organizations.[1] This essentially reformist administrative approach, which led some critics to believe he no longer desired a radically restructured society, distinguishes his first phase in the Ministry from his second.

1. *JB*, Jan. 26, 1963, pp. 1, 3; Jan. 30, p. 10; Jan. 31, p. 3; Feb. 1, p. 10; personal communication from Almino Afonso, March 18, 1972.

Almino took no public stand on the Three-Year Plan in the first months of 1963, but in March, as the effects of the austerity program began to generate dissatisfaction from almost all sides, he began to speak out against it. This firmed up left-wing support, but it implied opposing the president, who still hoped that the Three-Year Plan would cure Brazil's economic maladies without precipitating the withdrawal of any elements in his coalition.

Almino turned against Goulart at a moment when Almino was undisputed leader of the left wing of the PTB. His principal rival for that position, Leonel Brizola, had absented himself from the Chamber to carry the reform campaign to the streets in an effort to revive his flagging popularity.[2] Political commentator Carlos Castelo Branco observed that Almino's combination of administrative efficiency with leftist mobilization of the masses spelled the end of traditional clientelism and clientistic politicians. As the chief influence behind a new radical and demanding power base which maintained operational political linkages with the masses, he stood in a position to engineer a far-reaching transformation of the political system.[3] This view was seconded by another veteran political correspondent, who noted:

> Minister Almino Afonso personifies the essence of the present contradictory situation in the government, because he is splitting the president's own party. Seeking to assert himself through authentic leaders who have emerged from direct contact with the lower strata, the labor minister represents the point of no return on the dividing line between two versions of the PTB.[4]

The first sign of friction between the labor minister and the president came in April. Goulart was struggling to minimize his dependence upon radical organizations like the General Labor Command (CGT), because CGT leaders had challenged his authority and provoked a national crisis in a series of street demonstrations later dubbed the Battle of Guanabara (discussed in Chapter Seven). Almino chose this moment to initiate a process designed to confer official recognition upon the CGT. He replaced a ministerial regulation of 1954, which outlawed peak labor organizations above the confederation level, with one which stated that the CGT, while not an officially recognized body in terms of Brazilian labor law, was not specifically illegal. He further irritated the president by recommending that Goulart ask Congress to give the CGT legal status.[5] Goulart played for time and let it be known that he would not act before Labor Day (May 1). When he let Labor Day pass without acting, Almino called a conference to modernize the Consolidation of Labor Laws; its participants then urged that the CLT be amended to provide for a central body which would complete the truncated organizational pyramid of the corporative system.[6]

2. Brizola's loss of popularity is documented in *JB*-Marplan polls in *JB*, April 28, 1963, p. 19.

3. Carlos Castelo Branco in *JB*, April 21, 1963, p. 4.

4. Evandro Carlos de Andrade in *ibid.*

5. *OESP*, April 2, 1963, p. 8; *JB*, April 4, p. 4.

6. *JB*, April 7, 1963, pp. 1, 5; *OESP*, April 6, p. 3.

By April 9, Almino had begun declaring to labor groups that labor and mass pressure was necessary to balance that of big economic groups, thus reinforcing the pressure which the Battle of Guanabara had put on Goulart that week.[7] A week later Almino reiterated this, but he focused it on radical reform, stating that only mass pressure could overcome the drag of the status quo and make the structural changes which further national development required.[8]

Almino's exhortations and Brizola's street demonstrations sought to force Goulart to take a stand for structural reform. They succeeded. Soon Goulart gave his blessing to these popular movements.[9] The president's stand, however, proved to be a tactical move. Once it became clear that the CGT and other radical leftist groups were planning another general strike and had enlisted the support of revolutionary noncommissioned officers as well, Goulart tried to pull the props out from under them and Almino by supporting a rival labor organization, the União Sindical dos Trabalhadores (UST). (Chapter Seven details this episode.)

The president first tried to divest his cabinet of Almino in mid-April. Hoping to win the acquiescence of the labor left in the ouster, he suggested that he would appoint former Labor Minister João Pinheiro Neto, another favorite of the nationalist left, to the post from which he had displaced him four months earlier. Goulart acted too late, however, for Almino had just appointed Clidenor Freitas, a nationalist from the PTB's left wing, to the presidency of the State Employees' Welfare and Assistance Institute (IPASE). Nationalists and the labor left immediately defended Almino, therefore, declaring that they would consider his removal a hostile act.[10] This crisis arose as Goulart was preparing to depart for Chile on an official trip of state. Since he could ill afford a domestic crisis while he was abroad, he left Almino in the post.

When Almino returned two weeks later from the Inter-American Conference of Labor Ministers in Bogotá, where he had denounced the Alliance for Progress as ineffective and called for its radical reformulation, CGT leaders met and acclaimed him.[11] This was precisely the moment when they were threatening a general strike for the reforms and Goulart was trying to weaken them. Almino declared that he would not impede the general strike because the Constitution guaranteed the right to strike, thus backing radical labor against Goulart. Almino further angered the chief executive in mid-May by proposing the collective resignation of the cabinet. He claimed that it would allow the president flexibility in choosing a new cabinet, one which would presumably exclude War Minister Amaury Kruel and Finance Minister San Tiago Dantas and would thus be more capable of enacting radical reforms. This increased the tension of an already tense moment, when congressional debate on the agrarian reform bill had raised political passions and the nationalist sergeants had just held a rally

7. *OESP,* April 10, 1963, p. 4.
8. *JB,* April 19, 1963, p. 4.
9. *JB,* April 23, 1963, pp. 4, 6.
10. *OESP,* April 18, 1963, p. 3; *JB,* April 19, p. 3.
11. *OESP,* May 4, 1963, p. 3; *JB,* May 10, p. 3.

which their superiors judged subversive. Almino, by underscoring his position as champion of the left, had in effect reduced the president's flexibility, because the man Goulart had been trying to remove from his cabinet since April was Almino Afonso and not Dantas or Kruel.

As the general strike threat evolved into a strike of commercial pilots, the labor minister took the side of the president of the air transport workers' sindicato, who had been illegally fired. He thus encouraged the airline stoppage at a time when Goulart was trying to avoid any catalyst to another general strike.[12] Almino even made it difficult for the technical officials of his ministry to penetrate his circle of personal advisers in order to give him complete information on that strike, thereby prolonging it.[13] The minister's role in the pilot' strike was brilliantly played. Not only did he defend trade-union integrity against a law-breaking employer, he also postponed the cabinet shakeup for nearly a month, since Goulart could not remove him before it was settled.

The president sought to weaken Almino by undermining his main institutional constituency, the CGT. Although the effort did not ultimately change Goulart's labor base, it figured significantly in Almino's ouster, since it caused his allies in labor to withdraw from the public eye and act cautiously during the period when he could have most used their assistance. By postponing the cabinet shakeup until June 21 and thus allowing the crisis to lose pressure slowly, Goulart denied Almino the martyrdom he might have won if he had been ousted in April or May.

Goulart also acted to block Almino's efforts to sink political roots in São Paulo. Almino, preparing for the coming elections, had taken advantage of the ministerial powers of patronage and appointment to establish an independent electoral base in Brazil's major industrial state. In response, Goulart attempted to thwart him by withdrawing ministerial control of that base. The president moved to re-establish an old convention between the state of São Paulo and the federal government which would have eliminated the Labor Ministry's Regional Labor Office in São Paulo⁻ and allowed the state Secretariat of Labor to undertake supervision and control there. As part of the deal, Governor Adhemar de Barros would have let Ivete Vargas' PTB control the secretariat, thereby keeping the labor machinery in the hands of a Goulart ally.[14] However, pressure for a cabinet shift became great enough that Goulart ousted Almino directly, eliminating any need for the deal with São Paulo.

Almino's six months in the Ministry bring to mind the brief period which Goulart himself spent in this office in 1953-54. Goulart used the post to gain publicity and strengthen his labor base, a tactic which later served him well in his rise to power. Almino attempted the same strategy. However, unlike Goulart, who was cooperating with his chief executive, Almino was acting in opposition to the president's austerity measures and economic policy.

12. *OESP,* May 22, 1963, p. 6.
13. José Machado in *JB,* June 2, 1963, p. 10.
14. *OESP,* May 22, 1963, p. 3.

Jango left the Ministry under military pressure and as a martyr. Moreover, his honor was vindicated when Vargas himself decreed the 100-percent minimum-wage increase which Goulart had proposed and which served as the catalyst for his ouster. Almino, by contrast, was not vindicated by the chief executive, for it was Goulart who wished to remove him. He was not lionized as a martyr, because the president was undermining the CGT and thus isolating Almino from his major power base among the masses.

Patronage: Traditional Means for a Radical End

Almino's brief ministry had important political repercussions, because his conception of the political system and the role of politicians, parties, and constituencies within it differed fundamentally from established practice. Goulart, as labor minister and later as president, had wanted to grant advantages to labor in a paternalistic sense. The party provided a vehicle for more or less like-minded politicians who benefited from each other's cooperation. These politicians garnered the votes needed for election by distributing patronage and favors to their personal clienteles.

Almino opposed the clientelistic style and content of the PTB so long as it did not serve a radical purpose. He acknowledged that all politicians choose their profession to gain and exercise power. What differentiates among them, he argued, is the purpose for which they use that power. Almino sought to use political power to benefit Brazil's workers and poor.[15] As this section will demonstrate, his personnel policies reflected both his sensitivity to the realities of political power and his desire to serve the mass of citizens.

He relied upon new spokesmen for the masses who were somewhat autonomous of him and much more closely connected to their constituencies than were the wardheelers and patronage conduits who served Brazil's politicians of an earlier mold. He sought to use these new spokesmen to remodel the PTB. Their constituencies were more clearly definable in a functional sense – e.g., workers, peasants, sergeants, students – than those of the earlier period when the principal common bond was patronage distributed by the party leader. These new constituencies may be differentiated from the old ones, therefore, because they articulated demands for whole classes or categories of people.

The old clienteles, on the other hand, were not militant and did not make demands for specific occupational or functional groups, because politicians – not the affected social sectors themselves – had created them. These earlier clienteles, in other words, consisted primarily of passive recipients of patronage that politicians distributed to them as individuals, not as members of a specific class. Although at this moment it was still too early to speak of a real class consciousness among Brazilian workers, the labor leaders to whom Almino appealed manifested a much clearer conception of class interest and consciousness than their predecessors. They made demands not only so they could

15. Personal communication from Almino Afonso, March 18, 1972.

personally enjoy the material benefits of patronage, but also so they could increase their power and win benefits for their constituents.

Almino attempted to break down the old patronage system, which simply tied votes to jobs and favors handed out paternalistically and individually to an amorphous constituency. He did not do without patronage, as will become very clear, but he infused it with ideological content by using it to bind an electoral base to a program posited upon structural reform. In the Brazilian context, however, this was a revolutionary goal and was the principal reason for his ouster.

Patronage politics, therefore, could serve either system-maintenance or radical-reform purposes. In Chapter One we noted that politicians had generally used patronage in the labor structures to maintain the system by buying off potential counterelites with jobs and perquisites. In this chapter, it will become clear that Almino Afonso used patronage for an entirely different purpose. By placing representatives of the radical, nationalist left in important posts in his bureaucratic domain, he provided them with resources and leverage for mobilizing large numbers of people on behalf of fundamental political reform.

The two phases which characterized Almino's general behavior in the Ministry — i.e., emphasis on sound administration within the existing political system, followed by the subsequent attempt to work fundamental reform on that system — are also evident in his use of the patronage power. Almino's appointment practices provoked sharp public debate between his supporters and opponents, because the participatory populism which he sought to institutionalize would have changed the nature of the political game in Brazil, taking resources from some sectors to redistribute to others.

Among the opponents to the first phase were the leaders of the CGT as well as the traditional PTB machines of São Paulo and Guanabara. Both party branches controlled powerful positions in the social security apparatus. As his focus shifted toward radical nationalism and basic reforms, he won the CGT leaders as allies and alienated the more conservative elements in Brazilian politics. But again the traditional PTB machines of Guanabara and São Paulo found their prerogatives trammeled. Thus, demands for redress by the traditional politicians of these two organizations provided most of the material for this case study.

Shortly after taking office, Almino's hiring policies drew the attention of interested parties. The minister appeared to be breaking with established custom when he bypassed members of the Guanabara PTB in making key appointments. A number of his appointees had maintained ties with the late Deputy Fernando Ferrari and his Labor Renovation Movement (MTR) or with the Communist Party of São Paulo.

Almino apparently wished to establish an electoral base in São Paulo before the coming gubernatorial elections. Through frequent trips to the industrial center of Brazil, he broadened and deepened his contacts with labor, student, and nationalist leaders, and through his calls for efficiency he appealed to the moralistic followers of Jânio Quadros as well. In a statement designed to win the Janistas' support, he proclaimed his adherence to the much-neglected merit system in hiring, and he began to employ people who had qualified in competitive civil service examinations but had been passed over in appointments to the benefit of unexamined members of previous ministers' clienteles. He claimed with pride that he placed 20,208 functionaries who had passed the examination.[16]

First elected from the state of Amazonas as a member of the Socialist Labor Party, Almino had recently entered the PTB, and he was far to the left of the São Paulo branch of his new party. In São Paulo the PTB was merely one of many small parties, holding only 9 of the state's 59 seats in the Chamber and 12 of the 115 seats in the State Assembly,[17] and patronage motivated it more than program or ideology. At its head was Deputy Ivete Vargas, niece of the former dictator and president.

At this political juncture, the São Paulo PTB appeared vulnerable to the attack of a dynamic minister who would concentrate on administrative efficiency rather than patronage and spoils. The Paulista electorate seemed to be despairing of the old politics and searching for something new. This despair manifested itself in the election for the Chamber in 1962, when more than a quarter of the electorate had cast blank ballots, and blank and null ballots together totaled 29.8 percent.[18] Most of the established parties had been declining in São Paulo, and the PTB was on shaky ground, swinging from 8 to 5 to 9 seats in the Federal Chamber, and from 8 to 6 to 10 in the State Assembly, in the elections of 1954, 1958, and 1962. Renewed internal dynamism did not account for the rise in 1962, either, for an electoral study attributes it in part to support by the Communists.[19]

While the PTB showed little strength or dynamism during these years, dynamic new parties were cutting into the electorate of the more established ones. The Christian Democratic Party, for example, rose from 1 to 4 to 9 deputies in the Chamber, and from 4 to 11 to 13 in the Assembly, in these three elections. Thus, there was no question that São Paulo was ripe for political movements which would diverge from the traditional format. Almino's program was designed to do just that, as well as to give him control over the PTB.

While undermining the traditional leadership of the PTB, Almino also sought the support of the rank-and-file laborers and lower-level union leaders. He invited them to collaborate with the authorities by reporting infractions of the law at the workplace, because inspection officials in the Regional Labor Offices were insufficient in number and inadequately trained.

Aiming to win significant support from the moralistic middle- and working-class elements that supported Quadros, Almino publicized plans to instill real

16. *JB,* June 23, 1963, p. 3.
17. *Anuário Estatístico do Brasil,* 1963, p. 428.
18. Oliveiros S. Ferreira, "A Crise de Poder do 'Sistema' e as Eleições Paulistas de 1962," *Revista Brasileira de Estudos Políticos,* XVI (January 1964), 216.
19. *Ibid.,* p. 222.

efficiency in the social security system. At that time it insured nearly seven million persons and disposed of an annual budget larger than that of any state government except São Paulo.[20]

Almino's relations with the CGT reflected the two phases of his short ministerial career. Before he combined social security personnel shakeups with outspoken advocacy of nationalistic basic reforms, his administrative cleanup aroused the vocal opposition of the CGT leadership. Right after his appointment and in the period of confusion caused by his credit-of-confidence comment, a delegation of CGT leaders showed up at the Ministry expecting to be received warmly. Instead, they cooled their heels in an antechamber for three hours and left without seeing the minister. When they came back the next day, they were again ignored. Outraged, they demanded Almino's ouster, but Goulart got them all back on speaking terms, thereby renewing their access to policy makers and patronage.[21] By mid-April, when Goulart first attempted to replace the young minister, these very same CGT leaders, now Almino's staunch supporters, came to his defense with a general-strike threat.[22]

Almino's proposed social security reforms had initially disquieted these labor leaders, for they believed the minister would replace the tripartite directorates with a neutral administration of experts, thereby withdrawing their principal source of patronage. The minister, however, did not follow such a plan. Rather, he found that the existing structures could aid his attack on the traditional sectors of the PTB, for he could use these agencies to transfer power to friends and allies who adhered to his concept of radical nationalism.

After all, the radical nationalist interests of the CGT and the plan for reducing inefficiency and eliminating corruption in the social security apparatus were not mutually exclusive. Indeed, the CGT leaders backed Almino precisely because his drive on corruption served to purge the institutes of elements aligned with their political rivals, thus extending the control of the radical left over this important source of patronage. This strategy, therefore, appealed both to Quadros supporters and to the CGT, because it emphasized efficiency while it increased the political power of radical labor. One of Almino's subsequent tactical errors was to shift his public emphasis almost entirely to the basic reform campaign while he neglected the more conservative elements which he had been courting earlier.

Almino's drive for control of social security patronage came into the open following the Battle of Guanabara in April, when the forces of the radical and nationalist left seemed to be on a very rapid upswing. The optimistic flush of the moment made it appear a most appropriate time to challange the party's old guard with a much more radical program.

The new minister's appointment policies followed a consistent pattern. He transferred the traditional PTB machines' control over patronage to radical

20. *Anuário Estatístico,* 1965, p. 470.
21. *JB,* Feb. 15, 1963, p. 3; Feb. 16, p. 3; José Machado in *JB,* Feb. 17, p. 15.
22. *OESP,* April 18, 1963, p. 3.

nationalists while emphasizing improved, honest, and rational service for the Brazilian working class. He first highlighted the notorious inefficiency and corruption of the social security institutes in order to discredit their directors. For example, he berated the bureaucrats for self-indulgence, citing the flagrant example of the doubling of the institute treasurers' salaries two years earlier. He then decreed these increases null and void, and ordered the excess returned to the public coffers. [23] This type of stratagem simultaneously garnered popular support and made a case for subsequent personnel transfers. He strengthened his own constituency of radical nationalists in each shakeup.

Most frequently, he discovered a scandal involving the director of the administrative council or regional office of an institute and ordered an investigation which incriminated the man and thus forced his resignation. Almino then replaced him with a man who was personally loyal and not connected with the leaders of the PTB of São Paulo or Guanabara. He concentrated particularly on representatives of the government on the tripartite councils, because appointment of their replacements fell within his prerogatives.

The first institute to come under attack was the giant Industrial Workers' Social Security Institute (IAPI), with 28,015 employees (in 1966), 3,235,171 persons insured, and a budget of 167 billion cruzeiros. [24] After implicating Ezar Zacarias André, president of the IAPI's administrative council, in a web of corruption, Almino persuaded Goulart to replace André with a Paulista personally loyal to Almino himself. This is important because André was Ivete Vargas' man in the social security system, and his departure meant she would lose control over one of her principal sources of patronage and political leverage. [25] Almino further drew Ivete's wrath when he appointed a man outside the PTB as director of the Emergency Home Medical Assistance Service (SAMDU) in São Paulo. This provoked her to complain that the cleanup was a mere pretext to purge her own people. PTB members from São Paulo, she claimed, could assist in the reform just as well as those outside the party. [26]

At the same time that he confronted Ivete in São Paulo, he challenged the leadership of the PTB in Guanabara. The PTB floor leader in the State Assembly, José Saldanha da Gama Coelho Pinto, controlled this branch of the party. He also was an oldtime clientelistic politician who built a following more on patronage than on the material results of programmatic effort and administrative efficiency. Saldanha Coelho's man in the social security apparatus was José Firmo, president of the State Employees' Welfare and Assistance Institute (IPASE), whom Almino wanted to replace with ex-Deputy Clidenor Freitas. The IPASE employed 11,832 civil servants (in 1966) and insured 379,879 people. [27]

23. *JB,* April 24, 1963, p. 6.
24. Employee data from *Censo dos Servidores Públicos* (ch. 4 above, n. 26), p. 11; insured and budget data from *Anuário Estatístico,* 1965, p. 367.
25. José Machado in *JB,* March 17, 1963, p. 5.
26. *OESP,* April 17, 1963, pp. 3, 4.
27. As in n. 24, employee data from *Censo dos Servidores Públicos,* p. 11; insured data from *Anuário Estatístico,* 1965, p. 368.

The Guanabara branch of the party reacted rapidly and thought it had persuaded Goulart to name Freitas prefect of Brasília, thus deflecting Almino's thrust. [28]

This ploy only delayed the substitution process for a month, however, and on April 19 Freitas took the oath of office as president of the IPASE in a ceremony conducted by Almino and witnessed by high government officials and representatives from most of the nationalist groups, including dozens of CGT members, a delegation from the Parliamentary Nationalist Front, and representatives from the First Army, whose commander supported the nationalists.

Freitas' inauguration before so many radical guests served as a show of force to the PTB wheelhorses, and it illustrated the militant and demanding base upon which Almino would rebuild the PTB if he managed to gain control of it. In his address, he stressed that his program was complementary to the program of basic reforms which the president had submitted to the legislature. Accordingly, he called upon Congress to pass the reforms. [29]

Almino also took on the second-largest institute, the Commercial Workers' Social Security Institute (IAPC), with 17,242 employees (in 1966) and 1,707,323 insured (in 1963). Charging financial imprudence, he canceled a Christmas bonus which the administrative councils of the IAPC and the Transport Workers' Social Security Institute (IAPETC) — with 13,298 employees (in 1966) and 631,243 insured (in 1963) — had given to their functionaries. This provided his entering wedge against those directorates. [30]

Next he aired a scandal in the IAPC involving the son-in-law of its president. An earlier investigation into this had been aborted, presumably with the complicity of the two government representatives and the president, who represented the employers. The scandal publicly discredited the president, forcing his resignation, and it also justified Almino's replacement of the two government appointees by men loyal to him and his policies. [31] By mid-May, with a cabinet shakeup imminent, Almino declared that replacement of the government representatives on the remaining social security councils was under study, and he announced his plans to dynamize the Social Welfare Food Service (SAPS) and SAMDU by replacing the government representatives there also. [32]

The PTB old guard protested bitterly as Almino gained the upper hand. Following Freitas' appointment to the IPASE, Saldanha Coelho sent a message to the president through Ivete, denouncing Almino's conduct in the Ministry as injurious to the PTB in the state of Guanabara. [33] Ivete also attempted to mobilize the PTB caucus in Brasília to break with the minister, but Almino had shown such skill in office that his colleagues refused. Rather, 71 out of the 109 of them in the Federal Chamber put their names to a document urging Goulart

28. José Machado in *JB*, March 17, 1963, p. 5.

29. *OESP*, April 20, 1963, p. 5.

30. José Machado in *JB*, March 17, 1963, p. 5; employee data from *Censo dos Servidores Públicos*, p. 11; insured data in *Anuário Estatístico*, 1965, pp. 365-366.

31. José Machado in *JB*, April 21, 1963, p. 11.

32. *JB*, May 19, 1963, p. 14.

33. *JB*, April 17, 1963, p. 3.

to back Almino in the face of attempts to remove him. Drumming up such support was a very able move by Almino, for it made his replacement extremely difficult in mid-April — the very moment when Goulart wished to oust him.[34]

In this struggle between old and new guards, Ivete enjoyed the support of all but one — Rubens Paiva — of the 9 Paulistas in the Federal Chamber. In Guanabara, however, Saldanha Coelho's PTB was by no means unified, facilitating Almino's incursion. The Guanabara branch demonstrated a great deal more vitality than its São Paulo counterpart, holding 10 of the 21 seats in the Chamber and 13 of the 55 in the State Assembly.[35] It counted more nationalists than the São Paulo branch, including Deputy Sérgio Magalhães as well as Vice-Governor Elói Dutra, who planned to run for governor in the coming elections. Saldanha thus could not convince a majority of the PTB caucus in the Assembly to break with the minister.[36] The PTB radicals of Guanabara, who included several members of the CPOS, the Rio de Janeiro branch of the CGT, even protested the efforts of their more traditional brethren to place a Saldanha man at the head of the regional IAPI delegacy.[37]

As Almino pursued his course, the São Paulo PTB leaders finally confronted Goulart to voice their outrage at being deprived of social security positions. In a textbook illustration of the use of patronage to disaggregate political issues and groups in order to keep political protest under control, Goulart quieted them by putting 73 federal appointments at their disposal.[38]

In his battle with the oldline party machines, Almino even challenged Dante Pelacani who, though he was secretary-general of the National Confederation of Industrial Workers (CNTI) and vice-president of the CGT, also maintained close ties to Ivete Vargas and the São Paulo PTB. Dante held the post of director-general of the Social Welfare Department (DNPS), an office directly subordinate to the minister. By creating the Coordinating Council of the Social Security System as an advisory board which would operate parallel to the DNPS, Almino threatened Dante's prerogatives in the domain of social security. His announcement that he would initiate lawsuits against debtors to the institutes also challenged Dante's competence, since the DNPS had already issued a regulation to this effect.[39]

Deploring the appointment of a social security inspector in São Paulo who had recently been dismissed from another Ministry department for malfeasance, Almino forced Dante to transfer the inspector to a lesser post while the investigation was in process. He used the incident, moreover, to remind the director-general that the DNPS was a subordinate organ of the Labor Ministry

34. *OESP,* April 18, 1963, p. 3; April 19, p. 3.
35. *Anuário Estatístico,* 1963, p. 428.
36. *OESP,* April 18, 1963, p. 3.
37. *OESP,* May 23, 1963, p. 9.
38. *OESP,* May 9, 1963, p. 4; Graham, *Civil Service Reform* (ch. 4 above, n. 35), pp. 155-156.
39. *OESP,* March 30, 1963, p. 11; *JB,* March 25, p. 4.

and thus Dante was under his authority in the hierarchy. Although Dante was relatively secure in the post until his elective term expired at the end of the year, he avoided further public confrontation by announcing his annual vacation and leaving the country to let tempers cool.[40] He had been in a weak position because Almino's appointment policy had won the backing of a number of left-wing organizations, leaving them unwilling to rally to Dante's support.

Conclusion

Brazil's significant postwar industrial expansion and economic development had led, by the 1960's, to extensive social mobilization and modernization. Recognizing the growing actual and potential power of the newly mobilized social groups — most notably the working class and peasantry — Almino Afonso endeavored to replace the classical populism of his predecessors with a much more radical, participatory form of populism. Had he succeeded, the nature of Brazil's political constituencies would have changed dramatically. The amorphous, individualized clienteles held together by personal contact and patronage would have given way to functionally specific constituencies organized around clearly definable social classes or sectors, e.g., organized labor. It would have been much more difficult to buy off these constituencies simply by distributing modest amounts of patronage to their leaders. Such a change, therefore, would have accorded a far greater measure of power to organized labor than the classical populist model allowed, and it would have ratified in more formal terms the increasing political leverage which labor leaders had accumulated in the immediately preceding years. Thus strengthened, labor organizations would have used their new power and status, gained largely through *distributive*, patronage-type activities, to seek *redistributive* policies — that is, to change resource allocation among groups and classes.

Previously, the lower classes had played a dependent role in Brazilian politics because they lacked cohesive organization and a sense of class consciousness. The dominant political elites had originally designed the sindicato structure to prevent autonomous organization and the development of such a consciousness. In contrast to past practice, however, Almino lent support to those labor leaders who were struggling to create a class consciousness as well as strong labor organizations with a degree of autonomy. Had he been given more time, he might have effected a fundamental change in labor organization and the class structure of Brazil. Vitalized by the emergence of aggressive nationalistic labor leaders, such class organizations could have enabled the workers to articulate their interests more forcefully in the national political process. Stronger and more vigorous organizations would necessarily have increased labor's autonomy.

One should not conclude from this that Almino was laying the groundwork for a pluralist system of the liberal democratic variety. Considering Brazil's

40. *OESP,* April 16, 1963, p. 4; April 19, p. 4; April 20, p. 6; José Machado in *JB,* April 21, p. 11.

corporative political heritage, the emergence of liberal democracy would have been very unlikely. It is improbable, moreover, that such pluralism could have developed while Brazil was still undergoing the crises of modernization and industrialization, even if the nation's heritage were not corporative. The necessary social bases, such as universal literacy, generalized economic well-being, and autonomous social and political organizations for all or most sectors of society, clearly were not present to provide the substructure for such a system.

In view of Brazil's corporative heritage, let us outline, hypothetically, the system which might have evolved if Almino had succeeded. The formal framework would have continued to be corporative or semi-corporative. However, had he captured the PTB in São Paulo, and had similar movements met with success in other important states, the party also might have been remade along corporative lines with particular emphasis on labor and the peasantry. Given the deference to "authority" shown by so many Brazilian workers, the constituencies could not be expected to be entirely autonomous, but they would have been better able to articulate functionally specific sectoral interests than the amorphous clienteles of the preceding period. Such an evolution in its broadest lines might not have been dissimilar to the structuring of Mexican politics and the Mexican official party during the Cárdenas era, although the historical backdrop for that period — particularly the role of the Revolution in generating political legitimacy — gave the Mexicans decidedly more favorable circumstances.[41]

In his conscious employment of patronage for radical ends, Almino represented a significantly more modern stage in Brazilian political development than most other nationally prominent politicians. This is particularly evident when he is compared with João Goulart. When Jango rose to political prominence, politicians were using patronage to establish a national party system with a broader social base than the Old Republic (1891-1930), whose parties had been dominated exclusively by the rural oligarchies. He facilitated this limited expansion of political participation because, as he recognized himself, he had a great talent for reconciling diverse interests or factions.[42] In the sixties, however, his instinct for conciliation did not prove adaptable to the transformed conditions of the political system.

Goulart showed no awareness that recent changes in the political system — precisely those changes which Almino Afonso perceived and sought to embody in a new political style — required adaptation on his part. On the one hand, Jango did not seek to distribute patronage in a manner which would have enabled him to bring about modernizing change in the national political system; and when Almino tried to do this, the president frustrated the effort by ousting the ambitious minister. Subsequently, Goulart even went so far as to attempt,

---

41. On the role of revolution in political development, see Samuel P. Huntington, *Political Order in Changing Societies* (New Haven: Yale University Press, 1968), pp. 311-334.

42. Aurélio de Limeira Tejo, *Jango: debate sôbre a crise dos nossos tempos* (Rio de Janeiro: Andes, 1957), pp. 109-110.

albeit unsuccessfully, to annul most of the appointments of social security personnel made by Almino or by the nationalists Almino placed on the institute governing boards.[43]

On the other hand, Jango, unlike Kubitschek, proved incapable of using patronage to support dynamic legislative programs. Kubitschek had distributed patronage so as to build winning congressional coalitions for his proposals. Goulart, by contrast, almost completely lost control of the patronage machinery to local units of the PTB and to officials such as Almino, so the old politics could not function effectively either.[44]

In view of this loss of political control and direction, Brazil in the early sixties illustrates the difficulties which industrialization poses for political systems of the type David Apter calls reconciliation systems. The generally democratic political structure of such systems hinders authoritative control over manpower and natural resources. Lacking the authority to prevent ever more numerous political interests from diverting resources to their own narrow goals, such weak democratic polities ultimately decapitalize the nation's economy and contribute to its breakdown. Then, the political system itself collapses during the struggle over the dwindling resources still available. The collapse is usually followed by what Apter terms a mobilization system, whose authoritarian characteristics render it capable of mobilizing resources in order to reach mature industrialization.[45]

Prior to the early 1960's, Apter would have called the Brazilian political system a neo-mercantilist regime − a limited democracy with authoritative economic controls − for state planners guided the economy and did possess the authority to direct resources for development.[46] Manipulation of interest groups through the corporative structures kept most important economic issues out of the arena of mass politics and in the hands of a limited number of technocrats, facilitating Brazil's outstanding economic growth in the postwar period.

The system began to change, however, when radical nationalists and participatory populists moved into the power vacuum that developed under Goulart. The demands of the radical populists were redistributive in nature and thus heightened tension on the political system. Moreover, the cost of attending to these demands required more economic resources than were available, for policy errors by the technocrats had precipitated an economic crisis.[47] Thus, the simultaneous downturn of the economy and increase in political participation destroyed this neo-mercantilist system's authoritative control over resources, giving it the characteristics of a vulnerable reconciliation system.

43. Carlos Veríssimo do Amaral, "As Controvertidas Nomeações" (ch. 4 above, n. 27), pp. 30-33.

44. Graham, *Civil Service Reform*, pp. 153-158, 171-177.

45. David E. Apter, *The Politics of Modernization* (ch. 2 above, n. 26), pp. 39-42, 225-227.

46. *Ibid.*, pp. 408-416.

47. Leff, *Economic Policy-Making and Development* (ch. 1 above, n. 11), pp. 163-168.

Before self-sustaining industrialization can be achieved in Apter's framework, the reconciliation system ultimately gives way to a form which will concentrate political authority. The options pursued by Almino would undoubtedly have led to an authoritarian regime of the left, had he been successful. Goulart, however, was unwilling to assist him in this endeavor, and the ultimate collapse of the reconciliation system led instead to an authoritarian regime of the right under military auspices.

PART III

The Political Power
of the Labor Leaders

Chapter 6

POLITICAL STRIKES IN BRAZIL, 1960–1964:
STRENGTHS AND WEAKNESSES
OF ORGANIZED LABOR

Observers of pre-1964 Brazil generally agreed that the two social forces with the greatest impact upon the political process were labor and the military. Conservative spokesmen, for example, believed that labor leaders wielded enough strength to help President João Goulart overthrow the nation's liberal democratic political structures and establish in their place a "syndicalist republic." The events of 1964 and the years since then, however, have demonstrated that the military were far stronger than labor and that estimates of union leaders' political strength had been overdrawn by their allies and opponents alike.

The Brazilian political system, as we have seen, is corporative and was expressly established in the 1930's to provide the political elites with institutionalized controls over such social forces as organized labor. Despite this, labor leaders had gained two major sources of political power by 1960: (1) positions allocated to them in the official corporative institutions, which gave them access to state patronage; and (2) offices in the sindicatos, from which they led major strikes whose economic and political impact increased their bargaining power with the president and other political actors.

The following pages evaluate the sources of political power which derived from the strike as well as the limitations upon that power. While many contemporary observers correctly described the sources, they almost universally failed to notice the limitations. Significantly, the military embodied one of the greatest limitations.

This chapter presents 5 brief case studies of political strikes, in order to highlight the key variables in context. It concludes by summarizing the relevant variables for these 5 along with 12 other major political strikes or strike threats between 1960 and 1964[1] (see Table 20, at the end of this chapter). For our purposes, "political" strikes are those which were called to demand action from the government and public administration or which otherwise had important political implications. The 17 strikes or threats were selected on the basis of the importance given them in the political commentary and journalism of the time. This period of strikes, moreover, represents the most intensive strike activity since the Revolution of 1930. Coupled with the burst of political activity by many other reformist organizations in the period before the coup of 1964, it is clearly one of the "periodic and sudden expansions in the size, strength, and activity of social movements" which Eric Hobsbawm defines as social "explosions."[2] The reader should be aware, however, that another serious strike wave occurred in the immediate postwar period and that a number of important economic strikes broke out in the 1950's. The explosions of the postwar years and of the early sixties bear many similarities, and both ended in repression by the government.

The essential commodity of politics is power, and this analysis will endeavor to determine (1) the power which labor leaders wielded within the national political process, and (2) the extent of the power which they exercised over the rank and file in strike situations. It will be seen, particularly in the Goulart presidency, that the radical nationalists who came to dominate the Brazilian labor movement in the sixties were able to convert the power which accrued to them as a result of their control over strikes into real political power. They then used that power to exact concessions from the President of the Republic.

In analyzing the role of labor leaders at the level of the political system, we will employ the concept of power advanced by Dahl, i.e., that coercive influence constitutes power. "Negative coercion is based on the threat of extreme punishment, whereas positive coercion is based on the prospect of very large gains."[3] In the strikes under study here, the labor leaders exercised power over President Goulart by threatening to withdraw support which he desperately needed, as well as to dislodge other elements from the coalition upon which his government rested. The strike leaders were practicing dissensus politics as defined by Piven and Cloward:

> A cadre, acting on behalf of a minority within a coalition, engages in actions which are designed to dislodge (or which threaten to dislodge) not only that minority, but more important, *other significant constituent groups in that same alliance.* Through the cadre's ability to generate defections among other groups in a coalition, its impact becomes far greater than the voting power of the minority. If the strategist of con-

1. Detailed analysis of the remaining 12 strikes or threats appears in Kenneth Paul Erickson, "Labor in the Political Process in Brazil: Corporatism in a Modernizing Nation" (doctoral dissertation, Columbia University, 1970), pp. 185-270.
2. Eric J. Hobsbawm, *Labouring Men* (Garden City: Doubleday Anchor, 1967), p. 149.
3. Robert Dahl, *Modern Political Analysis* (Englewood Cliffs, N.J.: Prentice-Hall, 1963), p. 51.

sensus looks for issues and actions to bring groups together, then the strategist of dissensus looks for issues and actions which will drive groups apart.

Tactics to provoke dissensus are probably most effective at times when widespread social or economic change has already undermined a majority coalition, making it vulnerable to attack. Since the leaders of the coalition will tend to resist realignments of power and policy as long as possible, the disrupters must expose the underlying political tensions being produced by changing conditions. Then, confronted with actual or threatened electoral realignments, majority leaders will make concessions in an attempt to restore a weakening coalition or reorganize a shattered one.[4]

In the Goulart period, the nationalist left, with labor as its most important sector, used such a strategy of dissensus politics to extract material and deferential concessions from the president. However, the process finally culminated in the military overthrow of Goulart's coalition and a restructuring of the system to exclude the left-wing groups from participation in the political process.

To turn now from the question of power in the national political system to the power of labor leaders to call the workers out on strike, this chapter argues that the labor movement was much weaker than many contemporary observers thought and that union heads had relatively little organizational control over the rank-and-file. The success of political strikes, measured by the degree to which they disrupted economic activity, thus depended upon two factors independent of labor leaders' organizational control.

First, we hypothesize that the workers' economic situation strongly conditioned the success of a walkout, particularly when the content of labor leaders' demands appeared more political than narrowly economic.[5] During the period under study, wages were regularly increased by large percentages, but severe, spiraling inflation rapidly eroded their purchasing power. The curve of real wages (Table 16) therefore followed a saw toothed pattern. If union leaders called the strike when wages were at the low end of the curve, its prospects for success were good; however, if they called it shortly after a minimum wage hike and if their demands appeared to the workers as essentially political rather than directly related to their bread-and-butter needs, its chances for success were minimal.

A second major hypothesis concerning the success of important strikes relates to the disposition of the military toward the strike. During this period, the Brazilian military did not constitute an institution apart from civilian society. Military officers reflected to some extent the lines of cleavage within the broader society, and they generally intervened in politics at the behest of civilian groups.

4. Frances Fox Piven and Richard A. Cloward, "Dissensus Politics," *New Republic,* April 20, 1968, p. 22.

5. Leôncio Martins Rodrigues, in his study of the labor movement in São Paulo, finds that the great majority of strikes there were concerned with the erosion of wages by inflation and not with broader political, social, or professional matters. Rodrigues, *Conflito industrial e sindicalismo no Brasil* (São Paulo: Difusão Européia do Livro, 1966), p. 53.

TABLE 16

Real Minimum Wage in the State of Guanabara, 1952-1964

(in cruzeiros of February 1964)

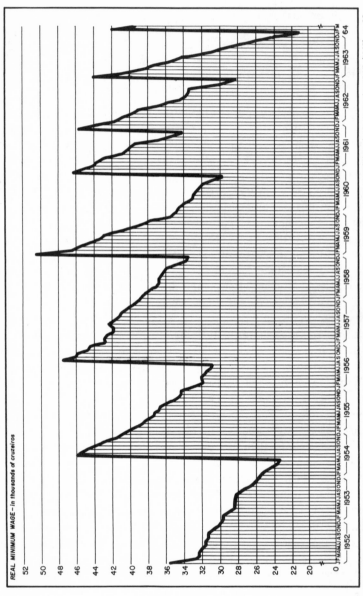

Source: Brazil, Ministério do Planejamento e Coordinação Econômica, Programa de Ação Econômica do Govêrno, 1964-1966 (Síntese), Rio de Janeiro: IBGE, (1965), p. 86.

Critics of the military often assume a natural affinity between the officers corps and right-wing interests, and these critics conclude that the left should seek an apolitical military institution. In Brazil, however, hardly any relevant civilian group has desired a purely apolitical, neutral military establishment.[6] Indeed, most civilian groups have sought its support, and we will see below that even labor leaders of the radical left appealed, sometimes successfully, to key officers.

Acts of omission or commission by the military directly affected the outcome of these strikes. The military generally assumed a position of benevolent neutrality or active support for the strikers in the period prior to 1963, but from that point onward most key commanding officers declared their opposition to strikes. In the period studied below, the leaders of the labor left appealed to officers generally described as "nationalists," who shared with them nationalist and radical reformist values. These labor leaders sought to use the officers to protect the strike movements from police repression and to enlist military support behind their demands for a radical restructuring of society. By mid-1963, their appeal to the officer corps had clearly failed, so they then mounted a campaign to win the backing of sergeants and noncommissioned officers.

Success of a strike, therefore, depended not only upon economic factors and the effectiveness of the picket line, but also upon what Brazilians call the *dispositivo militar.* This term refers to a military base of support at the disposal of someone, usually the President of the Republic, who would use it to protect strikers and their leaders from repression. As the military posture toward strikes shifted from benevolence to hostility in 1963, strike success diminished markedly.

In connection with the role of the military, the importance of the Brazilian federal system should be highlighted. Prior to 1964, there existed a variety of military and police forces at the disposal of differing political actors in Brazil. Outside the federal armed forces, the most important of these were the militias and police forces under the control of the state governors.[7] The governors of Guanabara and São Paulo, where the labor force was the most active, were particularly hostile to the radical labor leaders, and they often used force to crush strikes. They also attempted to exacerbate tensions during strikes in order to discredit the federal government, which usually supported the strikers.

One other variable deserving a word of explanation is the role of João Goulart. He had cultivated an image as benefactor of the working class since his short radical populist period as labor minister under Vargas, and in his own words, his major talent lay in conciliating diverse social sectors and political factions.[8] As vice-president (1956-1961) and later president (1961-1964), he was a major political actor in the strikes to be examined.

6. Alfred Stepan, *The Military in Politics: Changing Patterns in Brazil* (Princeton, N.J.: Princeton University Press, 1971), pp. 67-84.
7. Since 1964, the military rulers have concentrated the control of the most important of these units in the federal government.
8. Tejo, *Jango* (ch. 5 above, n. 42), pp. 109-110.

This analysis focuses on the following variables, and Table 20 summarizes them for all 17 strikes and threats:

1. the political situation, i.e., relevant aspects of the political situation at the moment of the strike
2. the economic situation, i.e., the relative level of the real minimum wage and specific wages in the involved sectors at the moment of the strike
3. the disposition of the military with regard to the strike
4. the goals of the striking sectors
5. success of the work stoppage
6. sectors involved
7. whether it was an actual strike or a threat
8. benefits to the strikers
9. the political actor who is the ultimate object of the pressure
10. the political beneficiary of the strike
11. the role of João Goulart

In the five case studies below, examination of these variables will shed light upon the process by which labor leaders generated and extended their considerable power in the political process; the foundations upon which this power rested; limitations upon it; and the connection between this process and the breakdown of the political system in 1964. This analysis rests principally upon journalistic coverage of the strikes, particularly in the daily and left-wing press. Confidential interviews with labor leaders, politicians, Ministry of Labor and labor-court officials, and other participants corroborated press observations in cases of weak or contradictory reporting. The footnotes below cite such interviews only when no press coverage exists. Because of general concern that Brazil was in a pre-revolutionary stage, however, journalists devoted much attention to these strikes, and their coverage was usually penetrating and thorough.

Parity Strike, November 1960

Wage parity between military and civil servants has provided a constant source of political tension in Brazil. One of the most important expressions of this tension appeared in the colonels' memorandum which forced João Goulart out of the Ministry of Labor in 1954 after he proposed a 100-percent raise in the minimum wage. The hike threatened to alter civil-military parity substantially.[9]

The parity strike of 1960 is another example of a political crisis caused by these tensions. This three-day strike of rail, port, and maritime workers took place due to the salary disparity which arose when the legislature raised military pay in July 1960 without attending to corresponding demands of the civil servants. The strikers worked in state-controlled enterprises and were paid

9. Text of memorandum in Oliveiros S. Ferreira, *As fôrças armadas* (ch. 4 above, n. 17), pp. 122-129.

according to the civil service scale. President Kubitschek ignored his campaign promise to prod the legislature, so strikers tied up national rail and maritime transport in early November.[10]

Vice-President Goulart, who had been reelected in October, did not play his accustomed role as conciliator of class conflicts. Rather, he remained in his home state of Rio Grande do Sul for the duration of the strike. He avoided the role because the strike represented the will of the mass of workers, who were in a decidedly ugly mood. He recognized that the strike had escaped from the control of the labor leaders and that it could not be brought to a halt without significant concessions. Thus, his appeal for a settlement would probably have been ignored, damaging his reputation both with the workers and with conservatives who felt it was in his power to bring any strike movement under control.

The strike, which coincided with a dispute over appointments in the social security system, precipitated the resignation of Labor Minister Batista Ramos. His replacement, Alírio de Sales Coelho, threatened to repress the strike with force and to fire the strikers, but such threats had little effect.[11] Indeed, the minister was bucking public opinion, for in the press an almost universal editorial reaction laid the blame at the doorstep of the legislature.[12]

The nation's executive and legislative institutions thus appeared incapable of resolving the crisis, so the military moved in to fill the leadership vacuum. Military drivers and vehicles took the place of public transport and minimized the disruptive effect of the strike.[13] Moreover, military pressure on the president and legislature brought the strike to a close and thus helped the workers win their raise. On the second day of the strike, the military ministers urged Kubitschek to come to Rio from Brasília, because the strike center was in Rio and a telecommunications walkout had isolated the capital. When the president arrived, these cabinet officers were on the verge of establishing military control on their own authority, because they feared the strike might be converted into an uprising.

At a cabinet meeting dominated by the military ministers, Kubitschek was convinced to submit a bill requesting a state of siege, which would allow him to rule by decree. This action served to ratify the *fait accompli* of the military ministers, while at the same time it prevented them from openly overstepping the bounds of the constitutional system. The legislators, still in Brasília, found themselves at a serious bargaining disadvantage, for a state of siege would temporarily close Congress and deprive them of a public forum, and they were already cut off from Rio by distance and the telephone strike. Party leaders therefore sped the parity bill through. The siege request was never formally presented to Congress.[14]

10. *CM,* Nov. 6, 1960, p. 6.
11. *DC,* Nov. 9, 1960, p. 1.
12. See Nov. 9, 1960, editorials in: *JB,* p. 3; *CM,* p. 6; *DC,* p. 4; and *DN,* Nov. 8, p. 4.
13. *HAR,* X, no. 11 (January 1961), 837.
14. Nov. 15, 1960: *JB,* p. 4, and *OESP,* p. 3; and *DN,* Nov. 10, p. 1.

This strike also highlights tensions which existed between the old *pelegos* and the Communists and other left-wing activists within the labor movement during the postwar period. Labor Minister Sales Coelho summoned the pelego directors of the workers' confederations in industry, commerce, land transport, and marine and air transport. Even though these confederation officers conceded the justice of the strikers' cause, they condemned this leftist-led walkout and jointly resolved to lend "unrestricted solidarity to the government of the Republic with respect to the measures taken to weaken the illegal strike called by rail, port, and maritime workers."[15] Throughout the period under consideration, the same two groups disputed the leadership of the labor movement, but dominance soon passed from the old pelegos to the left-wing directors of the striking unions and their allies in other sindicatos. The dynamism of these new leaders introduced a new factor into Brazilian industrial relations; this group played a major role in the explosion of labor activity in the early 1960's. Indeed, this strike was one of the early manifestations of this explosion. And as a result of their successful collaboration in this strike, radical rail, port, and maritime leaders set up a coordinating body, the Pact for Unity and Action (PUA), which figured prominently in subsequent strikes.

In conclusion, we now see that the strike, though political in method and impact, was definitely economic in content. In this case the pattern of pressure upon the legislature may be summarized as follows: labor struck, threatening domestic tranquility and weakening the national economy; the military, fearing disorder, threatened the executive if tranquility were not restored; the executive in turn frightened the legislators with a siege request which would substantially reduce their powers or even close Congress. Therefore, the legislature passed the bill which the strikers desired. In this particular instance, the pattern of pressure is similar to that found in Peru by James Payne.[16]

Succession Crisis Strikes, August-September 1961

When Jânio Quadros stunned Brazil with his resignation on August 25, 1961, the nation went through a bizarre civil-military crisis which saw a number of sectors of organized labor strike to defend Vice-President João Goulart's constitutional right to the presidency. Key military officers played a central role in the crisis. The military ministers sought to block Goulart. Favoring the vice-president, on the other hand, were some "constitutionalist" military officers, many politicians, and varied sectoral organizations ranging from the Medical Association of Guanabara to trade unions. Public opinion overwhelmingly supported the legal succession.[17]

15. *DC,* Nov. 9, 1960, p. 11.
16. James L. Payne, *Labor and Politics in Peru* (ch. 3 above, n. 16), pp. 8-11.
17. A Brazilian Institute of Public Opinion poll in Guanabara found that 81 percent of the electorate backed the legal succession, 10 percent favored the parliamentary compromise which ultimately was established, and only 9 percent desired Goulart's removal from office. *JB,* Sept. 2, 1961, p. 1.

Workers' organizations struck sporadically during the ten-day crisis, with greatest impact in the greater Rio region. Hardest hit were transport and certain manufacturing sectors. Politically, the transport sectors have a multiplier effect, because a great many of the workers in the city of Rio de Janeiro commute from working-class suburbs in the state of Rio via ferryboats and trains. When they cannot reach their place of employment, large numbers of idle workers roam the streets and easily lend themselves to demonstrations or disruptions of public order. Indeed, widespread rioting erupted in Niterói, the capital of the state of Rio, after the state militia wounded four people at a pro-Goulart demonstration. The army then put the city under military control.[18]

Work stoppages therefore disrupted public tranquility and dramatized the advantages of a rapid constitutional settlement to the crisis. Although strikes were by no means generalized throughout the economy or the nation, they played a significant role. Economic factors again predisposed the workers toward participation, for inflation had consumed 29 percent of the real minimum wage since its revision the previous November.[19]

In this context of national unrest, Governor Leonel Brizola successfully built up the morale of Goulart's supporters in his state of Rio Grande do Sul. Local governments and trade unions there showed their support by meeting in permanent session, and it appeared that these forces would split the nation and force a civil war if a constitutional solution to the crisis were not found.[20] Brizola thus shaped events and ultimately influenced Third Army Commander Machado Lopes to defy War Minister Denys.[21] The Third Army is the largest of Brazil's four armies, so its opposition to Denys carried great weight in inducing the military ministers to compromise.

The compromise allowed Goulart to take the presidency, but only under the provisions of an "Additional Act," which amended the Constitution to transfer most of the nation's executive powers to a prime minister who would henceforth be head of government. Due to overrepresentation of the most conservative, rural states in the legislature, the Additional Act thus provided a conservative constitutional check upon Goulart's radical populism.

The strike again marked the conflict between the old pelegos and the much more dynamic forces of the labor left. Even though the issues here were not openly economic, many important sectors went out on strike despite the fact that the pelegos heading the workers' confederations in industry, commerce, land transport, and maritime and air transport urged their workers to continue working and to remain calm.[22] Those confederation leaders had been prodded by their mentors in the American labor movement, who were in Rio at the time

18. *Ibid.,* p. 5.
19. Calculated from Getúlio Vargas Foundation data on cost of living in Guanabara, in *Conjuntura Econômica.*
20. *JB,* August 27, 1961, p. 4.
21. *HAR,* XIV (October 1961), 747.
22. *NR,* Sept. 1, 1961, p. 2.

attending the Fifth Convention of the Inter-American Regional Labor Organization (ORIT). Distrusting Goulart and Quadros, these visitors did not desire their return to power, as one of them acknowledged.[23]

Although the strikers won no direct economic benefits, their political gains were quite clear. The chief beneficiaries were the leaders of the labor left, because President Goulart subsequently threw the influence and patronage of his office behind them, enabling them to replace the cold-war generation of pelegos in top labor offices.

The pelegos' behavior in the succession crisis proved that they would not support Goulart when the chips were down. He and they had been at loggerheads since 1953 when, as labor minister, he had tried to oust some of them. More recently, in May 1961, he had attacked them at the Second National Encounter of Labor Leaders, one of several meetings which signaled an awakening and invigoration of the Brazilian labor movement. A broad range of leaders contributed to this awakening. One major group, which included Communists and other left-wing nationalists, chose to work within Brazil's corporative institutions and to collaborate with populist politicians like Goulart. The other major group, dubbed "renovators," sought to free labor from governmental domination. This group felt such populist compromises ultimately weakened labor, because they diverted union heads' attention from their own rank-and-file. The dynamics of populist politics in the corporative system, the renovators claimed, caused labor leaders to seek their main constituency among politicians instead.[24] Goulart, logically, put his weight behind the first group.

The opportunity for the definitive ouster of the most unpopular pelegos came at the National Confederation of Industrial Workers (CNTI) biennial election in December, when Goulart put the power of the presidency behind the men who had backed him three months earlier. This election provides an insightful case study of the mechanisms of governmental influence in labor affairs in this corporative state. Goulart came to Rio for the CNTI congress, where he organized the ouster of the pelegos. These incumbents exercised power over the voting delegates because their confederation offices enabled them to distribute travel opportunities, jobs, and other favors. Goulart's labor adviser, Gilberto Crockatt de Sá, countered the pelegos' offers with even more attractive promises from the president. To those who would vote for the left-wing slate, he offered good appointive posts for friends and relatives as well as substantial payments in cash. He assured them, moreover, that if the pelego slate won, Goulart would have the Ministry of Labor intervene in the confederation and call a new election which the opposition would win. Under such conditions, the election of the opposition slate appeared certain, so it would have been foolish of the swing

23. Serafino Romualdi, *Presidents and Peons* (New York: Funk and Wagnalls, 1967), pp. 285-286.

24. Timothy Fox Harding, "Political History of Organized Labor in Brazil" (ch. 1 above, n. 9), pp. 330-350.

votes to refuse the benefits they could reap from merely accepting the inevitable.[25] Of the 52 votes, the pelegos had been assured of 22 and the challengers 17. The remaining 13 were undecided. The final tally was 29 to 23, indicating that all but one of the swing votes went to the victorious slate.[26]

To conclude, the succession-crisis strike movement was at least moderately successful, because it followed considerable erosion of mass purchasing power and because military opinion was divided over the political issues and strikes. Its beneficiaries were Goulart, who acceded to the presidency, the labor leaders of the radical left, who took credit for the speedy increase in the minimum wage and who soon gained control of the nation's most powerful labor confederation, and the many workers earning the minimum wage, who soon got a raise.

Cabinet Crisis General Strike, July 1962

Goulart devoted his first eight months in office almost exclusively to pacifying the various political forces. He claimed that this task, plus the restrictions of the parliamentary system, prevented him from implementing a program of fundamental reform.[27] The left-wing leadership of labor also remained quiescent, to avoid provoking a right-wing military reaction while Jango consolidated his power. However, the climate was ripening for labor agitation, as inflation subtracted an ever-increasing portion of labor's paycheck. On Labor Day (May 1), against this inflationary backdrop, labor leaders kicked off a campaign for basic structural and nationalist reforms and for increasing economic benefits. This culminated in the July 1962 general strike for a cabinet which would support these measures.

The cabinet crisis which occasioned the strike arose due to the lack of foresight of the Additional Act's framers. The Act failed to alter the constitutional provision of the presidential system, which required legislators who intended to run for reelection to relinquish all appointive posts 90 days before the election. Retaining such a provision under cabinet government in a parliamentary regime was absurd, for it required the resignation of the cabinet, which is theoretically the executive, three months before an election. Government would then rest with an interim cabinet composed of legislators who did not intend to pursue their political careers in the September elections.

Piqued by Goulart's Labor Day call for a plebiscite to reestablish presidential supremacy, the legislators wished to spite the president. They stubbornly rejected his proposed constitutional amendment to eliminate the provision in question. Thus the cabinet had to resign in July, and the selection of a new one occasioned a national crisis. Goulart's first choice for premier was San Tiago Dantas, a man committed to the basic reform program of the nationalist left. The Congress rejected him. Senator Auro de Moura Andrade, the president's

25. Confidential interviews.
26. *NR*, Dec. 15, 1961, p. 2.
27. *NR*, May 4, 1962, p. 1.

second choice, proposed a cabinet unsympathetic to the reforms – one which even included as military ministers three officers who had opposed Goulart's legal succession in August. Unwilling to compromise, the president refused to ratify the suggested cabinet, and he vowed to reject any list which would not favor his reform program.[28]

In the meantime, the workers, who had been threatening a general strike for the previous three weeks, finally readied their strike apparatus to oppose Auro's unacceptable policies. Faced with Goulart's adamancy and the threat of civil disorder inherent in the general strike, Auro resigned as premier without ever having his cabinet officially confirmed by the Chamber. It was already too late, however. The crisis culminated in a general strike, rioting, and the ultimate appointment of a premier whose reformism was substantially similar to San Tiago's.

By the time Auro resigned, the strike machinery had already been called into action for July 5, the following day. Goulart vainly sought cancellation of the strike order, a move which, if successful, would have made him look eminently moderate and reasonable in this moment of acute political passion and intransigence. However, his appeals to the strike leaders, through four top-level emissaries, failed.[29] Dante Pelacani, then acting president of the CNTI and head of the strike movement, replied to presidential emissary Leocádio Antunes: "We are on the side of President Goulart but not under his command. If we don't hold the strike, it will break our morale."[30] Thus, they demonstrated their strength as well as their independence of Goulart.

The strike was considered a success, although its effectiveness varied considerably from one part of the country to another. Hardest hit was the transport sector. Throughout the nation, airline, maritime, and dock workers struck; and, in the Rio area, many other public, commercial, and industrial sectors were affected.[31]

The walkout occurred during a period of food shortages in the state of Rio, and the days preceding it had witnessed marches and demonstrations demanding that the government make available such staples of the Brazilian diet as black beans, rice, and sugar. With transport effectively paralyzed, the strike meant that the residents of these working-class suburbs would go hungry for one more day. Lacking transportation to their jobs in the city of Rio, moreover, large numbers of workers milled around in the streets until violent riots and looting shook four of the state's main population centers, leaving a toll of more than 40 dead and 700 injured.[32]

28. *JB,* July 4, 1962, p. 1.
29. The emissaries were Gilberto Crockatt de Sá, Leocádio Antunes, San Tiago Dantas, and General Osvino Ferreira Alves.
30. *JB,* July 5, 1962, p. 3.
31. Jover Telles, *O movimento sindical* (ch. 3 above, n. 19), pp. 178-179; *JB,* July 6, 1962, p. 4; *NR,* July 13, 1962, p. 3.
32. *DC,* July 3, 1962, p. 7; *JB,* July 6, p. 1.

Deteriorating economic conditions help explain the breadth of the walkout. The real minimum wage curve was again at the low end, accounting for the favorable response among the rank-and-file. Real wages were 26 percent below the previous high of November 1961, and at a point they had fallen below for a total of only 10 months over the 6 years since July 1956.[33] In addition, some of the principal participating sectors, such as teamsters, stevedores, maritime workers, and metalworkers, had specific economic or workplace grievances which were not directly tied to the minimum wage.

Pelacani's comment cited above suggests that control over the rank-and-file was rather tenuous, making it difficult to call a halt to the strike. Thus, this case supports the hypothesis that economic factors were more important to its success than the organizational power of the labor leadership. Further evidence emerged the following day, when rumors of another strike call precipitated a walkout which forced business to close early in Rio. Afterward, the strike leaders admitted that they lacked the organizational strength to hold the workers at the workplace once rumors began the sudden work stoppage.[34]

The strike gave Jango a chance to test his *dispositivo militar,* and it showed considerable support for the president himself and, consequently, for the general strike. He denounced the action of the same anti-constitutional forces that tried to block his legal succession, and the commanders of all four armies responded by professing their support for him and pointing out that their armies were being maintained in a state of readiness against any attempted coup.[35]

Vital to the operation and success of the strike was the support of General Osvino Ferreira Alves, a nationalist who commanded the First Army in Rio. The labor leaders had been acting with caution until Osvino's statements suggested that he would support them. In a speech to his troops ten days before the general strike, he denounced an offensive of the extreme right which aimed at establishing a dictatorship, and he likened it to German Nazism and Italian Fascism.[36] Only after Osvino repeated his strong stand in favor of Goulart on July 4, however, did the strike organizers activate their plans for the following day.[37]

The strike leaders already knew Goulart could guarantee the support of the civilian branches of the federal government. He had instructed the Labor Ministry to refrain from pronouncing the strike illegal, and the rail and port workers, who are employed by the government, knew they would not be docked any pay during the stoppage. Thus, it is significant that they hesitated until they had the assurance of military protection. In Guanabara, they needed the First Army to protect them from repression by Governor Lacerda's state police. The

33. Calculated from Getúlio Vargas Foundation data on cost of living in Guanabara, in *Conjuntura Econômica.*
34. *JB,* July 7, 1962, p. 4.
35. *JB,* July 5, 1962, p. 1.
36. Text of speech in Telles, *O movimento sindical,* pp. 160-161.
37. *Ibid.,* pp. 174-178; *JB,* July 5, 1962, p. 3.

Army added to the strike's success in Guanabara, for the high command refrained from substituting military vehicles for idled public transport, even though this had been customary during past transport strikes.[38] Military officers even helped end the strike, for it was officially called off at midnight on July 5 after they had assisted in negotiating the release of labor leaders jailed by the Guanabara police.[39]

The principal immediate goal of the strike was to pressure Congress to approve a prime minister whose cabinet would support the basic reforms; indeed, they attained their objective. Regarding the cabinet, the strike leaders demanded a labor minister who would look favorably upon them. A week after the strike, they met with Goulart and the new premier in Brasília, where they discussed suggestions for labor minister, rejecting several names before accepting Hermes Lima.[40]

In his inaugural address, Minister Lima then called for labor's active and direct participation in the leadership and debates which would determine the specifics of Brazil's nationalist development. Lima's speech shows that the strike leaders had begun to increase their political influence and power in national politics. While in Brasília, these union heads accompanied the president as he signed the year-end bonus bill, which provided each worker with an annual bonus equivalent to one month's pay (called the "thirteenth month" in Brazil). This law, the result of several years' campaign, further augmented their prestige.

Following the strike, labor leaders worked to sustain their movement's momentum. Three thousand union delegates at the Fourth National Labor Encounter in August institutionalized the temporary General Strike Command on a permanent basis as the General Labor Command (CGT), a body which later provided one of the most important organizational underpinnings for the basic reform campaign. The delegates endorsed principles and programs for structural change, arguing that only through such reform could Brazil emerge from its economic, social, and political stagnation. They threatened another general strike for the reforms, if necessary.[41] And they forced Jango to promise to support these principles and programs before they agreed to back his campaign for a plebiscite to reestablish presidential rule.[42] Goulart's reluctant acquiescence showed the growing power of the labor leaders, because at this moment he wished to project a moderate image in order to secure the broadest possible support for the plebiscite.

In this strike, the pattern of pressure took the following form. The president played a major role, for he first urged workers to strike for a reform-oriented cabinet. Like the parity strike of 1960, this walkout aimed to pressure Congress by demonstrating the power of the masses and by discrediting the legislators in

38. *DC,* July 7, 1962, p. 1.
39. *JB,* July 6, 1962, p. 1; July 7, p. 4.
40. *JB,* July 17, 1962, p. 5.
41. Text of principal manifesto in Telles, *O movimento sindical,* pp. 184-186.
42. *Visão,* Aug. 17, 1962, p. 15.

the public eye. It succeeded on both counts. It seriously disrupted public tranquility and the national economy, and even newspaper editorials which did not approve of it condemned the legislators' vain inaction for precipitating the crisis. This enabled the labor leaders of the radical left to expand their already growing political power: when the president asked them to cancel the strike, they rebuffed him.

General Strike over Plebiscite, September 1962

The general strike of Saturday, September 15, 1962, was a sequel to and an outgrowth of the July strike. Goulart had taken a strong stand for the basic reforms, and he blamed the parliamentary system for blocking his proposals. He therefore urged Congress to call a plebiscite on the regime jointly with the congressional elections of October 7. When the prime minister failed to obtain such a bill, his cabinet resigned on September 13.

This prompted the CGT, which had readied the general strike machinery as a threat to Congress, to call the walkout for Friday evening, September 14. Labor pressure had crystallized several days before the strike in a nine-point ultimatum to the president, cabinet, and legislators: (1) a plebiscite on October 7; (2) revocation of the National Security Law; (3) reform of the electoral law to grant the right to vote to all citizens, including soldiers and illiterates; (4) 100 percent minimum wage hike, with corresponding increases for those above the minimum to maintain the wage hierarchy; (5) approval of the most favorable right-to-strike bill pending in Congress; (6) immediate retraining and placement of all civil servants, regardless of the results of government manpower studies; (7) radical distributive agrarian reform; (8) rejection of the pending bank reform bill, and the delegation of power to the cabinet to draw up a new one and all others necessary for national emancipation; (9) an immediate prize freeze on the most necessary foods.[43] Once the strike was under way, the CGT leaders added demands for a personal meeting with Goulart, the right to organize sindicatos among the peasants, and strict enforcement of the profits remittance law.

In this crisis, the president demonstrated considerable skill at manipulating public opinion and both military and labor dispositivos. The legislature conceded defeat and passed a compromise bill which called a plebiscite three months after the election and allowed Goulart to appoint a caretaker cabinet for the interim.

The CGT admitted that the strike was less effective than the one in July. Called on a Friday afternoon and continuing into Saturday, it came on a most inappropriate day because many plants and workplaces are closed during the weekend anyway.[44] As in July, Rio was hit the hardest. Transport and certain manufacturing activities were most seriously paralyzed, but by Saturday, even in Rio, few sectors showed its effect.

43. *JB*, Sept. 11, 1962, p. 3; text in *O Semanário*, Sept. 13, p. 1.
44. *JB*, Sept. 18, 1962, p. 4; Sept. 28, p. 3.

Despite its hasty calling and the inopportune day, economic deprivation made it a partial success. The real minimum wage had dropped 34 percent from its previous high in November 1961.[45] The delegates to the August meeting had demanded its readjustment, and the CGT pressed for it during the strike. Some transport workers had specific economic grievances that predisposed them to strike, while maritime officers and engineers had already tied up shipping in pursuit of their own economic demands.[46]

As in the July strike, labor found valuable allies in the military. Since the strike's objective was very dear to the president, Goulart used labor and military institutions to bring pressure on Congress. The armed forces not only protected the strikers, as they had in July, but military leaders even ran a campaign of their own to seek the plebiscite. The minister of war, beginning in late July, announced that his sounding of military opinion found a consensus favoring an early plebiscite. The ministers of the Air Force and Navy soon rallied behind him. Ultimately, the commander of the Third Army made public a memo envisioning a "fratricidal struggle if Congress failed to set a date for the plebiscite."[47]

In their active campaign for a plebiscite, military leaders naturally supported the striking workers who sought the same goal. When Governor Lacerda sent his police out to break up the strike, troops from the First Army prevented some arrests, secured the release of some of those detained, and even imprisoned two of Lacerda's security officers who attempted to invade a radio station which was broadcasting communiqués and news from the strike command. In São Paulo, the Army convinced the police to exercise moderation, and only one union leader was arrested there. The Air Force lent protection to the union headquarters of the striking air transport workers.[48]

CGT leaders again received a number of significant benefits for their role in the crisis. As in July, the political gains were impressive, particularly with respect to their power vis-à-vis the president. Again, Goulart tried unsuccessfully to terminate the strike once he had made his own personal political gain. In the early hours of September 15, the legislature approved the compromise Capanema-Valadares bill to hold a plebiscite on the regime in January. Goulart immediately appealed to the CGT, personally and through Labor Minister João Pinheiro Neto, to cancel the strike, but his appeal fell upon deaf ears. The strike continued, although ineffectively, until its scheduled termination at midnight. [49] Thus, once more, the radical labor left had proved that it would not be his handmaiden. In these negotiations, Pinheiro Neto, whom Goulart had just

45. Calculated from Getúlio Vargas Foundation data on cost of living in Guanabara, in *Conjuntura Econômica.*

46. *JB,* Sept. 15, 1962, p. 4; Nov. 7, p. 10.

47. *JB,* July 29, 1962, p. 10; Aug. 7, p. 1; Aug. 8, p. 3; Sept. 12, p. 1; Sept. 13, p. 3, including text of memo; Sept. 14, p. 1.

48. *JB,* Sept. 15, 1962, p. 1.

49. Sept. 16, 1962: *DC,* p. 1, and *JB,* p. 9; and confidential interview.

appointed labor minister, assured the strike leaders that their demands regarding the revision of the minimum wage and the organization of rural sindicatos would be satisfied.[50]

At the beginning of the following week, the president had the Air Force fly the four most important strike leaders to Brasília, where they discussed the cabinet he was about to appoint. In these exchanges, Goulart had to argue strenuously to win acceptance of his choices for the Ministries of Finance and Agriculture. And he agreed to hasten the revision of the minimum wage and to try to hold or reduce soaring prices on articles of primary necessity. In return, he won a 30-day moratorium on the political general strike while he pursued the reforms through established channels.[51]

In the months that followed, CGT leaders showed their increased influence by meeting frequently with the labor minister while pressuring for an early raise in the minimum wage. Since CNTI Secretary-General Dante Pelacani also headed the executive body of the national social welfare system, he lent a team of statisticians to the Labor Ministry to speed the raise.[52] The strike, therefore, prompted the readjustment, even though it was not enacted until January 1. Without a strike, however, the raise probably would have come still later.

In another gesture which symbolized the growing power of the strikers, Labor Minister Pinheiro Neto came to CNTI headquarters, where he signed a new ministerial regulation to facilitate the organization of rural workers. The radical labor leaders had opposed the previous regulation ever since Labor Minister Franco Montoro, a Christian Democrat, had instituted it in 1961, because they felt it restricted their power in rural areas, to the advantage of Christian Democrats and other moderates.

In return for Goulart's pledge to pursue the reforms, the CGT campaigned to turn out the worker vote in January's plebiscite. Goulart assisted by conveniently raising the minimum wage a few days before the polling. By a five-to-one margin, the electorate rejected the parliamentary system.

The pattern of political pressure again resembles that of previous strikes. The president, relying on his military and labor dispositivos, pressured the Congress, and again, Congress issued the bill he desired. Moreover, the CGT leaders again proved their strength and further augmented their growing leverage over Goulart.

Santos Strikes, September 1963

The restoration of full presidential powers deprived Jango of his excuse for failing to check inflation and to restore dynamism to the flagging economy. The credit of confidence which he had enjoyed before the plebiscite soon dissipated, causing political initiative and power to disperse among other political actors.

50. *JB*, Sept. 16, 1962, p. 9.
51. *JB*, Sept. 20, 1962, p. 3.
52. *NR*, Sept. 27, 1962, p. 2.

Though he had won an increase in power in formal terms, he began to suffer losses in the realities of informal political bargaining.

The nature of the strike process changed after the plebiscite, reflecting the diffusion of political power. The *dispositivo militar-sindical* broke up, and a fundamental opposition between its two components emerged. In the drive for the plebiscite, President Goulart had brilliantly controlled political initiative, particularly by influencing the actions of labor and the military. Once military misgivings about the increasing power of labor surfaced in late 1962, however, the two began to assume political initiative themselves, and they pursued their conflicting interests quite independently of the president's desires.

During this period, moreover, many sergeants and noncommissioned officers became increasingly radicalized and alienated from the military hierarchy. They had become so outspoken in their advocacy of radical political and social reforms, for example, that at a rally co-sponsored by the CGT one sergeant threatened, in the name of the radical sergeants' movement, to take up arms alongside radical labor and other forces in order to implement the reform program.[53] This process quickly intensified the officers' hostility to radical labor and the strikes.

The overtly anti-strike role of the military and the consequent reduction of labor leaders' power may be observed in several strikes and strike threats after late 1962, but the Santos strikes of September 1963 most graphically exemplify this. These strikes occurred at a moment of high military tension, because the Supreme Court was preparing to rule upon the political status of sergeants. Indeed, when the Court ruled the following week to sustain their ineligibility to vote or run for office, sergeants in Brasília rose up in arms.

Tension was also rising in radical labor circles. At a rally in August to commemorate the death of Vargas, CGT representative Rafael Martinelli warned Goulart, who was also on the podium, that strikes were about to become more intensive and widespread until the basic reforms were achieved. Not two weeks after the rally, an economic strike by nurses and hospital employees in Santos evolved into a citywide solidarity strike, which brought the developing confrontation between labor and the military into the open.

Negotiations failed in the hospital strike, so the Forum Sindical de Debates (FSD), the CGT coordinating body in that city, called the general strike in sympathy. As soon as port and other principal activities in Santos came to a standstill, Governor Adhemar de Barros sent in his armed state police. Using tear and nausea gas, they broke up a meeting of the FSD in the port workers' *sindicato* and arrested 250 participants.[54]

This action by the state government typified the activity of Adhemar and

53. *O Semanário,* May 16, 1963, p. 8, including text of speech; *OESP,* May 12, p. 9; *JB,* May 12, pp. 1, 3, 4.

54. *JB,* Sept. 3, 1963, p. 3. For a detailed and insightful case study of one of the most active unions in Santos, that of the stevedores, see Ingrid A. Sarti, "Estiva e política: estudo de caso no porto de Santos" (master's thesis, University of São Paulo, 1973).

Carlos Lacerda, whose governments constituted mainstays of civilian legal and extralegal opposition to Goulart. Both generally attempted to turn political strikes and labor agitation to their advantage by obstructing negotiations and peaceful solutions. Thus increasing the likelihood of disorder, they aimed to frighten the center and right and further alienate them from the president.

The PUA responded to the arrests by threatening a national general rail and port strike if the federal government did not resolve the situation in favor of the strikers within 24 hours. At the same time, military leaders warned Goulart that they would not condone such a strike, and they threatened to repress it with force if necessary. Second Army Commander Peri Bevilacqua, in a joint press conference with Adhemar, made clear his opposition to the strike.

This confrontation signaled the definitive demise of the *dispositivo sindical-militar.* Goulart acquiesced to military pressure by dispatching Labor Minister Amaury Silva to Santos to terminate the strike peacefully. The state government, however, by ordering its political police to arrest the president of the textile workers' *sindicato,* immediately destroyed the peaceful solution which the labor minister had negotiated. The FSD, predictably, continued its sympathy strike, with the adherence of the Santos-Jundiaí Railroad and other sectors. [55] At this point the military made good its threat to quash the strike. War Minister Jair Dantas Ribeiro sent the chief of staff of the Second Army, with supporting troops, to act as interventor in Santos. He was instructed to use force, if necessary, to maintain order. The general easily convinced the FSD to call off the strike, and the PUA also decided to avoid confronting the military with the national general strike they had threatened.[56]

Important as economic deprivation may be to the success of a walkout, the Santos experience suggests that the disposition of the military is a factor of even greater weight. The real minimum wage had fallen 47 percent since the January readjustment, the contracts in many sectors earning more than the minimum were about to terminate, and Clodschmidt Riani, president of the CNTI and CGT, was threatening a national general strike to raise the minimum.[57] Still, the general strike never extended beyond Santos, due to the military threat to crush it. The military had effectively isolated the radical labor leaders, to whom Goulart was unable or unwilling to offer any encouragement. The military threat prevented another walkout when the sergeants rebelled the following week.

Conclusion

In Brazil between 1960 and 1964, labor leaders derived political power from their positions in the corporative framework and from their control over major

55. *JB,* Sept. 4, 1963, pp. 1, 4.
56. Sept. 5, 1963: *JB,* pp. 1, 3, and *CM,* p. 5; Sept. 6: *UH,* p. 2, and *CM,* p. 1.
57. Real minimum wage calculated from Getúlio Vargas Foundation data on cost of living in Guanabara, in *Conjuntura Econômica; JB,* Sept. 1, 1963, p. 29.

strikes. We have discussed 5 major strikes here in order to illustrate the relationship between the strike process and the political power and influence of labor leaders. Our concluding section is based on data from those 5 cases and 12 other major political strikes or strike threats between 1960 and 1964. (Table 20, at the end of this chapter, summarizes the relevant data for all 17 cases.)

First, it becomes clear that, by controlling strikes during this turbulent period, labor leaders gained considerable political power, most notably over President João Goulart. Our case studies show that CGT leaders rejected Goulart's requests to cancel the two general strikes of 1962, and, by trading on their apparent success in these strikes, they successfully influenced his choice of new cabinet members after each stoppage. Later, in February 1964, these labor leaders submitted, on behalf of rebelling sailors, a list of candidates from which the president selected the new Navy minister.

Radical statements by labor leaders and their allies on the left, their impact on cabinet formation, and the political demands of major strikes led certain observers, particularly hostile ones, to label these strikes as "merely political." [58] Such an interpretation implies that the labor leaders exercised effective control over the rank-and-file and could close the plants for purposes alien to the immediate well-being of the workers. The evidence from these 17 strikes and threats refutes this claim and supports the contention of CGT Vice-President Dante Pelacani:

> The so-called political strike, which has nothing to do with politics in the sense usually intended, is unleashed by the Brazilian workers with economic objectives and never partisan political objectives. Politics, as workers understand it, is the art of administering well. Thus, the workers demand the application of political measures with the goal of gaining better administration of the common weal, in order to assure greater economic tranquility to the proletariat. [59]

Summarizing our data in tabular form reveals more clearly the economic dimension of these political strikes. For our purposes, readers should include strike threats along with failures, because labor leaders did not go beyond the threat level when economic or military factors would have condemned a stoppage to failure. In other words, union leaders called their workers off the job only when they believed that the workers' economic situation was grave enough to predispose them to strike. And they withheld the strike call when the military clearly planned to repress or undermine the stoppage.

Table 17 supports Pelacani's contention that economic factors motivated the strikes of this period. Walkouts successfully paralyzed economic activity only when workers felt severe economic deprivation, as at the end of a contract period when inflation had substantially eroded their purchasing power: 9 of the

58. J. V. Freitas Marcondes calls them "merely political" in *Radiografia da liderança sindical paulista* (São Paulo: Instituto Cultural do Trabalho, 1964), p. 70.
59. *JB,* Dec. 29, 1963, Caderno Especial, p. 15.

TABLE 17

Initial Success of "Political" Strikes in Brazil, 1960-1964,
by Relative Economic Deprivation of Workers Involved

		Real wages low or other immediate economic grievance	No immediate economic grievance; or redress in process	Total
Success of strike in terms of work stoppage at outset	Very or moderately successful	9	1	10
	Strike threat which did not become strike	3	3	6
	Failure	0	1	1
	Total	12	5	17

10 moderately or very successful work stoppages occurred at moments when workers suffered an economic squeeze. The one exception was the strike after Varig Airlines violated the labor law and fired a pilot with tenure; if the company were not made to recant, other pilots could fear for their jobs, so this strike also relates to economic security.

One might ask why the 3 threats made at moments of relative economic deprivation did not become strikes, for one would expect workers to respond under such circumstances. The explanation rests with the second major variable, i.e., the attitude of key military officers toward the strike movement (Table 18). In each of the 6 threats which did not result in work stoppages, key officers had threatened to crush the movement if the workers took to the streets.

Pursuing the military variable further (Table 19), we find that officers wielded decisive influence on the strikes' outcomes in 14 of the 17 cases. The one apparently anomalous entry, where the workers won a favorable settlement in the face of military opposition, was the parity walkout of 1960. Seeking in that case to prevent disruption of public order, the military ministers pressured the president and legislature to pass the bill sought by the workers. The military therefore tailored this strike's outcome as well, even though it favored the workers. In all other cases where a unified officer corps opposed a strike, they shaped its outcome to fit their own desires.

In ultimate testimony to these findings, the general strike called to prevent Goulart's overthrow fizzled completely. CGT leaders called it only five weeks after the minimum wage had been doubled, so relative economic deprivation did not motivate the rank-and-file. And the military administered the coup de grâce, arresting those leaders who did not go underground and crushing what little worker resistance could be found.

TABLE 18

Initial Success of "Political" Strikes in Brazil, 1960-1964,
by Attitude of Key Military Officers Toward Them

		Military favorable, indifferent, openly split	*Military opposed to strike*	*Total*
Success of strike	Very or moderately successful	7	3	10
in terms of work stoppage	Strike threat which did not become strike	0	6	6
at outset	Failure	0	1	1
	Total	7	10	17

To be considered in conjunction with the military is the role of important state governors such as Carlos Lacerda in Guanabara and Adhemar de Barros in São Paulo. As opponents of strikes in general and of Goulart in particular, they expended considerable energy during this period to increase the disruptive appearance of these strikes. Adhemar provided the clearest illustration of this when he sabotaged the Santos general strike settlement. The governors pursued this course to build a strong public reaction against strikes and the CGT. They were thus taking advantage of what Skidmore calls "the 'democratic' process of opinion formation within the Brazilian high command."[60] The longer and more disruptive the strikes could be made, the more the growing anti-strike current in the military would deepen.

The assertion that these strikes were "merely political" assumes that labor leaders possessed strict control over their rank-and-file. The evidence from these 17 strikes and strike threats does not support such an assumption. On the contrary, the data support Henry Landsberger's generalization that in Latin America, "With rare but, of course, important exceptions, labor is not automatically responsive to orders from its top leadership. . . ."[61] The mass of workers in these Brazilian strikes only followed strike calls when they were undergoing temporary economic hardship.

Many observers ascribed great political power to these labor leaders, but they failed to notice substantial limitations upon that power. The principal limitation

60. Thomas E. Skidmore, *Politics in Brazil* (ch. 1 above, n. 9), p. 210. General Golbery do Couto e Silva also stressed the importance of public opinion on political action by the military; see Stepan, *The Military in Politics* (n. 6 above), p. 97.
61. Henry A. Landsberger, "The Labor Elite: Is it Revolutionary? " in Seymour Martin Lipset and Aldo Solari (eds.), *Elites in Latin America* (New York: Oxford, 1967), p. 258.

TABLE 19

Ultimate Outcome of "Political" Strikes in Brazil, 1960-1964, by Attitude
of Key Military Officers Toward Them, and Officers' Influence Upon
Their Resolution

		Military favorable, indifferent, or openly split	*Military opposed to strike*	*Total*
Military did not influence out- come	Settlement favorable to workers' demands	3	0	3
Military influenced outcome	Settlement favorable to workers' demands	4	1	5
	Military undermine, crush, or force settlement unfavorable to workers' demands	0	3	3
	Strike threat which did not become strike	0	6	6
Total		7	10	17

was internal to organized labor, i.e., the fundamental weakness of Brazilian labor organizations. Few union heads possessed strong, institutionalized ties to the mass of workers. Sindicato membership was generally low. In greater São Paulo, the most industrialized area in Brazil, for example, only 13 percent of the workers in the important sectors of metallurgy, mechanical and electrical equipment, and textiles were active members with dues paid up-to-date in 1961. [62] The município- rather than plant-based structure of the sindicatos, and the social service mentality which Brazilian labor law fosters, prevented labor leaders from converting the unions into effective mass organizations.

The leaders failed to institutionalize and strengthen their ties with the base, furthermore, because their positions of importance within the corporative framework absorbed most of their attention. As contacts with politicians helped them pyramid their power, many labor leaders simply diverted their focus from their

62. Leôncio Martins Rodrigues, *Conflito industrial* (n. 5 above), p. 93.

union constituency to a new, political, constituency. Their neglect of ties with the base did not, however, prevent them from regularly calling successful strikes, because spiraling inflation constantly eroded purchasing power and predisposed angry wage-earners to walk off the job. These strikes, in turn, created the illusion that the union heads exerted strong control over a politically important mass, and politicians therefore accorded them increasing power within the councils of state. Labor leaders apparently took their own weakness into account, for they usually called "political" strikes when real wages were low.

The second important limitation was external, i.e., the attitude of key military officers toward the strike movement. As we have seen, the most successful general strikes enjoyed military support and, later, when a unified officer corps began systematically opposing walkouts, most threats did not escalate to strikes; and those that did were ultimately crushed.

The fundamental economic nature of these strikes, however, should not obscure the relevance to the workers' well-being of the political demands articulated by their leaders. Some scholars have characterized Brazil as a dual society in which the rural agrarian and the urban industrial sectors are relatively independent.[63] The labor leaders of the nationalist left during the early 1960's, on the contrary, premised their thought and action on the fundamental *interdependence* of these two sectors.[64] In an excellent discussion of the politicization of labor movements in developing areas, sociologist Leôncio Martins Rodrigues found that Brazilian labor leaders perceived a functional interrelationship between the two sectors. These union heads then concluded that Brazil's agrarian structure posed the principal obstacle to improving the workers' standard of living. In other words, the traditional rural sector, which controlled a majority in the Brazilian Congress, was holding back economic development and the benefits it would bring to the workers.[65] Labor leaders therefore demanded agrarian, tax, economic, educational, and administrative reforms. These they expected to provide a basis for more rapid industrialization, now that import substitution had outlived its usefulness as a means to self-sustaining economic development.

The lack of strong ties between labor leaders and the body of workers is the reflection of Latin American populism on the level of labor organizations. Brazilian workers do not possess the degree of class consciousness which could contribute in an important way to the success of strikes, even when the economic situation of the workers has deteriorated. In a plant level study, sociologist Juárez Rubens Brandão Lopes ascribes the low level of class consciousness of São Paulo's industrial workers to their rural origin. Two-thirds of

63. Jacques Lambert, *Le Brésil* (Paris: Armand Colin, 1953), *passim.*
64. A more explicit and highly developed example of this type of argument appears in André Gunder Frank, *Capitalism and Underdevelopment in Latin America* (New York: Monthly Review Press, 1967), pp. 145-150.
65. Rodrigues, *Conflito industrial,* pp. 36-41, 55-56. A labor document reflecting this point of view is "O operário e a questão agrária," *Boletim do DIEESE,* I, no. 3 (July 1960), 1 and 11.

the work force in his study had migrated from the interior and had first worked on the land before coming to the city. In rural areas, social relationships are generally of a patron-client nature – that is, vertical rather than horizontal or class-based. Since these recent arrivals to the city still held traditional attitudes which limited collective action to one's family and friends, these migrants tended not to join the sindicatos.[66] Furthermore, Brazilian sindicatos do not generally maintain active factory-level units which might attract these workers.

Therefore, the success of a strike derives not from an internalized sense of duty to one's class, but rather from economic deprivation and from the force of external authority, in this case a picket line to keep workers from entering the factories. Given this lack of class consciousness, Leôncio Martins Rodrigues notes that

> *. . . for the authority of the management of the enterprise to be challenged, it follows that the challenge be made by another "authority," that of the sindicato leadership which must bear the responsibilities and consequences.* The importance of "higher authorities" for the success of strike movements can be judged by the presence of politicians, deputies, and personalities alien to the labor movement who participate in the general assemblies of the workers and even in the picket lines, offering with their presence protection against the measures of repression and lending the union activity a "legal" character.[67]

The pickets not only aimed at keeping the workers off the job, but they also tried to force the management to lock the worke.s out. Circulating from one factory to the next, they prevented workers from entering and threatened violence against the plant as well. This latter threat often caused management to declare a lockout or holiday with pay, which automatically swelled the picket line. The pickets then proceeded to the next factory to repeat their performance. The snowball effect was very important and generally functioned most effectively when prestigious outsiders had lent the movement legitimacy. Throughout the period under study here, these characteristics typified the strikes.

The case studies show that certain economic sectors and geographic areas are more prone to strike than others. In particular, the transport sectors show high strike turnouts. Their strategic position increases their capacity for economic and political dislocation and, hence, the likelihood that they will be satisfied. In addition, many transport workers were on the federal government payroll and generally could count on receiving pay for days lost. Similarly, the Rio area, where over 30 percent of all federal employees were based,[68] had the highest levels of adherence. In some measure the same holds true for Santos, a port city linked to the rest of São Paulo state by a federal railroad. In the capital of

66. Juárez Rubens Brandão Lopes, *Sociedade industrial no Brasil* (São Paulo: Difusão Européia do Livro, 1964), pp. 33, 69.
67. Rodrigues, *Conflito industrial,* pp. 61-79; quote, p. 73.
68. *Anuário Estatístico do Brasil,* 1967, p. 732.

Brazilian private industry, São Paulo, successful walkouts generally required a higher degree of deprivation.

Let us close by turning from the internal mechanisms of the strike to its relation to the political system in general (Table 20). Insofar as labor's disruptive tactics threatened the president, this process bears a good deal of similarity to the pattern of "bargaining by violence" which Payne highlights in his study of labor in Peru.[69] Indeed, this is the way dissensus politics works. By the mere threat of driving the military and the right out of the coalition, CGT leaders increased the attention given them by the president. They believed, moreover, that if they succeeded in removing the military from among Goulart's close collaborators, they could force him to rely even more upon radical labor as the mainstay of his government.[70] While they sought to drive a wedge between the high command and Goulart, they did not wish to provoke a military coup; witness, for example, their cautious behavior in the strikes after Quadros' resignation and again in late 1963. That their strikes did ultimately contribute to military intervention must be attributed to miscalculation.

The dangers for those who push dissensus politics to the extreme are evident in Charles Anderson's description of Latin American political systems in the populist era. He notes that for new power contenders to gain admission to the political arena: (1) their power capability must be sufficient to pose a threat to the existing contenders, and (2) they must be willing to abide by the unwritten rules of the game, which forbid the exclusion of any existing power contenders from the system.[71] Brazilian labor leaders during this period fulfilled the first condition by demonstrating their capacity to paralyze vital economic and social functions. Throughout the period under study, their power increased vis-à-vis the president and within the political system as a whole. There can be no doubt that they proved themselves serious political power contenders.

The system described by Anderson, however, requires the new contenders to tolerate the others and vice versa. Implicit in radical labor's demands for a fundamental restructuring of economy and society was the exclusion of some of the power contenders present at that time. Unless the radicals achieved power quickly and removed some of the already participating political sectors, the latter were likely to react as the Anderson model predicts, by eliminating the challengers.[72] They did just that in 1964, repressing radical political and labor leaders and excluding organized labor from effective participation in the political process.

---

69. Payne, *Labor and Politics in Peru* (ch. 3 above, n. 16), pp. 10-11.

70. See, for example, the excerpt of a speech to this effect by Rafael Martinelli of the CGT, in the following chapter.

71. Anderson, *Politics and Economic Change* (ch. 1 above, n. 21), p. 105.

72. *Ibid.*, pp. 105-106. José Nun presents a number of reasons why the insecure position of the middle class in the social structure of most Latin American countries causes it to align with the status quo; see his "The Middle-Class Military Coup," in Claudio Veliz (ed.), *The Politics of Conformity in Latin America* (New York: Oxford University Press, 1967), pp. 87, 101-104.

TABLE 20

"Political" Strikes in Brazil, 1960–1964: A Summary

Incident	Strike or threat	Success of work stoppage	Sectors involved	Political situation	Economic situation	Disposition of military
1. Parity strike, November 1960	S	Total in sectors on strike	Rail, port, maritime	Kubitschek govt., demoralized after 1960 election, neglects to resolve civil-military wage parity crisis	Wages central issue in strike	Opposed to disruptive aspects, but help strikers extract material gains from Congress
2. Succession crisis, August 1961	S	Transport heavy; Rio area heavy; São Paulo little except Santos-Jundiaí railroad; Salvador some effect	General, national	Quadros resignation; military wish to keep Goulart from presidency	Real minimum wage down 29% since November 1960	Military ministers opposed to strike and Goulart; officers divided
3. Cabinet crisis, July 1962	S	Transport heavy; Rio area heavy; elsewhere weak	General, national	Congress forces cabinet resignation and labor demands nationalist cabinet	Real minimum wage down 26%; other sectors have specific economic grievances	Favorable to strikes
4. Plebiscite crisis, October 1962	S	Transport heavy; partial closing in Rio; rest of country light	General, national	Goulart trying to force bill for plebiscite	Real minimum wage down 34%; some other key sectors have specific grievances	Protect strikers and back plebiscite

TABLE 20 (continued)

Incident	Strike or threat	Success of work stoppage	Sectors involved	Political situation	Economic situation	Disposition of military
5. Cuban missile crisis, October 1962	T	Not called	Rail, port, maritime	Missile crisis	Sectors involved earning above minimum wage	Intransigently opposed
6. Pinheiro Neto ouster, December 1962	T	Not called; bank workers strike for economic reasons	General	Minister of labor fired for criticism of IMF and U.S. ambassador	Minimum wage low but about to be revised	Abstain
7. Merchant marine strike, December 1962-January 1963	S	Relatively successful at outset; loses adherents with time	Maritime	Not relevant for strike; plebiscite held	Strikers want wage parity reestablished	Oppose and break it
8. Strike threat for basic reforms, April-June 1963	T	Not called	General, national	Left demanding basic reforms; military and civil service wage hike demanded; cabinet crisis coming	Minimum wage revised in January; most contracts in mid-term; no generalized economic grievances	Oppose; control shifting away from left
9. Pilots' strike, May-June 1963	S	Successful	Air transport	Same as above	Same as above; no data on pilots	Abstain

TABLE 20 (continued)

Incident	Strike or threat	Success of work stoppage	Sectors involved	Political situation	Economic situation	Disposition of military
10. Stevedores, Santos, June 1963	S	Successful	Stevedores in Santos	Same as above; state govt. intervenes in Santos sindicato	State pressure hurts Santos stevedores	Intervene in favor of strikers and against state government
11. Santos general strike, September 1963	S	Nearly total success	General in Santos	Labor and left angry with Goulart and trying to force him left	Real minimum wage down 47% and São Paulo contracts nearing end	Oppose, and threaten to crush it
12. General strike in solidarity with Santos	T	Not called	General, national	Same as above	Same as above	Intervene and prevent strike
13. Sergeants' rebellion, September 1963	T	Not called	General, national	Sergeants deprived of political rights by constitution; rebel in Brasília and plot elsewhere	Same as above; workers preparing economic strikes	Threaten to crush it
14. Bank workers' strike, September 1963	S	Intermittent in 7 states, as planned	Selected banks	Continuing crisis, as above	Bank workers seek wage increase	Hostile to all strikes

TABLE 20 (continued)

Incident	Strike or threat	Success of work stoppage	Sectors involved	Political situation	Economic situation	Disposition of military
15. Seige crisis, October 1963	T	Not called except for 3-hour warning on Leopoldina RR	General, national	Military ministers request state of siege and CGT opposes	Minimum wage low and São Paulo contracts terminating	Oppose and threaten to crush it
16. São Paulo general strike, October 1963	S	Moderate success	São Paulo industrial sector	Continuing crisis	São Paulo contracts terminate	Oppose, in state of readiness
17. Overthrow of Goulart	S	Spotty and put down by military	General, national	Military overthrows Goulart	Minimum wage revised 5 weeks earlier, high	Oppose and crush it

TABLE 20 (continued)

Incident	Strike or threat	Goals of striking sectors	Benefits to labor	Ultimate object of pressure	Political beneficiary	Role of Goulart
1. Parity strike, November 1960	S	Wage increase—parity with military increase	Wins wage hike	Legislature and president	Left wing in labor, which founded PUA	Abstains, refrains from conciliating
2. Succession crisis, August 1961	S	Ensure Goulart's accession, prevent military coup	No specific economic benefits, though minimum wage raised in November	Legislature and military	Goulart returns; labor left aided by Goulart to win CNTI election in December	Abroad, trying to return
3. Cabinet crisis, July 1962	S	Appointment of nationalist cabinet committed to reforms and protection of labor union freedom	Wins nationalist cabinet and chooses new labor minister; shows strength in refusing to call off strike at Goulart's request	Legislature and public opinion	Left wing in labor demonstrates power over Goulart and institutionalizes CGT	First encourages strike, then tries unsuccessfully to stop it

TABLE 20 (continued)

Incident	Strike or threat	Goals of striking sectors	Benefits to labor	Ultimate object of pressure	Political beneficiary	Role of Goulart
4. Plebiscite crisis, September 1962	S	100% minimum wage hike; basic reforms; plebiscite	Govt. promises to raise minimum wage and satisfy other labor demands; labor gets voice in cabinet composition; shows strength by refusing to call strike off early for Goulart	Legislature	Labor left increases strength over Goulart	First encourages strike, then unsuccessfully to stop it
5. Cuban missile crisis, October 1962	T	Demonstrate opposition to U.S. blockade of Cuba	None	U.S. govt. and Brazilian military	None	Abstains
6. Pinheiro Neto ouster, December 1962	T	Retain fired labor minister in office	None	Pres. Goulart	None	Does not cede to pressure but makes other concessions
7. Merchant marine strike, December 1962-January 1963	S	Raise pay in their sector	None	Pres. Goulart	None	Opposed

TABLE 20 (continued)

Incident	Strike or threat	Goals of striking sectors	Benefits to labor	Ultimate object of pressure	Political beneficiary	Role of Goulart
8. Strike threat for basic reforms, April-June 1963	T	Get reforms passed, get pay hike	None	Pres. Goulart and legislature	None	Opposes and weakens CGT with UST
9. Pilots' strike, May-June 1963	S	Job security for fired president of pilots' union	None	Pres. Goulart and labor courts	Labor Minister Almino Afonso	Pressured by circumstances to be mediator
10. Stevedores, Santos, June 1963	S	Prevent admission of new members, which would lower members' wages	Keep membership down on compromise	Pres. Goulart and state govt. in São Paulo	No real beneficiary	Supports sindicato with military against state govt.
11. Santos general strike, September 1963	S	Solidarity strike with striking hospital workers	Hospital workers gain wage hike	Executive branch, to bring pressure on hospital to raise pay; Pres. Goulart for minimum wage hike	Hard line in military	Forced to accede to military intervention
12. General strike in solidarity with Santos	T	Gain basic reforms and oppose Adhemar	None	Pres. Goulart, to intervene against São Paulo state govt.	Hard line in military	Forced to condone military intervention to convince leaders to call off strike

TABLE 20 (continued)

Incident	Strike or threat	Goals of striking sectors	Benefits to labor	Ultimate object of pressure	Political beneficiary	Role of Goulart
13. Sergeants' rebellion, September 1963	T	Support sergeants and oppose military coup	None	Pres. Goulart, legislature, military	Military	Forced to accede to military view, as opposed to labor
14. Bank workers' strike, September 1963	S	Wage increase	Win subsequent pay raise	Banks	None	Conciliates the opponents
15. Siege crisis, October 1963	T	Prevent state of siege which might allow military to crush them	None	Pres. Goulart, legislature, military	Left and labor	Withdraws siege request and moves left
16. São Paulo general strike, October 1963	S	Wage raise and collective contract for all industrial workers in state	Wage hike of 80%	Labor courts and labor minister	Left wing makes some organizational gains	Seeks conciliation
17. Overthrow of Goulart	S	Oppose military coup	None; their organizations broken	Military	Military and right wing	Flees to exile

Source: Kenneth Paul Erickson, "Labor in the Political Process in Brazil: Corporatism in a Modernizing Nation" (doctoral dissertation, Columbia University, 1970), pp. 185-270.

Chapter 7

LABOR POWER IN NATIONAL POLITICS: THE CGT VERSUS PRESIDENT GOULART

In this book we have shown that, by manipulating political strikes and controlling important sources of patronage and policy in the corporative state framework, radical nationalist labor leaders gained considerable political power in Brazil in the early 1960's. We have demonstrated how they skillfully used these mechanisms to increase their political leverage. To probe the role of labor in policy making and to illustrate the national political power structure during this period, the present chapter examines four cases in which the interests of the president and the CGT leaders came into conflict.

The definition of power used in Chapter Six applies here as well: coercive influence such as the threat or use of sanction or severe deprivation constitutes power. Organized labor could subject the president to two types of deprivation. On the one hand, since Goulart was trying to hold together a broad coalition of diverse elements, labor spokesmen could threaten to withdraw their support from him. On the other hand, they could go farther by taking the type of action likely to dislodge *other* elements from the coalition as well. This is the function of dissensus politics as described in Chapter Six.

The four cases below document the mutual dependence and antagonism which existed between the president and the General Labor Command (CGT) officers. This peculiar relationship resulted from contradictions inherent in the combination of corporatism with liberal democracy; corporative institutions made labor leaders dependent upon the state, while electoral democracy, which facilitated the development of radical populism, enabled them to seek greater power vis-à-vis the state.

These crises received considerable public attention, facilitating documentation. The final one illustrates not only the activity of labor organizations within the national political process, but also the internal workings of these labor bodies. The reader should bear in mind the political events of the preceding chapter, for they form the context for the cases below as well.

The Battle of Guanabara

By early 1962, only six months after the right had almost deprived him of the presidency, Goulart had proven himself such a successful consensus-builder that one of the leading national news magazines commented: "Now, more than ever, one is forced to ask: 'Where is the opposition?' In truth, political opposition no longer exists in Brazil."[1] It was this same ability which gained the president his five-to-one margin in the plebiscite in January 1963.

This situation reversed itself almost immediately after the plebiscite. During the first half of 1963, Goulart found himself struggling to keep his coalition together in order to implement the austerity program of the Three-Year Plan. The austerities were required by Finance Minister San Tiago Dantas' agreement with the International Monetary Fund (IMF), which postponed Brazil's foreign debt repayments.

In April, rising opposition to the Three-Year Plan triggered a series of incidents dubbed the Battle of Guanabara. This episode enabled the nationalist left to highlight the crumbling of the left wing of Goulart's grand coalition. Although this period witnessed some minor strikes and a general strike threat, its importance for our study lies in the worsening relations between the president and his *dispositivo sindical.*

The Battle of Guanabara began with a hemispheric conference to express solidarity with Cuba. Goulart, struggling to hold his coalition together, attempted to deprive the conference of national and international visibility by screening out prominent participants. He ordered the Ministry of Foreign Affairs to refuse visas to such applicants as Janet Jagan, Lázaro Cárdenas, and various Russian citizens.[2]

Governor Lacerda, however, made a public issue of the conference and refused it a permit to convene in Rio on the grounds that it would violate the constitutional provision prohibiting propaganda for war, class struggle, and subversion of the constitutional order.[3] The participants, therefore, shifted to the shipyard workers' union across the bay in Niterói, bringing the event the publicity Goulart had sought to deny it.

A collision between Goulart and the governor of Guanabara was unavoidable, for Lacerda, in a televised statement, had prohibited the conference in terms most insulting to the chief executive. Outraged spokesmen for the Parliamentary Nationalist Front (FPN) demanded that the president intervene in the state government to guarantee the safety of the convention at its original meeting spot. General Osvino Ferreira Alves declared his willingness to occupy strategic points in Rio if ordered to do so. When the workers of the Central do Brasil and Leopoldina Railways struck to manifest their opposition to Lacerda and their sympathy with municipal transit workers in Rio who had walked out for a pay

1. *Visão,* April 20, 1962, p. 12.
2. *JB,* March 27, 1963, pp. 1, 4, 6; *Visão,* April 5, p. 14.
3. *JB,* March 26, 1963, pp. 1, 5.

hike, one person died in a riot at the Central do Brasil terminal. The First Army seized the excuse to deploy troops in the city, alleging the need to protect federal property and prevent further violence. This made federal intervention appear increasingly likely and provoked more deputies to bring pressure on Goulart to confront the right-wing governor by transferring the conference back to Rio.[4]

Without intervening in the state, Goulart retaliated by sending his chief labor and military advisers to call a popular demonstration in Rio to defend his honor and defy the governor. In keeping with his policy of moderation and consensus, the president condemned the extremes of both right and left, and he specifically excluded the CGT, the National Union of Students (UNE), and radical deputies of the FPN from the organizers of the rally.[5] The plan miscarried, however, for Osvino failed to give it the backing he had at first promised, and Lacerda's police turned back the two advisers as they descended on the city from working-class areas in the surrounding hills.[6]

Disillusioned by Goulart's support of the austerity program and his lack of enthusiasm for the pro-Castro conference, the leaders of the CGT, UNE, and FPN boldly announced that their absence had caused the low turnout for the anti-Lacerda demonstration, and they threatened to withdraw all support from Goulart's government if he kept up his centrist posture.[7]

The leaders of the CGT then set out to demonstrate to the president that his control over labor and the masses was waning. To prove their own power, they laid plans for a street rally in Rio which would show how they could muster mass support in the face of Lacerda's opposition. They claimed, ironically, that it would be a demonstration of redress for the president who had been wronged by the governor. Osvino lent support by announcing that he would give it military protection.[8]

It then became apparent that the radical nationalists were succeeding in polarizing the national political situation and that this could break up Goulart's coalition. Osvino's promise of military support for the demonstration posed a threat to Army unity, and Minister of War Amaury Kruel reacted strongly. He met with Goulart on April 8 and threatened to resign if the president refused to let him punish Osvino for taking sides in a nonmilitary political issue.[9]

Hoping to allow passions to subside so he could hold the cabinet together, Goulart disavowed the demonstration and urged its organizers to cancel it. In a telegram to Clodschmidt Riani, president of the CNTI and CGT, he expressed appreciation for labor's solidarity and support, but he asked that the demonstration be postponed because it would fall in the middle of Holy Week. The

4. *JB*, March 28, 1963, pp. 1, 4, 5.
5. Hermano Alves in *JB*, April 14, 1963, p. 5; *JB*, March 31, p. 1.
6. *OESP*, April 5, 1963, p. 3.
7. *OESP*, April 7, 1963, p. 3.
8. April 7, 1963: *JB*, pp. 1, 4; *OESP*, p. 6.
9. *JB*, April 10, 1963, pp. 1, 3.

disgruntled Riani threatened to hold it anyway.[10] However, Goulart's brother-in-law, Brizola, and his allies in the FPN managed to win the postponement. It was delayed twice and then forgotten as the CGT began to plan for the Labor Day rallies on May 1.

Leftist distrust of Goulart had been mounting since early April when he denounced the extremes of right and left alike. The outcome of the Battle of Guanabara — indefinite postponement of the demonstration and the threat of punishment for the top nationalist in the army — created a coup scare, and the CGT instructed its strike organizers to be vigilant. Riani declared his organization independent of the president, whom he accused of involvement with right-wing military forces, and he demanded that Goulart disprove the charge by replacing Kruel with Osvino, whose compulsory retirement would force him out of the command of the First Army in a few months anyway.[11]

Goulart was the loser in this crisis, for it augmented the left-wing nationalists' distrust of him and drove them to practice more intensively the politics of dissensus. The radicals did, in fact, succeed in putting Goulart on the defensive with their show of strength, and they consolidated their ad hoc coalition in the form of the Popular Mobilization Front (FMP). This body provided a permanent organizational framework for the cooperation of radical groups committed to the basic reforms, such as the CGT, FPN, UNE, Brazilian Union of Secondary Students, women's groups, sergeants, and others. Prior to the crisis, these groups had all espoused the same nationalist goals and reforms, but their shared mistrust of Goulart now drove them into much closer collaboration.

Jango Undermines the CGT with the UST

The Battle of Guanabara made it clear to Goulart that the CGT was willing and able to work at cross-purposes to him and that it would henceforth refuse to do his bidding without compensation. The disintegrative effect of its recent activities on his broad but shaky coalition was indisputable, and, most important of all, it threatened to dislodge the *dispositivo militar.*

Campaigning vigorously against Jango's financial policies, moreover, the CGT demanded that he declare a moratorium on the foreign debt, jettison the Three-Year Plan, and reject the conditions imposed by the IMF. The CGT won Almino Afonso to its cause, and in April he came out strongly against the plan despite his membership in the cabinet. If Goulart sacked Almino now that the minister and the CGT were strong allies, the labor organization might take to the streets in defense of Almino, further weakening the president's coalition. Subsequently, the CGT helped organize a rally at which incensed nationalist sergeants threatened to carry out the basic reforms, with their weapons if necessary.

Goulart, therefore, undertook a delicate maneuver to save the coalition.

10. *OESP,* April 9, 1963, pp. 3, 44.
11. *OESP,* April 9, 1963, p. 3.

Seeking to eliminate his dependence upon the CGT while still maintaining a strong organizational base in labor, he attempted to supplant the CGT with the União Sindical dos Trabalhadores (UST), a central labor organization founded in São Paulo the previous September by Domingos Álvares, president of the Federation of Metalworkers of that state.

Although the UST eschewed partisan politics and ideology, it adamantly defended labor activism and the use of the strike to achieve justice in labor relations. Like the CGT, it called for basic reforms. It did not oppose the presence of Communists in labor unions, though it stood firmly against their use of sindicatos for their own partisan ends. Differentiating it from the CGT was the fact that the UST leaders were not trying to pressure Goulart to the left against his own short-range interests. Thus, the backing of the UST would retain labor support for Goulart's coalition as well as his program.[12]

For Goulart, the UST was the only viable alternative to the CGT, because the one other organized interunion force was the Movimento Sindical Democrático (MSD), a grouping founded by the bitterly anti-Goulart pelegos. The MSD, a nonmilitant organization which preferred to settle industrial disputes in the labor courts rather than through strikes, refused membership to Communists and remained silent on the issue of basic reforms.[13]

In their drive to create a central labor organization of importance, the leaders of the UST could not resist the temptation of government backing. Such support implied perquisites, sinecures, and benefits which would help them extend their influence. They hoped that, as their organization grew, the CGT would lose its government support and, consequently, its power and following, leaving the UST at the pinnacle of organized labor in Brazil.

Immediately after the rally of disgruntled sergeants, Goulart moved to reduce his dependence on his former labor allies.[14] He dispatched his labor adviser, Gilberto Crockatt de Sá, to lend the prestige of the presidency to the UST and to indicate in plain language that the president was displeased with the conduct of the CGT's radical leaders. Crockatt called them "the dictators of the CGT . . . who will hand everything over to the reactionaries," and he made bitter allusions to their connections with the rebellious activities of the sergeants. He suggested that constant pressure and seditious activities from the left would play into the hands of the right, provoking a military coup and bringing widespread repression down upon the society in general. He also brought the clash between Goulart and Almino Afonso into the open, calling the labor minister young and inexperienced.[15]

Taking advantage of the situation, the UST held a meeting of labor leaders in late May to plan for a national labor congress. The congress, scheduled for August, would bestow the sanction of significant constituency support upon the

12. Osvaldo Peralva in *JB,* Aug. 18, 1963, Caderno Especial, p. 6.
13. *Ibid.*
14. *OESP,* May 12, 1963, p. 9.
15. *OESP,* May 19, 1963, p. 25; *JB,* May 21, p. 13.

UST, thus letting it claim to be the most important central labor organization in the country. The UST leaders' euphoria over the possibility of becoming the chief central labor organization was so great that, when several of the moderates in the CGT proposed that the two bodies unite their strength in one, they refused. The president of the UST even announced that he planned to challenge the CGT leadership frontally by running against incumbent Riani for the presidency of the National Confederation of Industrial Workers (CNTI), the main organizational base of the CGT.[16]

The bubble burst soon afterward. Goulart realized that the labor leaders with a real and powerful organizational base were those in the CGT, and he began to renew his contacts with them again following their visit to Brasília in late June. The UST leaders only became aware that they had been abandoned when their funds began to dry up and Minister of Labor Amaury Silva ignored their demands for appointments in the Ministry bureaucracy.[17]

The CGT leaders dealt the final blow to the UST in early August. They deliberately organized the National Basic Reform Week and the Day of Protest Against the High Cost of Living to coincide with the national meeting of the UST. This left the UST the option of collaborating with the CGT in a street rally or else appearing uninterested in the fate of the inflation-wracked working class: the real minimum wage in Guanabara had declined by 37 percent in the seven months from January to July.[18] The UST leaders chose not to collaborate. Thus, by the time the Day of Protest rally was held on August 7, the UST was an all-but-forgotten acronym on the national political scene.[19]

The rapidity of its demise suggests that the UST never did have the organizational strength of the CGT. A large number of non-Communist labor leaders affiliated with the CGT had shunned the UST, since they felt it would be no more than a personal vehicle for Goulart and would not have given them or their unions any particular rewards.[20] The CGT, regardless of its ideological content, had demonstrated power in bargaining with the president, so these independent leaders felt it served their interests to remain affiliated with it rather than with the UST. In this matter, therefore, Goulart found himself alienating some of the most radical leaders of the CGT, no closer than before to the intransigent anti-Communists of the MSD, and without much effect on the non-Communist independents. He therefore elected to lend his prestige to the CGT once it had been chastened.

Despite the brevity of the UST episode, it did serve some important short-run purposes for the president. By threatening to withdraw support from the CGT, Goulart managed to shift its balance back toward the more moderate line of Riani and Pelacani, reducing the influence of its radical wing, which was

16. *JB,* June 27, 1963, p. 13; June 2, p. 5; and July 5, p. 10.
17. Paulo Rehder in *JB,* July 14, 1963, p. 16.
18. Calculated from cost-of-living figures in *Conjuntura Econômica.*
19. Paulo Rehder in *JB,* July 7, 1963, p. 15, and July 14, p. 16.
20. *OESP,* July 17, 1963, p. 6; and Sept. 3, p. 10.

composed of transport-sector representatives like Rafael Martinelli of the Rail Workers' Federation and Osvaldo Pacheco of the Port Workers' Union.

The temporary weakness of the CGT prevented a pilots' strike from extending to other sectors and caused postponement of a national general strike, threatened for late May, and its subsequent transformation into a caravan of labor leaders to Brasília. In the capital, they briefly disrupted the legislature while demonstrating for the basic reforms, but the national economy was spared another costly paralysis. Furthermore, this was the period of the conflict between Jango and Almino Afonso, and the UST issue served to weaken and alarm the CGT leaders so much that they dared not resort to disruption to defend the minister. Although this is one of the most significant moments of the Goulart presidency, most studies of the period have neglected it.

For Goulart's future tenure in the presidency, the "Battle of Guanabara" was of major importance. He demonstrated an awareness that the CGT leaders constituted a potential threat to his coalition, yet he did not take full advantage of his position in the corporative-state framework to assure his independence of them.

Labor-Left Pressure on Goulart, August 1963

The cabinet shift which Jango finally carried out in late June removed the left from most of its institutional strongholds in the government. Political commentator Carlos Castelo Branco concluded: "In both civilian and military sectors, the government of João Goulart has finally linked its destiny to the orientation and direction of the nation's ruling groups (*classes dirigentes*)."[21]

Following the cabinet shift, the FMP and FPN assumed a very hostile attitude toward Goulart, and Deputy Neiva Moreira of the latter body declared that his group would henceforth consider Jango an adversary. Two groups of leftists, considered "moderates" and "extremists," collaborated within the CGT at this time, but the extremists held a majority on its executive board. Riani and Pelacani, labeled moderates, occupied the two top posts on the directorate, but radicals from the transport sector and the Bank Workers' Confederation filled the other six slots.[22] CGT leaders, therefore, simultaneously pursued both radical and moderate lines of rhetoric and action. The CGT itself held to the moderate line, while the radicals worked through its affiliates, the Guanabara-based Permanent Committee of Trade-Union Organizations (CPOS) and the rail and port workers' Pact for Unity and Action (PUA).

By removing Almino in the cabinet shakeup, Goulart reduced the access of radical labor leaders to official institutional power bases. These labor leaders, therefore, considered alternative means to influence government policy. Hoping to repeat their successful pressure on Congress in the two general strikes of the

21. Carlos Castelo Branco in *JB*, June 22, 1963, p. 4.
22. *JB*, June 30, 1963, p. 15.

previous year, the PUA and CPOS moved to carry the reform campaign to the streets. They therefore proclaimed the National Basic Reform Week, culminating in the Day of Protest against the High Cost of Living on August 7. The CGT proper, however, maintained its ambivalent stance, as the moderates refrained from antagonizing the president. This policy ultimately bore fruit, for Goulart reinstated that organization at the peak of his dispositivo sindical.

At the outset of the Reform Week, the FMP made a clean ideological break with Goulart, blasting his politics of consensus and conciliation.[23] The Day of Protest was marked by violence, as Lacerda's state police broke up a workers' march in front of the Leopoldina Railroad Station and invaded the textile workers' sindicato, attacking Hércules Correia dos Reis, the president of the CPOS. After the clash between workers and police, the First Army sent in troops to maintain order and protect the demonstrators and federal property.[24]

The CGT reacted to the police violence and the arrest of some of their members by calling another giant public rally to condemn Lacerda's "atrocities," and they demanded that Goulart honor it with his presence.[25] They hoped, with this invitation, to exact a definition of policy from the president. Indeed, Goulart's politics of conciliation had just taken an alarming turn when he asked General Kruel, who had just left the War Ministry in the cabinet shift, to head his military household. This suggested that the president was moving to contain Brizola and the radical leftists.[26]

Political polarization thus strained Goulart's coalition, forcing him closer to a choice he hoped to avoid. On the center-right, the Social Democratic Party (PSD), the largest party in the legislature and an important component in the president's coalition, began to split. One of its factions wished to break with Goulart and join the parliamentary opposition. In an attempt to hold the party together, the PSD factions agreed on a "minimum program" for Goulart to approve in order to retain their unified parliamentary support. The program, which espoused objectives not unlike those of the Three-Year Plan, was obviously designed to widen the gap between the FMP and the president.[27]

On the left, FMP policy also reflected this polarization. It rejected a more centrist program which would have helped Goulart maintain his coalition intact. The radicals believed that his policy of centrist conciliation was bound to fail and that he would eventually adhere to their program of radical reform.

The left went ahead with its plans for the rally, which was being organized by Hércules Correia of the CPOS and CGT and José Gomes Talarico. Both belonged to the left wing of Goulart's Brazilian Labor Party (PTB), in Guanabara. Goulart agreed to address the assemblage, but he forbade the presence of Brizola, who

23. Derly Barreto in *JB,* Aug. 2, 1963, p. 4.
24. *JB,* Aug. 8, 1963, pp. 1, 4.
25. *JB,* Aug. 9, 1963, p. 3.
26. Aug. 4, 1963: *OESP,* p. 3; and Edísio Gomes de Matos in *JB,* p. 3.
27. *JB,* Aug. 15, 1963, p. 6.

absented himself from Rio that day to protest his brother-in-law's politics of conciliation.[28]

Goulart's exclusion of Brizola was the latest in a series of actions which had caused the left to fear a coup from the president. His plans to promote nine colonels to general aroused suspicions, for the new generals would greatly strengthen his dispositivo militar. In cooperation with the moderate leadership of the Army enlisted men's association, he planned to authorize the construction of an enlisted men's clubhouse; this would undermine the position of leftist activist Jamil Amidem within that constituency. Minister of War Jair Dantas Ribeiro had made it clear that if the Supreme Court annulled the mandates of the sergeants in Congress, the officer corps would brook no protest from within the ranks.

On the labor front, Crockatt still sought to create an alternative labor base to the CGT, and during a milk producers' lockout to force prices up in mid-August, Goulart backed down from his promise to give military cover to CGT volunteer milk transport convoys. The government had intentionally weakened the communications network of the radical left by ordering the state oil monopoly to cancel its new program on Brizola's radio station, thus withdrawing one of that station's most important sources of revenue.[29]

Finally, Goulart seemed to be embarking on a program of conservative reformism by completing plans to purchase the American and Foreign Power Company's utility holdings for a generous sum. He was reported to be renegotiating another Food for Peace agreement with the United States, which would generate counterpart funds for the Americans to spend in Brazil. Thus, the left began to fear that the president might take advantage of the anti-Lacerda sentiment to pull a coup against the extremes of both right and left, much as Getúlio had done in 1937.[30] With Brizola and Almino both deprived of official support in recent months, Miguel Arraes, governor of Pernambuco, remained the sole important leftist commanding executive and administrative institutions. He became the standard-bearer of the left as they began organizing contingency plans to block any attempt at a coup.[31]

The rally, held to commemorate Vargas' death in August 1954, reflected the increasing political polarization of the period. The left sought to increase the polarization, hoping it would precipitate the breakup of Goulart's coalition. Although the FMP had officially decided not to participate, some of its leaders appeared under the standards of other organizations. Rafael Martinelli, president of the National Sindicato of Railroad Workers, for example, represented the CGT.[32]

28. *JB*, Aug. 20, 1963, p. 5.
29. Paulo Rehder in *JB*, Aug. 25, 1963, p. 5; and Derly Barreto in *JB*, Aug. 18, p. 4.
30. Derly Barreto in *JB*, Aug. 18, 1963, p. 4.
31. Wilson Figueiredo in *JB*, Aug. 18, 1963, p. 4; *JB*, June 30, p. 15.
32. *JB*, Aug. 22, 1963, pp. 1, 3.

Goulart, in his address, demonstrated that he was not yet ready to take a stand with the radical left and that he still valued the support of the PSD and moderates within the legislature. He emphasized that the reform program must be carried out within the confines of the legislative and constitutional process.[33]

The speech, witnessed by 40,000 civilian spectators and 15,000 soldiers which the First Army had assigned to protect the rally from the hostile state police, was interrupted by chants from the disappointed crowd demanding *"definição"* — the clarification of whose side Jango was really on in the struggle for the basic reforms. The crowd reserved its ovation for the speeches of Martinelli and José Serra, president of the radical National Union of Students (UNE) and for the names of Brizola and Arraes, who were conspicuously absent.[34]

Speaking in the name of the workers, Martinelli demanded revision of the minimum wage, immediate adoption of the basic reforms, and nationalization of crucial economic activities such as electric power, air transport, and the pharmaceutical and meat-packing industries. He put his strongest emphasis on the reforms and, underscoring labor's role in Goulart's political rise and promising such support in the future, he exhorted the president to implement the reforms immediately:

> ... we need to be sure that you, with the support of the workers, will implement structural reforms immediately, without further delay. Didn't we go to the streets throughout Brazil to put into practice the patriotic ideals of Vargas' letter of testament? Didn't we prevent the enemies of the *Pátria* from carrying through their attempts to establish a dictatorship? Didn't we ensure your accession? Didn't we secure full constitutional powers for you? The message we bring from all the workers and from the entire nation, Mr. President, is that for these homages to be worthy of the sacrifice and political testament of Vargas, they must mark the victory of the basic reforms.[35]

The applause for Martinelli was much more enthusiastic than for the president, because the cause championed by the railroad workers' leader had broad public support. Indeed, a public opinion poll revealed that 73 percent of the population in Guanabara and 70 percent in São Paulo were in favor of the agrarian reform.[36]

In the name of the working class, Martinelli promised a more demanding relationship with management. His speech marked the official CGT break with Jango and its reintegration into the policy line of the FMP. This further sapped Goulart's hopes for political tranquility, because the FMP had announced plans

33. *Ibid.,* p. 1.
34. *JB,* Aug. 24, 1963, pp. 1, 3.
35. *JB,* Aug. 23, 1963, p. 3.
36. Brazilian Institute of Public Opinion poll cited in *CM,* Aug. 25, 1963, p. 9.

to pressure Congress directly, using the civil rights march on Washington that week as a model.[37]

As a result of recent political polarization, therefore, the president discovered he was standing alone. The left was countering his conciliatory pattern with a highly successful display of dissensus politics, and CGT leaders in particular tried to demonstrate to the president that they had the strength to assist him, should he override the legislature and decree the reforms. So great was the polarization that both right and left feared a coup, and the tensions of the period made it appear that Goulart would, in fact, be forced to opt for one side or the other. It is a tribute to his ability to regain political equilibrium, as well as a commentary upon his inability to understand the deeper systemic reasons for these political crises, that he did not make a definitive option for the left until the CNTI election in January, if he made one at all.

Social Security and
Labor Confederation Elections, 1963-1964

With respect to his relations with left-wing labor, Goulart finally crossed the Rubicon in January 1964. After vacillating inconclusively during elections in the National Confederation of Commercial Workers (CNTC) and in the social security institutes, he cast his lot with the CGT ticket in an electoral showdown in the CNTI. The disloyal opposition considered this a definitive declaration for the radical left, so the plotters grew in numbers. However, Goulart had made so many tactical political zigzags that, to him, presidential assistance to the labor left in the CNTI may have seemed a short-range, tactical maneuver rather than a definitive commitment.

Available evidence from Goulart's career suggests that he had no fundamental comprehension of socialist ideology and that his primary interest was to remain in office rather than to implement such an ideology. His views toward the working class were essentially paternalistic and humanitarian, not socialist. His semi-official biographer described his laborism (*trabalhismo*) as "basically senti-mental," rather than intellectual, and he traced this to Jango's experience as a fazendeiro and cattle dealer.[38]

Furthermore, when faced with the choice between socialism on the one hand or populism in a capitalist system on the other, Goulart chose the latter. In the cabinet shakeup of June, he moved to the right, ousting Almino Afonso, who did indeed espouse a socialist ideology and aimed to lay the political foundations for a new social and political order.

If these assumptions about Goulart's goals are correct, it would have been in his interest to ease the crisis of legitimacy which threatened his government. He

37. Paulo Rehder in *JB,* Aug. 25, 1963, p. 5.
38. Tejo, *Jango* (ch. 5 above, n. 42), pp. 100, 132; see also pp. 90-133.

could have used the power of his office as he did in 1961 to bring about a change in the leadership of the labor *dispositivo* as well as to reduce radical labor's control of important organizations in the social security system.

The president vacillated, first ousting Dante Pelacani and other radicals from the top spots in the social security system, then opting for the radical left in the subsequent CNTI elections. This latter act confirmed his alliance with what the right perceived as communism; it therefore played a major role in touching off the coup.

The first round of confederation elections came in the CNTC in October. The slate of unpopular President Antônio Pereira Magaldi, who had been using the CNTC to further the ends of his anti-Communist Movimento Sindical Democrático (MSD), was tied 10 to 10 by the leftist challengers. Minister Amaury Silva declared the body under ministerial intervention, in order to prevent Magaldi from using his office to twist the arms of opposition voters prior to a second balloting several months later. As a runoff would not be held until February, when a fusion ticket was elected, the CNTC elections did not provide any clear clues to Goulart's definitive posture with regard to labor.[39]

In late December, the social security board elections took place. Government officials made it known that customary policy called for rotation of the top slot among the sectoral representatives (government, labor, and employers). Board members were in the third year of four-year terms, so rotation meant their removal from the command posts but not from the boards. In the central coordinating office of the system, the National Social Welfare Directorate, employers' and government delegates teamed up to remove CGT Vice-President Dante Pelacani from the director-general's post and to replace him with a government delegate. The government representative turned out to be José Pessoa Cavalcanti, the official substitute for Gilberto Crockatt de Sá, Goulart's personal labor adviser. Since the UST affair, the CGT saw Crockatt as an enemy. Therefore, the election of his substitute as director-general of the entire Social Welfare Department (DNPS) provoked extremely bitter denunciations, for Crockatt would subsequently have the right to reassume his position and wield all of the patronage and power of that office. It thus appeared that Jango was turning against the radical labor base and that he wished to assume personal control of these political levers.

All of the social security institutes held elections, and the government representatives took the presidency of the bank workers' and industrial workers' institutes, i.e., the two sectors with the most radical confederations. Workers' representatives were elected president only in the commercial workers' (IAPC) and the railroad and public utility workers' (IAPFESP) institutes, but these two did not enhance the power of the CGT. The commercial workers were by no means radicals of the CGT type, and the CNTC was under intervention in the wake of the inconclusive elections, so the government could figure on influ-

39. *OESP,* Oct. 22, 1963, p. 17; *CM,* Jan. 10, 1964, p. 8; *JB,* Feb. 28, p. 10.

TABLE 21

Distribution of Offices, by Sector, in
Social Security Apparatus
After 1963 Election

Organization	President*	Vice-President*
DNPS	G	—
IAPI	G	E
IAPETC	G	W
IAPC	W	E
IAPB	G	E
IAPM	G	W
IAPFESP	W	G
SAMDU	W	G
SAPS	G	E

Source: OESP, Dec. 24, 1963, p. 7; *JB*, Dec.
24, 1963, p. 9; and information supplied by the
respective offices.

*G = Representative of the government
E = Representative of the employers
W = Representative of the workers

encing that organization if the need arose. The IAPFESP itself was under intervention because of a patronage scandal, so the government could control it as well. Table 21 presents the breakdown of the top social security offices after the 1963 elections. Goulart's steps to weaken the radical left in the social security system naturally gave hope to the moderates and anti-Communists that, in the coming CNTI elections, Jango would favor them and sever his ties with the radicals.

Pelacani's ouster drew more attention than the changes in the other institutes. As one of the nation's most visible and effective labor leaders, he had often personified the new autonomy of labor organizations vis-à-vis the government. This, of course, had given Goulart good reason to reduce Dante's institutional leverage. Dante's negotiations to create a winning slate for the CNTI elections, for example, had recently irritated Goulart, because the labor leader, using the name of the president, had promised to reward supporters with labor court judgeships and other posts.[40] In mid-December, he stated to the Pact for Joint Action (PAC) in São Paulo, a CGT affiliate, that Jango wanted the release of two metalworkers still imprisoned in the sergeants' rebellion case. This so angered the president that he stopped receiving Pelacani in the presidential

40. *OESP,* Dec. 4, 1963, p. 15.

palace. Finally, Dante had refused to participate in a moderate slate which Crockatt was promoting for the coming CNTI elections.[41]

The president, still mindful of Dante's inadequacies in lining up labor support for a state-of-siege request in October, found the CGT leader an easy target, because Dante's prestige had declined after he was implicated in a housing construction scandal.[42] Goulart also counted on the eager collaboration of the employers' representatives, because the DNPS, at Dante's direction, had initiated investigations on which it would base lawsuits against employers who had failed to pay their statutory contributions.[43]

Following his defeat, Pelacani bitterly denounced Goulart for his alliance with the employers against the workers, and, in the name of the sindicatos, he declared an open struggle against the president who had forsaken them. Other CGT spokesmen approved his break with the president, but within a few days their intransigence had withered, and they issued a note denying that they had ever severed relations with the president or the government.[44]

Shortly after the election, the labor leaders and the president had come to terms again. José Barbosa, the government representative elected to the presidency of the bank workers' institute (IAPB), resigned to take another post in public service. Since Barbosa was a member of the PTB in São Paulo and a longtime Janguista, he obviously stepped down at Goulart's request. It was expected that Edgard Rocha Costa, a workers' representative and incumbent president, would be reelected in new balloting.[45]

At this time, the industrial workers were preparing for the CNTI election on January 6, 1964. The importance of this election should not be underestimated, for the CNTI encompassed half of the organized workers in Brazil and provided the CGT's principal organizational and financial base of support. As the CGT had no independent source of revenue, the CNTI covered its expenses and housed the CGT offices.[46]

Even before the social security elections, rumors filled the trade-union milieu as both incumbents and a more moderate challenging slate claimed presidential support. Crockatt, acting in Goulart's name, had first tried to form a fusion ticket on which incumbents, opposition, and government would name an equal number of directors, with the specific exclusion of Ari Campista on the right and Hércules Correia on the left. The left refused. After this rebuff, Crockatt set out with determination to promote the challengers against incumbent Riani's slate.[47]

Once his labor adviser began assembling a slate of non-Communist CNTI

41. Dec. 24, 1963: *OG,* p. 6; *UH,* p. 2.
42. *OESP,* Dec. 21, 1963, p. 11; Dec. 25, p. 17.
43. *UH,* Dec. 24, 1963, p. 2.
44. *OG,* Dec. 24, 1963, p. 6; Dec. 26, p. 6; Dec. 28, p. 7.
45. *JB,* Dec. 28, 1963, p. 4.
46. "Os 'Generais' da Derrota," *O Cruzeiro,* May 2, 1964.
47. *CM,* Dec. 28, 1963, p. 6.

leaders, Jango let it be known that he had authorized Crockatt to speak in his name.[48] Crockatt was lining up support among the federations from the small states, through emissaries who promised sinecures and favors. The CNTI directorate countered by sending dental equipment and jeeps for those federations to use in their social-service programs.[49]

However, Goulart's support of the moderates began to waver when the CGT threatened to break relations with him, following the social security elections. Furthermore, Labor Minister Amaury Silva was beginning to favor the incumbents. He planned to run for governor of his native state of Paraná, where the bank workers provided one of his electoral bases. They were closely affiliated with the Riani-Pelacani group and the CGT, and Silva pointed out to Goulart that they might turn on him if he supported another slate. Since incumbent governor Nei Braga, a Christian Democrat, was of questionable loyalty to the president, Amaury Silva's successful candidacy would also serve Goulart's own interest. The labor minister thus directed the Trade Union Tax Commission, whose head was Nilo Isidoro Biazzeto, a former officer of the Paraná bank workers, to take funds from the labor congress account and make them available to the directorate of the CNTI to cover the expenses of delegates to the convention.[50]

During the week preceding the election, Goulart did not disavow the efforts of either his labor minister or his personal labor adviser, both of whom continued to claim that they enjoyed his confidence. The first concrete clue to the president's preference came three days before the election, when the delegates to the CNTI convention approved the accounts of the incumbent slate, a blow to Crockatt and his forces.[51] The day before the election, Minister of Justice Abelardo Jurema arrived in Rio and declared that the president had chosen to support the Riani slate.[52] The electors were then taken individually to the chief executive, who explained that it was in the interest of the government that they elect Riani.[53] Arrangements were worked out during the day, and the incumbents had the delegates committed to them spend the night in the CNTI headquarters because of rumors that Lacerda's police planned to arrest some of them in an attempt to prevent Riani's election.[54] This also had the advantage of isolating them from agents of the other slate, who might offer a higher price for their vote. The incumbent slate won, 33 to 20, with one null vote. The breakdown shows that 14 of the 15 undecided delegates voted with the 6 Janguistas and 13 radical leftists and Communists to form the majority.[55]

48. *OESP*, Dec. 4, 1963, p. 15.
49. *OESP*, Dec. 17, 1963, p. 22.
50. *OG*, Jan. 2, 1964, p. 2.
51. *JB*, Jan. 4, 1964, p. 12.
52. *OG*, January 7, 1964, p. 9.
53. *JB*, May 12, 1964, p. 14.
54. *NR*, Jan. 10, 1964, p. 7.
55. *OESP*, Jan. 8, 1964, p. 10.

Crockatt had gambled the last of his political capital and lost. His influence on the president in trade-union matters had obviously come to an end. Goulart accepted his resignation a few days later.[56] Crockatt's case illustrates Goulart's style in running political risks. Until the last few days before the CNTI elections, Crockatt was following Goulart's instructions in an attempt to loosen the president's dependency upon the left-wing nationalists. The labor adviser had behaved similarly in the UST affair as well. After a policy finally failed, Goulart merely sacrificed a lieutenant upon whom the onus for the policy could be heaped. The president, freed of both the unsuccessful policy and the lieutenant, remained unscathed by their failure. In the case of Crockatt, however, the task was not difficult, since the labor adviser's honesty, sincerity, and competence were questioned by many observers.[57]

In summary, Goulart had passed up his last chance to avoid complete reliance on the radical elements within the dispositivo sindical. The new slate lost no time in further frightening Brazil's conservative opposition by threatening a general strike for a 100-percent hike in the minimum wage and by visiting and expressing solidarity with the two imprisoned labor leaders who were accused of participating in September's sergeants' rebellion.[58] In the eyes of the right-wing opposition, therefore, this constituted weighty evidence that Goulart was going to bring the nation under a Communist dictatorship.

Since we assume that Goulart's principal goal was to stay in office, he had made a serious miscalculation. Had he followed through on the fusion solution and thus ousted the most radical leftist leaders, he would have reduced the provocative quality of the election in the eyes of his opponents on the right. After the Riani victory, the powerful Federation of Industries of São Paulo broke with the president.[59]

It should be noted, however, that he might have had equal difficulty dealing with the new leadership, for it would have included independents and members of the UST. They would have been less dependent upon him than the Communists, who were formally proscribed from the political system and thus needed presidential assistance to achieve readmission to the electoral arena. Hence, the new leaders might have turned out more intransigent than the CGT in the economic field. If they did lead campaigns for the economic betterment of the working class at a time of economic contraction, they also could have prevented Goulart from serving as a conciliator. Thus, they too could have divested him of his chief political function.

Given the worsening economic situation, Goulart may therefore have been in an untenable position, whichever faction headed the labor organizations. As his minister of justice later observed from exile, Goulart proved that it is impossible

56. *JB,* Jan. 12, 1964, pp. 1, 9.
57. See, for example, Edmar Morel, *O golpe começou em Washington* (Rio de Janeiro: Civilização Brasileira, 1965), pp. 15, 79.
58. *OESP,* Jan. 9, 1964, p. 13; Jan. 11, p. 7.
59. Confidential interview.

to fulfill the role of protector of the working masses and at the same time be President of the Republic. Consideration of broader national interests necessarily prevented him from attending to the demands of the workers to the extent they expected from an ally in his position.[60]

The election also illustrates the political deals and vote-buying which facilitate coalition-building within the labor movement. Crockatt and Amaury Silva both offered federal government posts in exchange for support.[61] An industrialist promised one of the candidates on the Riani slate 500,000 cruzeiros and a house of his own if he would switch to the challengers. Crockatt offered other delegates half a million cruzeiros and more for their votes, and he also paid two million for advertising in a daily read by the working class. It was run as news copy on the front page and predicted the victory of the opposition slate of João Wagner, for which it had high praise.[62] Financial inducements were not only a part of electioneering in the labor structure; they also underlay the general maintenance of good relations between labor and the president. For example, investigations following the coup of 1964 disclosed that the head of Goulart's civilian cabinet had written 14 checks on the presidential account to 8 labor organizations during the last seven months of his government. They totalled over 21 million cruzeiros.[63]

Conclusion

These four cases show how in pre-1964 Brazil, two contradictory principles of political organization – liberal democracy and elitist corporatism – gave rise to fundamental conflict. Vargas' corporative institutions, true to their purpose, subjected labor organizations to state tutelage and control. After the Constitution of 1946 established electoral democracy, however, populist politicians in search of working-class votes began to provide labor leaders with positions of political influence and patronage in the very state institutions which had been designed to control the working class. The labor leaders, seeking further to increase their political power, confronted populist politicians, including the nation's top populist, President Goulart, with strikes and demonstrations which they, the labor leaders (rather than the politicians), controlled. Goulart and the CGT leaders found themselves, therefore, locked in a relationship of mutual dependence and mutual antagonism, as they sought to outmaneuver but not destroy each other.

Goulart, as Chapter Six made clear, gave labor's radical leftists and nationalists control of an important political command post when he used his office to

60. Abelardo Jurema, *Sexta-feira, 13* (Rio de Janeiro: O Cruzeiro, 1964), p. 59.

61. Armando de Brito, "Relatório do delegado governamental, procurador da Justiça do Trabalho, Armando de Brito – no processo da CNTI-CGT" (Rio de Janeiro, May 5, 1964, mimeo.), pp. 23-24.

62. Jan. 7, 1964: *OG*, p. 9, and *UH*, p. 2; also, confidential interview.

63. *JB*, April 28, 1964, p. 5.

assure their victory in the CNTI election of 1961. Earlier chapters of this study document how these labor leaders, by effectively drawing advantage from strikes and their offices in the corporative structures, enhanced their power and developed a measure of autonomy. By early 1963, the CGT had strengthened its position so it could make certain policy demands upon the president. The left's all-encompassing demand — that the government enact the sweeping basic-reform proposals — constituted a major issue throughout the Goulart presidency. This issue and its corollary — that the government abandon the Three-Year Plan's austerity measures — dominated the Battle of Guanabara.

In that struggle the labor leaders demonstrated to Goulart that they formed a critical link between the president and a large part of his mass base, thereby highlighting their political utility to him. They made their point even more forcefully than in the general strikes of the previous year, because they first caused a rally on his behalf to fizzle by refusing to show up with their supporters, and then they underscored the point by calling a demonstration of their own to prove their control of the mass base. The degree to which they were bluffing remains unclear, for Goulart finally negotiated the cancellation of their demonstration.

In this episode and the others covered in this chapter, the labor left played dissensus politics very skillfully; i.e., they proved they could weaken the president's coalition by driving some other, usually more conservative, participants from it. They again brought the point home to Goulart when speeches at the CGT-organized sergeants' rally in May struck at the unity of the armed forces. This episode so seriously alienated Goulart's military support that he made a quick change in policy and began employing the levers of the corporative state to weaken the CGT. Characteristically, he focused on short-run gains and did not attempt to push his advantage to the point of destroying the CGT and placing new leaders at the head of his labor base. He repeated this indecisive pattern at the time of the social security and confederation elections. In both cases where he sought to weaken the CGT, therefore, his vision and actions were tactical rather than strategic. He always aimed to leave the leaders of the nationalist left in labor with enough power to assist him politically, while preventing them from gaining the upper hand.

Profoundly aware that left-wing labor leaders had played a key role in his political rise, Goulart dared not risk his labor clientele and the CGT leaders who controlled it. Indeed, he had acknowledged that he could not abandon that clientele without endangering his career.[64] He held to this belief right up through the military coup which overthrew him in March 1964. With the troops already moving, he rejected General Kruel's offer to try to save him if he would agree to take concrete measures to free his government from labor and the Communists.[65]

64. Pedro Gomes, "Minas: do diálogo ao 'front,' " in Alberto Dines et al. (eds.), *Os idos de março e a queda em abril* (Rio de Janeiro: José Álvaro, 1964), p. 78.

65. Eurilo Duarte, "32 mais 32, igual a 64," in *ibid.*, p. 144.

At the rally in August, Rafael Martinelli, trading upon Goulart's dependence upon his labor clientele, demanded a radical policy line from him. The CGT orator's pointed rhetorical questions — backed up by the growing CGT strength manifested in strikes and demonstrations as well as in threats to break with the president — hit their mark, leading Goulart to tie his own future even more tightly to that of his labor clientele.

Goulart's ultimate profession of allegiance to the CGT leaders proves that *he* perceived them as powerful. This case study demonstrates the utility of Charles Anderson's observations on the Latin American political process. Anderson writes that "... the most persistent phenomenon in Latin America is the effort of contenders for power to demonstrate a power capability sufficient to be recognized by other power contenders. ..." Once recognized, they may then negotiate with the existing power contenders.[66] He claims that new contenders frequently do not need to exercise their power capability; mere demonstration often wins acceptance from other contenders.

The shifting alliances and frequent threats of political reprisals by the CGT leaders and others, therefore, were not merely examples of the unpredictability of Latin American politics, even though the U.S. press cast them in that light. Rather, they constituted demonstrations of a power capability which the labor leaders felt should entitle them to positions of importance in the decision-making process. Their power lay not only in the capacity to paralyze national economic activity, but as well in the ability to touch off the explosive force of the urban mob. The riots during the cabinet-crisis strike in July 1962 offered a low-level example of the force of the mob.

Power relationships in pre-1964 Brazil were thus characterized by tentativeness. No single legitimate process transferred or definitively guaranteed control of the government as elections do in Western democracies. Goulart, in his effort to remain in office, thus perceived labor as an essential mainstay for his regime; the very fact of this perception automatically translated itself into real power for labor leaders. Believing that radical labor leaders could exert positive sanctions in the form of support for his government, as well as negative sanctions in the form of withdrawal at a moment when he would be unlikely to pick up equivalent backing from the right, the president clearly accorded them influence in national policy making. At the famous rally of Friday the Thirteenth (March 1964), for example, he incorporated the whispered suggestions of PUA head Osvaldo Pacheco into the policy guidelines he was announcing.[67] This event did not mark the inauguration of labor power in Brazilian politics; it was merely one further increment in its growth. Since 1962, Goulart's behavior had manifested an increasing respect for that power.

When there is a showdown among power contenders for control of the political system, the demonstration of a power capability differentiates itself

66. Charles W. Anderson, *Politics and Economic Change* (ch. 1 above, n. 21), p. 97.
67. Alberto Dines, "Debaixo dos deuses," in *Os idos de março,* pp. 311-312.

from actual possession. Confronted by the mobilized military in April 1964, the labor leaders saw their power vanish. This event supports another of Anderson's generalizations about Latin American populist politics: power contenders who do not appear willing to accept and tolerate the continued participation of already-established particpants in the political system will be excluded from that system by those established members. In the informal process of Latin American politics, traditional power contenders demonstrate a remarkable capacity for survival, and Anderson notes that in only three cases has revolution succeeded in eliminating certain power contenders from the political arena.[68]

In the recent period of industrialization and social change, what accounts for the tenacity of the traditional Latin American political system? Our study of labor in the Brazilian political process allows us to proceed further than Anderson by explicitly pinpointing some of the key mechanisms that protect the status quo. Most important among them are populism and the corporative nature of the state. Populism facilitated worker participation in the political process, but it prevented workers from organizing themselves autonomously. Their organizations thus could not withstand the challenge of armed force. Indeed, the military put a damper on their strike activity after August 1963 and completely wiped out their organizational base in 1964.

One may speculate that Almino Afonso's type of participatory populism might eventually have permitted labor autonomy to emerge. This would, of course, have required the development of autonomous organizations and the elimination of labor leaders' dependence upon state structures and offices. In view of Brazil's corporative state structure, such an achievement would be extremely difficult. The labor laws undermine the autonomy of the working class by imposing restrictive controls on its organizations and by coopting many of its representatives. Indeed, through the fifties, the system worked as intended. When it failed in the sixties, however, power contenders wedded to the status quo convinced the armed forces to intervene in the political process. As the next chapter demonstrates, the new government simply applied the state's existing corporative levers over labor organizations to remove union officers who manifested an inclination or ability to organize autonomously.

68. Anderson, *Politics and Economic Change,* pp. 104-111.

PART IV

The State and Labor
Since 1964

Chapter 8

THE CORPORATIVE SYSTEM SINCE 1964:
MODERNIZING THE ESTADO NOVO

The leaders of the civil-military coalition which overthrew President Goulart on April 1, 1964, justified their coup by pointing to economic decline, political instability, and, in particular, to the agitation of nationalist organizations like the CGT. Laying the blame on subversive activities by certain individuals rather than on defects and injustices within Brazil's socioeconomic system itself, the dominant military officers purged radical activists from the armed forces, civil service, labor organizations, student associations, political parties, teaching profession, mass media, and other sectors.

This chapter first describes the establishment of authoritarian rule by the military, examining the measures used to purge the national political elite and to bring labor organizations under strict control. It shows how the government has used the authoritarian corporative institutions to control workers while extracting resources from them for capital accumulation. It documents the hardships which workers have borne since 1964, and it discusses their attempts to devise, in the face of constant repression, new strategies of resistance and defense.

Military Rule and Democratic Institutions:
Unmaking the Populist System

Accusing the Goulart government of "deliberately bolshevizing" the nation, the new rulers drew Francisco Campos, the author of the Estado Novo Constitution, out of retirement to amend the Constitution of 1946 with an "Institutional Act." The Act left no doubt about either the low esteem in which the victorious officers held the nation's elected representatives or the relationship which they intended to maintain with Congress: ". . . this revolution does not seek to legitimize itself through the Congress. It is the Congress, rather, which receives its legitimacy from this Institutional Act, as a result of the exercise of the

Constituent Power inherent in all revolutions."[1] This Act and subsequent ones gave the government the right to annul or cassate (from the root *cassar*: to nullify, dismiss) the mandate of any of the nation's elective officers and to deprive them, as well as any other officials or citizens, of their political rights for ten years. The military rulers have made ample use of this weapon. They purged more than one-fifth of the federal legislators elected in 1962. And in a political crisis between December 1968 and October 1969, the executive removed 89 of the 409 deputies elected in 1966. This time, the government barred the deputies' legally elected substitutes from replacing them, thus keeping their seats vacant.[2] Such dramatic purges tamed the legislators, so the government annulled far fewer mandates in the following years.

Spelling out its powers in a series of subsequent Institutional Acts, all of which explicitly exempt their provisions and effects from judicial scrutiny or evaluation, the government now may make or change any rule it deems necessary for the pursuit of the national interest.[3] In 1965, for example, the parties most closely associated with the pre-1964 populist politicians defeated the pro-government candidates in important gubernatorial elections in Guanabara and Minas Gerais. A hard-line military faction reacted by forcing President Castello Branco to decree the Second Institutional Act. This document closed all existing political parties and created the conditions for the formation of an official "government" party and an official "opposition" party, respectively the National Renovation Alliance (ARENA) and the Brazilian Democratic Movement (MDB). Constrained by purges and intimidation, neither party appeared to threaten continued military rule; as the Rio wags put it, the difference between the two was that one said "Yes" and the other said "Yes, Sir!" After 1974, however, the MDB began to pose more serious problems for the military hard-liners, a topic briefly discussed in the next chapter.

To avoid direct elections of the kind which led to the embarrassing gubernatorial defeats of 1965, the Second Institutional Act removed the selection of Brazil's president, vice-president, and state governors from the hands of the electorate and transferred it to the corresponding legislative body. The military, easily in control of the legislatures, no longer need fear that the opposition will use popularly elected executives against the central government. To illustrate this control, consider an attempt at insubordination by the Rio Grande do Sul Assembly in the 1966 indirect elections for governor. Several ARENA deputies tried to support the MDB candidate, thus giving him a majority. Even though the opposition candidate, a respected jurist, could by no stretch of the imagination be considered subversive or corrupt – indeed, President Castello Branco was

1. The First Institutional Act is reprinted in Alberto Dines et al., *Os idos de março* (ch. 7 above, n. 64), pp. 401-403. See also Dines' commentary, pp. 356-357.

2. Ronald M. Schneider, *The Political System of Brazil* (ch. 1 above, n. 9), pp. 189, 275, 303; *OESP,* Jan. 18, 1969, p. 3.

3. The Institutional Acts (and all other Brazilian federal legislation) may be found by date in the *Coleção das leis do Brasil* (Rio de Janeiro: Departamento de Imprensa Nacional).

then considering him for appointment to the Supreme Court – the president viewed his impending victory as an embarrassment to federal authority. He therefore purged seven state deputies, shifting the balance back to the ARENA candidate.[4] By the 1970 gubernatorial elections, only one candidate ran in each state except for one, and party leaders chose him in consultation with the nation's president. This held equally true for the one state (Guanabara) where the MDB held a majority. In 1974, the process was repeated.[5]

The Second Act also abolished direct elections for mayors of state capital cities. Since 1965, each state governor appoints the executive of his capital city. This measure took away an institutional base which could have provided the MDB with resources and a tribune, for the opposition has consistently been strongest in the largest cities – which are, in Brazil, state capitals. Indeed, this measure deprived nearly 20 million persons, slightly over one-fifth of all Brazilians, of local self-government. Government legislative sleight-of-hand also deprived other politically sensitive *municípios* of elective local executive officers, in the name of "national security." This Act also extended the reach of the military courts to civilian offenses against the armed forces and/or the nation.

Finally, military and police forces have created a climate of fear in order to dampen any form of opposition. Torture of the most brutal and sadistic type is commonplace. Security officers deliberately perpetuate widespread insecurity by sweeping up large numbers of "suspects" in periodic dragnets. By arresting some 5,000 citizens in the weeks prior to the 1970 election, they certainly intimidated opposition leaders and voters alike.[6]

The government thus has ample means to control the composition of the national political elite. It has gone further, however, by sharply reducing the legislators' freedom in policy matters. The Institutional Acts, the military government's Constitution of 1967, and the military-imposed constitutional amendments of 1969 have altered the legislative process in ways evocative of de Gaulle's Fifth Republic. Congress must act upon all bills submitted by the president within 90 days (100 days under certain circumstances) or they automatically become law; and if a bill is designated "urgent," a joint session has only 40 days to reject it before it enters the books. Amid bitter protests from

4. Leônidas Xausa and Francisco Ferraz, "As eleições de 1966 no Rio Grande do Sul," *Revista Brasileira de Estudos Políticos,* no. 23/24 (July 1967/January 1968), p. 242; Schneider, *Political System,* pp. 178-179.

5. On 1970, see *OESP,* Oct. 3, 1970, p. 5; Oct. 4, pp. 1, 4, 5; the exception was Acre, where each party presented a candidate. On 1974, see Ronald M. Schneider, *Brazil: Foreign Policy of a Future World Power* (Boulder, Colo.: Westview Press, 1976), chs. 1 and 9.

6. *New York Times,* Nov. 22, 1970, p. 101; *OESP,* Nov. 7, p. 3; Carlos Castelo Branco in *JB,* Nov. 14, p. 4. On torture, see U.S. Senate, *Foreign Assistance and Related Programs Appropriations for Fiscal Year 1972; Hearings Before a Subcommittee of the Committee on Appropriations* (Washington, D.C.: GPO, 1971), pp. 1335-1412, and especially the article by Ralph Della Cava, reprinted from *Commonweal,* April 24, 1970, and an exchange of letters between Della Cava and Lincoln Gordon, former U.S. ambassador to Brazil, pp. 1340-1373. See also Amnesty International, *Report on Allegations of Torture in Brazil* (London, 1972).

many members of both parties, the government used this mechanism to win automatic enactment of the aforementioned bill which deprived politically sensitive municípios of elective local government. In this particular case, leaders of the government party urged their members to leave town during the last week of discussion on the bill so the lack of a quorum would prevent a vote and assure automatic passage. Although 106 of the 126 opposition members were present for the joint session, only 92 of 280 showed up from the government party. Indeed, ARENA leaders stood outside on the driveway urging their colleagues to return home.[7]

As ultimate weapon, the executive may suspend Congress at his discretion. President Castello Branco suspended the legislature for a month in late 1966 when deputies attempted to block his purge of six of their colleagues. And President Costa e Silva closed it from December 1968 through October 1969 after its members refused to waive one deputy's parliamentary immunity so the government could try him in a military court.[8]

The president exercises informal and formal controls over the media. Castello Branco warned the media in November 1965, for example, to refrain from giving press coverage to Carlos Lacerda, then a self-proclaimed presidential candidate who was beginning to support the opposition. If informal persuasion fails, however, the military may use the press law of January 1967 to imprison writers, editors, and publishers, regardless of the veracity of their material. The government seizes issues of newspapers which print news on taboo topics, and in May 1973 the censor's knife even deleted passages from the press law, which *O Pasquim* tried to print in its entirety.[9] Several Brazilian newspapers are under prior censorship, while most exercise self-censorship.

The Second Institutional Act packed the Supreme Court with 5 new judges in October 1965, and when that proved insufficient, the Fifth Institutional Act purged it of "subversive" judges in December 1968, bringing it back to its original number of 11. The Second Act also packed the Federal Appeals Court. As stated above, the Institutional Acts are expressly exempt from judicial review. The International Commission of Jurists, which studies and reports on the rule of law throughout the world, observed of Brazil in December 1969: "The role of the judiciary to protect individual rights has thus been rendered negligible. . . . The mere fact that the executive, legislative, and judicial powers are all wielded by the armed forces means that, even in trials where procedural formalities are observed, the fundamental rights of the individual are inadequately protected."[10]

Thus, the ruling military eliminated potential counterelites, reduced the

---

7. See *JB,* May 28, 1968, p. 3, and other journalistic coverage of the week.

8. The deputy in question subsequently wrote an insightful, *engagé* autobiographical essay on Brazil: see Márcio Moreira Alves, *A Grain of Mustard Seed* (Garden City, N.Y.: Doubleday Anchor, 1973).

9. *Latin America,* VII (May 11, 1973), 148-149.

10. "A Crisis for Democracy — Brazil," *Review of the International Commission of Jurists,* no. 4 (December 1969), 16-17.

autonomy of the nation's legislative and judicial institutions, and expanded the role of the executive agencies. Having thus subordinated the formal governmental institutions which allowed the rise of populism, the new rulers moved to tighten controls over the corporative system.

Military Rule and the Corporative System: Modifications in the Labor Law After 1964

One month after the overthrow of João Goulart, President Castello Branco's Labor Day speech addressed the issue of government control of the sindicato system. Once the brief period of intervention necessary to eliminate "corruption and subversion" in the sindicatos had passed, he said, the Ministry of Labor would respect their autonomy as they resumed "their normal function as authentic representatives of the workers."[11]

Despite Castello's assertion, the government has exerted every effort to limit the autonomy of workers' organizations. The long-standing direct and indirect controls established in the Consolidation of Labor Laws (CLT) facilitated this task. Furthermore, the military government, mindful of the autonomy which labor leaders gained in the fifties and sixties, enacted a considerable body of new legislation to tighten its grip. This legislation refined and supplemented the techniques of the Estado Novo in order to make the corporative system work better as an instrument of social control. It did not seek to free the labor movement from government tutelage. In a word, the coup initiated by the anti-Vargas tradition has resulted not in the destruction of the Estado Novo legacy but, rather, in an attempt to apply it more efficiently. This is in keeping with past Brazilian experience, for the overthrow of Vargas in 1945 and again in 1954 did not bring the destruction of the corporative labor structure.[12]

The government's new labor legislation serves three main purposes. Firstly, by tightening direct controls, it prevents the sindicatos from providing an organizational base from which to attack the existing social and political system or to oppose specific government policies. Secondly, it seeks to strengthen the sindicatos and the corporative system for their role in nation building and social cohesion. And thirdly, under the guise of inflation control, it transfers resources to industry by subjecting the working class to several types of forced saving programs. We will examine these three aspects of the legislation.

Claiming that subversion had caused political instability before 1964, the Castello Branco government intervened and purged the leadership of the most powerful and politically active union bodies.[13] Labor confederations and federations are by their nature and position more politically active than sindicatos, so

11. Humberto de Alencar Castello Branco, *Discursos, 1964* (Rio de Janeiro: Departamento de Imprensa Nacional), p. 23.
12. For a discussion of the pro- and anti-Vargas currents, see Skidmore, *Politics in Brazil* (ch. 1 above, n. 9), pp. 55-62.
13. Castello Branco, *Discursos, 1964,* pp. 22, 36-37.

one would expect more intense intervention at the upper levels. Indeed, the government intervened in 67 percent of the confederations, 42 percent of the federations, and only 19 percent of the sindicatos. Bank and transport workers' organizations figured prominently in the political strikes between 1960 and 1964, and they were hit harder, proportionally, than those in other sectors. And, significantly, large unions suffered more than small ones: the Ministry intervened in 70 percent of those sindicatos with 5,000 or more members; in 38 percent of those with 1,000 to 5,000 members; and in only 19 percent of those with fewer than 1,000 members.[14] The military government simply decapitated the radical labor movement.

The government then moved to tighten the legal straitjacket in order to prevent future radical mobilization of the sindicatos. The minister of labor, who had helped draft the CLT during the Estado Novo, added sharper teeth to old provisions or drew up new ones wherever he considered existing controls insufficient to guide workers' activity in appropriate directions.

New measures rigorously screen the channels to administrative and governing posts within the official labor organizations. Added to those forbidden to run for elective posts within the sindicatos are individuals whom the military government has temporarily or permanently deprived of their political rights as well as those who publicly defend the ideological principles of political parties or other bodies which the authorities have banned as contrary to the national interest.[15] This is aimed not only at the Communist Party but at all the pre-1964 political parties, which the government proscribed following its embarrassing defeat at the polls in 1965.

Prospective candidates, moreover, now must submit a declaration "that they will zealously work for faithful obedience to the Federal Constitution and national laws and that they will promise to respect the duly constituted authorities and carry out their decisions."[16] Both the Ministry and the political police scrutinize all candidates. On officially taking office, newly elected officials must repeat their oath to respect the Constitution and laws.[17]

Reflecting the belief that labor unrest prior to the coup was due to minority agitation, the new rules made voting mandatory for union members in order to prevent small cliques from taking over the sindicatos (art. 529). This measure also seeks to contribute to political socialization by increasing individual participation in approved social organizations.

In 1964, the government also regulated the constitutional provision guaranteeing the right to strike. The strike law prohibits political and solidarity strikes,

---

14. See the detailed study of government intervention in Argelina Maria Cheibub Figueiredo, "Política governamental e funções sindicais" (master's thesis, University of São Paulo, 1975), pp. 40-76. The second set of percentages is drawn from the 1510 workers' sindicatos (out of a total of 2049) for which Figueiredo obtained membership data.

15. CLT, art. 530, as amended by Decreto-lei 229 of Feb. 28, 1967, and portaria 40 of Jan. 21, 1965.

16. Portaria 40 of Jan. 21, 1965.

17. CLT, art. 532, as amended by Decreto-lei 229 of Feb. 28, 1967.

but it permits economic strikes by workers in most activities. Government application of the law, however, in conjunction with the official wage policy described later in this chapter, has rendered illegal and impossible all strikes except those to recover back wages which an employer has refused to pay. Strike data are scant for Brazil, but annual strike totals for the state of São Paulo show how thoroughly the government's enforcement of the strike law and complementary forms of intimidation have reduced work stoppages. Before the strike law, there were 180 strikes in 1961, 154 in 1962, and 302 in 1963. The total dropped to 25 in 1965, 15 in 1966, 12 in 1970, and zero in 1971.[18] Although no accurate count exists for more recent years, the number of strikes has risen slightly.

The government fundamentally restructured the social security system in order to prevent labor leaders or radicals from using its immense resources against the status quo. In 1966, a new law combined nearly all the institutes into one single National Social Welfare Institute (INPS). It thus implemented a plan advocated by social security technocrats but opposed by many affected sectors for over twenty years. This vast new agency, whose budget is second only to that of Brazil's federal government, counted an active insured population of 15 million in 1975, and a projected total of 26 million by 1980. In 1974, to consolidate "apolitical," technocratic control over social security activities, the government withdrew the INPS from the supervision of the Ministry of Labor and placed it under a new Ministry of Social Welfare. New legislation also reduced the government's contributions to a mere 5 percent of INPS revenues, thus shifting more of the burden to workers and employers.[19] To prevent this giant organization from being used against the status quo, the new rulers abandoned the principle of shared, tripartite executive control. A government-appointed director runs the INPS.

New laws also altered the composition of the board of directors of the National Social Welfare Department (DNPS), the policy-making body for the social security system. Although tripartite participation remains, the government's position on the board was strengthened; four directors are now appointed by the government and only two each from the employers and employees. Its president must be drawn from the government appointees. Thus the administrative state has reasserted its control over this important source of patronage and political power.[20]

Once the government achieved control of working-class organizations through careful screening of leadership, it aimed at using its leverage for two principal ends. One was to strengthen the corporative system by encouraging unionization, and the other was to enforce conformity with the official economic plan's wage squeeze.

18. Kenneth Scott Mericle, "Conflict Regulation" (ch. 3 above, n. 28), pp. 129-132, 248. The strike law is Lei 4330 of June 1, 1964, rectified June 18, 1964.

19. Malloy, "Evolution of Social Security Policy" (ch. 3 above, n. 13), pp. 18-27.

20. Relevant legislation is compiled in Ronaldo Waldemiro Groehs, *A lei orgânica* (ch. 4 above, n. 25).

The new rules sought to make union membership more appealing. The original CLT provision had given union members preference for jobs in companies with public contracts. Now they also enjoy preference in appointment to jobs in the civil service, ports, or similar activities, if their source of employment fails; in credit from public institutions for the purchase of their own home and for financing vehicles or tools for their trade; in purchasing or renting certain properties or apartments under public control; and in scholarships for secondary education or vocational training for themselves or their children.[21]

The government also sought to expand the sindicato structure in the countryside. After closing down the peasant leagues that flourished in the early 1960's and intervening in most rural sindicatos, it then began to cover the rural areas with a network of official (and, usually, rather inert) sindicatos under approved leadership, provoking one analyst to comment, "The last remaining uncorporatized arena that caused so much anxiety during the Goulart regime will then have been preempted and, presumably, placed beyond the reach of any future radical mobilization."[22]

Although the Labor Ministry's corporative theoreticians have amended the CLT to make union membership more attractive, national membership figures have not kept pace with the rise in employment in the economically expansive years since 1965. Union membership fell from 49 percent to 36 percent of the growing nonagricultural work force between 1965 and 1972. During this period, membership in the industrial sector fell from 45 to 39 percent of those employed, and in banking it fell from 52 to 47 percent. In commerce, however, it rose from 37 to 42 percent.[23] Government promises to revitalize the sindicatos by expanding their social-service activities thus had no positive effect upon membership rates by the early 1970's, probably because the same government was severely reducing workers' real wages and repressing any union activists who sought to mobilize workers in defense of their earnings.

The rise in additional family members holding outside jobs during this period may also help to explain the drop in membership rates. The falling real wages discussed below have forced a great many people into the labor market for the first time, and many of them, hopeful of returning to the household in future "better times," may view their working career as temporary. Therefore they would not join a sindicato.

Government officials, their grip thus reinforced, sharply reduced the real wages (actual purchasing power) of most workers; they imposed, through a new unemployment fund, a forced saving plan upon wage-earners, and they eliminated a welfare service for which workers still have to contribute through a payroll tax.

To justify the squeeze on workers, government planners cited the fight

21. CLT, art. 544, as amended by Decreto-lei 229 of Feb. 28, 1967.
22. Philippe C. Schmitter, "The 'Portugalization' of Brazil? " in Stepan (ed.), *Authoritarian Brazil* (ch. 2 above, n. 20), pp. 207-208.
23. See Table 4 above.

against an inflation which they blamed for the economic slowdown of the early 1960's. What is important to note, however, is that the planners, at least by 1967, applied anti-inflationary discipline *selectively* against the working class while they made credits and other benefits available to members of the middle and upper classes. It is the latter whose per capita income soared during the "economic miracle" from 1968 through 1974. While much of this new middle- and upper-class income went to increased consumption, it is significant that much also went into capital accumulation via the dynamic stock and bond markets which were reorganized and stimulated by new legislation in 1965. More than a device to control inflation, therefore, the squeeze on workers served principally to help industrialists accumulate capital.[24]

It was not easy for the economic planners to impose such drastic reductions in workers' real wages. The government began by setting ceilings for contractual wage increases. The sindicatos resisted and struck, many employers granted increases above official ceilings which even they considered unconscionably low, and labor court judges often approved contracts exceeding the guidelines' maximum. Once it became clear that these general guidelines would fail to hold the lid on wage increases, President Castello Branco gradually removed all flexibility from the parties by issuing a wage-construction formula with sanctions for its violation. This process, which we will now describe in detail, occurred during the first two years after the coup.

Although the new military government eliminated many of Brazil's most important labor leaders, their replacements frequently gained considerable nominal wage increases in the severely inflationary economy of 1964, even though in real-wage terms they often represented no gain at all or even a loss. To prevent a recurrence, the government in 1965 forced the purged and submissive legislature to establish norms for wage settlements. These laws directed labor court judges to aim at reestablishing the average real wage over the 24 months immediately preceding the expiration of a labor contract, conditioned by the following factors: repercussion of the readjustments on the national economy and society; confirmation that the readjustment satisfies the basic necessities of the wage earner and his family; addition of the real loss of purchasing power between the time the case was begun and the date of the decision; and the need to correct distortions in the wage hierarchy within a given economic sector to achieve social equity. Beginning in July 1966, judges were to add the productivity-increase index for the sector.[25]

Under these provisions, labor courts would only raise wages to the *average* of past years rather than to previous *peaks.* Thus the real wage curve, which has a sawtoothed pattern in a severely inflationary economy, would fall considerably *below the low point* of previous years before the next annual revision, leaving an annual average well under that of previous years. Technocrats responsible for the

24. Francisco de Oliveira, "A economia brasileira: crítica à razão dualista," *Estudos Cebrap*, no. 2 (October 1972), 59-82.

25. Lei 4725 of July 13, 1965, modified by Lei 4903 of Dec. 16, 1965.

TABLE 22

Effect of Government Wage Norms on Real Income, with
Constant 40% Annual Inflation (Hypothetical)

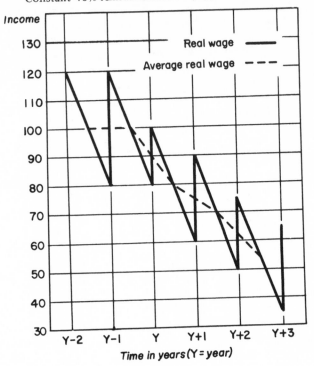

wage decision were well aware that real wages would fall, but they considered
that an acceptable outcome.[26]

To make the wage squeeze clear, Table 22 presents the impact of these laws
in hypothetical terms. It demonstrates that if we assign an index of 100 to the
average of the previous two years and assume constant inflation of 40 percent,
average real wages would decrease 30 percent from the base period over the
course of two years. Inflation did not remain constant but declined in the years
following the coup, so the guidelines dealt workers a slightly less severe short-run
blow than the one in our hypothetical example. Nevertheless, with cost-of-living
rises of 65.7 percent in 1965 and 41.3 percent in 1966, real wages plum-
meted.[27] Even so, wage settlements generally continued much higher than the
economic planners wished, because the guidelines were neither specific nor

26. Barry Ames, "Rhetoric and Reality in a Militarized Regime: Brazil Since 1964,"
Sage Professional Papers in Comparative Politics, IV, 32-33.
27. Increase in cost of living calculated from Getúlio Vargas Foundation tables for
Guanabara, in *Conjuntura Econômica,* XXI (November 1967), 167.

TABLE 23

Discrepancy Between Projected Inflation
and Actual Inflation, 1966-1975

12-month period ending in July	Projected inflation	Actual inflation	Discrepancy
1967	10%	30%	20%
1968	15	22	7
1969	15	21	6
1970	13	26	13
1971	12	18	6
1972	12	16	4
1973	12	12	0
1974	12	30	18
1975	15	27	12

Source: The projected inflation figures (*resíduo infla-cionário*) are those issued by the National Monetary Council before each of the twelve-month periods, as recorded in the files of the First Regional Labor Court (TRT) in Rio de Janeiro. Actual inflation shows the rise in the cost of living in Guanabara, as recorded by the Getúlio Vargas Foundation in *Conjuntura Econômica.*

binding enough to secure compliance by the labor court judges, who in most cases did not want to be party to such outright exploitation of the working class.

Consequently, when a presidential decree regulated these laws in January 1966, it made some concessions to those who decried the painful belt-tightening while it also sought to compel enforcement by the judges. In reconstituting the previous wage level, it added to the guidelines a factor equal to half of the estimated inflation for the coming year, as decreed by the National Monetary Council. In theory, this would have brought the average real wage up to that of previous years. The theoretical justice of this provision, however, was no more than a facade. In practice, the National Monetary Council has systematically underestimated inflation. By providing consistently low estimates to the labor courts, it has reduced the purchasing power of workers' wages in each new annual contract. Table 23 presents the gap between the council's projections and actual inflation from 1967 through 1975, a gap which averaged 9.5 percent per year.

The president stipulated, moreover, that, if the labor courts approved any wage agreement in excess of the terms of these laws, the corresponding percentage above the guidelines would be subtracted from the projected inflation factor in the next contract settlement. He also directed government authorities to consider invalid any contract in violation of these laws. Nonetheless, labor court judges still approved contracts which set wages above the legal limits.

Finally, government dissatisfaction over the lack of "the necessary uniformity in the construction (*apuração*) and application of the indices" resulted in a decree-law in mid-1966 which transformed the earlier guidelines into a rigid formula. This decree-law even required that the Supreme Labor Court issue binding instructions to compel the regional labor courts to apply the formula.[28] The government has thus forced the judges to keep the lid on contract settlements. One prominent labor-court judge observed wryly that the courts could now be replaced by a computer.[29]

In revising the *minimum* wage each year, however, the authorities have not even complied with the norms laid down in these laws. One study found that the five minimum-wage revisions from 1969 to 1973 averaged 3.6 percentage points below the raise that would have resulted from strict application of the formula.[30] The degree to which this affects the working class is readily apparent if we remember that about 40 percent of Brazil's workers earn the minimum wage, or only slightly more, or a specific fraction of it (as with "apprentices," who earn, by law, 50 percent of the miminum wage if they are between 14 and 16 years old, and 75 percent if they are between 16 and 18).[31]

Table 24 shows how the minimum wage policy has evolved from 1952 through 1975. The downward trend from the late fifties accelerated after 1964, so that by 1970 the minimum wage had lost nearly a quarter of its pre-coup purchasing power. By 1968, real wages had fallen so low that some economists blamed the wage squeeze for causing the economic recession of the mid-sixties. The government, desiring both to revive the economy and to prevent worker explosions such as the one that shook Minas Gerais in April 1968, took the exceptional step in June of declaring an emergency bonus of 10 percent, effective retroactively to May, for workers whose contracts had already run at least six months. The law excluded minimum-wage earners, whose paychecks had gone up on Labor Day.[32] This small, selectively applied increase did not, however, prevent another major explosion, this time in São Paulo in July.

Due to continued inflation, this raise did little for workers' purchasing power, but the beginning of the Brazilian "economic miracle" in this period caused working-class families' incomes to pick up a bit as additional family members found work and many workers began to put in overtime. By 1973 the boom had provoked such full employment in industrial São Paulo that a labor shortage even forced up the wages of unskilled workers.

With the world recession of 1974, however, foreign markets contracted, Brazilian economic activity began declining, and domestic inflation shot up,

28. Decreto-lei 15 of July 29, 1966; quote from preamble.
29. Mericle, "Conflict Regulation," pp. 247-249.
30. DIEESE, "Salário mínimo 1/74," April 25, 1974, p. 6.
31. Mericle, "Conflict Regulation," p. 255; Lei 5274 of April 24, 1974.
32. Jarbas Passarinho, *O Ministério do Trabalho e Previdência Social e o Plano Estratégico do Govêrno* (Rio de Janeiro: Ministério do Trabalho, 1968), pp. 10-19; Lei 5451 of June 12, 1968.

TABLE 24

Index of Annual Average of Real Monthly Minimum
Wage in Guanabara, 1952-1975

Year	Index (1960=100)	Year	Index (1960=100)
1952	95	1965	82
1953	83	1966	76
1954	115	1967	75
		1968	73
1955	113	1969	71
1956	105		
1957	134	1970	69
1958	101	1971	69
1959	115	1972	71
		1973	75
1960	100	1974	70
1961	115	1975	75
1962	100		
1963	92		
1964	90		

Source: The index numbers were derived by dividing the
legal minimum wage by the monthly cost-of-living figures for
Guanabara published regularly in *Conjuntura Econômica* and
then averaging the twelve months each year. The yearly figures were taken as proportions of the 1960 average.

again tightening the squeeze on the working class. During the election campaign
in 1974, therefore, the president declared a similar 10-percent emergency bonus.
It applied to minimum-wage earners, too, so most workers benefited from it.
Nonetheless, the economic decline continued. By August 1975, certain industrial
spokesmen, wishing to boost their sales, called for another, this time more
significant, wage raise.[33] In early 1976 the government appeared to be heeding
these appeals and the nation expected, on Labor Day, a minimum-wage increase
well in excess of inflation. These expectations were disappointed, however, when
President Geisel decreed a 44-percent hike, barely above the inflation rate.[34]

Another form of inflation control is a byproduct of a new, individualized
unemployment fund. One of the most highly prized benefits for Brazilian labor
prior to the overthrow of Goulart had been job stability or tenure, i.e., protection against being fired once a worker had reached ten years of service with an
employer, except in duly proven cases of *falta grave.*[35] Despite workers' feeling
for the stability law, it should be acknowledged that employers frequently

33. See Lei 6147 of Nov. 29, 1974; and *Latin America,* IX (July 25, 1975), 229-230.
34. *Latin America,* X (March 12, 1976), 87; X (May 7, 1976), 140.
35. CLT, art. 492.

flouted it by systematically dismissing workers before they achieved ten years of service and in other ways, as a survey of management in São Paulo revealed.[36]

Foreign investors objected strongly to the stability law. The Castello Branco government, despite its assurances that national social legislation would remain inviolate,[37] heeded these objections. In 1966 the president submitted a bill to abolish the previous form of stability, except for those employees who had already attained it (about 15 percent of the work force). To replace stability, the bill established a severance pay fund, the Fundo de Garantia do Tempo de Serviço (FGTS). The legislators, not wishing to support such an unpopular measure, abstained from acting on it. At the end of the waiting period fixed by the Institutional Act, it automatically became law.[38]

This extremely complex law requires that employers establish a bank account in the name of each of their employees and that they deposit therein each month the equivalent of 8 percent of the employee's wages. Employees may withdraw this money only in the event of their dismissal, retirement, or under other specified extraordinary circumstances. The legislation establishing the Fundo terminated several employer-funded programs designed to assist workers and it eliminated employers' statutory contributions to others.[39] In this way, the government's new programs reduced services previously available to the working class and thus further lowered workers' standard of living.

By eliminating job stability, the FGTS has had a marked impact on workers' lives. Firstly, it has heightened personal economic insecurity by facilitating very high involuntary turnover rates. In the state of São Paulo in 1970, for example, 35.5 percent of the work force had put in less than one year on the job, 55.6 percent had not yet reached two years, and 74.2 percent had not reached three years. Secondly, workers lacking stability are hesitant to complain against their employers in the labor-court system. One examination of labor court records for 1964, before the establishment of the FGTS, and for 1968, after its passage, found that grievances initiated by workers against their employers dropped from 39 to 17 percent of total grievances. Finally, turnover lowers workers' paychecks

36. Ary R. Carvalho, "Medidas Legais de Promoção e Contrôle," in Raimar Richers et al. (eds.), *Impacto da ação do Govêrno sôbre as emprêsas brasileiras* (Rio de Janeiro: Fundação Getúlio Vargas, 1963), pp. 137-142.

37. Document of Comando Supremo da Revolução, cited in A. F. Cesarino Júnior, *Estabilidade e Fundo de Garantia* (Rio de Janeiro: Forense, 1968), pp. 37-38.

38. Lei 5107 of Sept. 13, 1966; Alexandre de Souza Costa Barros and Argelina Maria Cheibub Figueiredo, *The Creation of Two Social Programs, the FGTS and the PIS: A Brazilian Case Study on the Dissemination and Use of Social Sciences Research for Governmental Policy Making* (preliminary version) (Rio de Janeiro: Escola Brasileira de Administração Pública, 1975), pp. 45-49, 58. On the politics of the passage of the FGTS, see pp. 26-67.

39. Cesarino Júnior, *Estabilidade*, pp. 59-61. This book is a thorough critique of the program by an eminent labor lawyer. See also "Encargos Sociais e Fundo de Garantia," *Conjuntura Econômica*, XXI (January 1967), 57-64, for a brief comparison of the provisions of stability and the Fundo.

compared to employees who stay with the same company over the long run. This occurs because most workers hire in at the minimum wage, and the annual raises in the minimum wage have been less than those set by the labor courts for continuously employed workers. Kenneth Mericle clearly demonstrates that if two workers began in the same trade with the same pay in 1965 and one of them remained continuously employed with the same firm while the other was fired each year and moved immediately to a new company, the paycheck of the victim of annual involuntary turnover would in 1972 come to only 83 percent of that of the stable worker.[40]

Shortly after the coup, the new regime abolished the controversial Fundo Social Sindical, whose funds were used for political gain by previous administrations. In its place was established a National Department of Employment and Wages (DNES), which receives the 20 percent of the imposto sindical formerly allocated to the FSS. For the first year these funds covered the expenses of setting up its office, but since then they have been placed in an account for Employment and Wages, which is transferred to the national treasury and ultimately returned to the general fund of the Ministry of Labor. Because of its fight against inflation, the government held these funds rather than spending them, so this reallocation of one-fifth of the trade-union tax implied yet another parcel of enforced saving imposed upon the workers.[41] In 1964 the captive Congress abolished the tripartite Minimum Wage Commissions and transferred their cost-of-living studies to the DNES, marking yet another technocratic, as opposed to political, solution.

The pre-1964 populist regime and the succeeding authoritarian regime held sharply contrasting attitudes toward the integration of the working class into the general social system, and the DNES and Fundo Social Sindical illustrate the contrast. The Fundo was designed to accommodate the working class in modern industrial society through social welfare projects. The DNES, on the other hand, aims at raising productivity. It formulates official vocational-training policies, undertakes manpower surveys, and handles job placement. Since 1964, military force has eliminated the need to make social and political compromises with the working class. Instead of integrating workers into the *society* and *polity*, the new technocratic programs integrate labor into the *economy* as a mere factor of production.

Let us now translate the cold statistics of falling real wages into the reality they reflect: declines in quantity and/or quality of food, housing, clothing, family unity, personal health, and workplace safety. One study in São Paulo found that in order to buy a marketbasket with a month's essential nutritive requirements for one person, workers earning the minimum wage in December

40. All data in this paragraph are from Mericle, "Conflict Regulation," pp. 185, 280-285.
41. Ames, "Rhetoric and Reality," p. 34.

1965 would have had to spend 87 hours and 20 minutes on the job; in December 1973, they needed to put in 158 hours and 42 minutes for the same market-basket.[42] This fall in purchasing power accounts for workers' generally inadequate nutritional intake, a pattern which is most aggravated at the lowest income levels.[43] Moreover, at the same time that official wage policies were driving down the disposable income of Brazil's working-class families, the federal government shifted the emphasis of its expenditures on public health from preventive to curative medicine, a move that necessarily benefits the rich and deprives the poor, for the poor have only limited access to doctors and hospitals.[44] Worse yet, these expenditures are already very meager: a World Bank study of 51 developing countries (including 12 Latin American and 2 English-speaking Caribbean countries) found Brazil spent only two-tenths of one percent of its gross national product on its health budget, or about 80 U.S. cents per person per year. This was the lowest proportion of all the 51 countries.[45]

These factors, in the context of skyrocketing urbanization which provoked the near-collapse of water and sewer systems, made the workers and the poor in general the principal victims of the epidemic diseases which have ravaged Brazil since 1973: meningitis, encephalitis, and polio. Infant mortality figures reflect the declining public-health picture. A University of São Paulo study found that in greater São Paulo in 1968, 68 babies out of 1,000 died during their first year, but by 1973 the figure had reached 93 out of every 1,000. In Recife in 1970, 148 babies out of every 1,000 died during their first year, and by 1973 the figure had reached 174.[46]

Family unity suffered because the declining real wages of family heads compelled additional family members to take outside jobs. Surveys of São Paulo working-class families found an average of one family member employed in 1958, whereas in 1969 two persons per family held outside jobs.[47] Poor nutrition and inadequate living conditions, excessive overtime, and consequent deterioration of health and reflexes have caused rising rates of workplace accidents. Official figures show that 14.6 percent of the labor force suffered workplace accidents in 1969, and this figure rose annually to reach 19.4 percent in 1973.[48]

42. DIEESE, "Salário mínimo 1/74," p. 8.
43. "Nível alimentar da população trabalhadora da cidade de São Paulo," *Estudos Sócio-Econômicos,* no. 1 (July 1973), 1-32.
44. Malloy, "Evolution," p. 29.
45. World Bank, *Health Sector Policy Paper* (Washington, D.C., March 1975), pp. 74-75; data were drawn mostly from the early 1970's, with more than half, including those for Brazil, from 1971.
46. *Latin America,* IX (May 23, 1975), 157; IX (Oct. 24, 1975), 330.
47. "Família assalariada: padrão e custo de vida," *Estudos Sócio-Econômicos,* no. 2 (January 1974), 25.
48. Ângela Mendes de Almeida and Michael Lowy, "Union Structure and Labor Organization in the Recent History of Brazil," *Latin American Perspectives,* III (Winter 1976), 115-116. A survey of São Paulo which clearly presents many of the social costs of Brazil's economic "miracle" is Vinícius Caldeira Brant et al., *São Paulo 1975: crescimento e pobreza* (São Paulo: Edicões Loyola, 1976).

Labor's Response

How have workers reacted to such an oppressive situation? Government control of the sindicatos has limited their reaction. As previous chapters have demonstrated, union heads had not consolidated strong organizational links with workers before the coup of 1964. After the coup, the most effective, militant, and/or radical labor leaders fled into exile or were jailed or harassed by the new government. The Ministry of Labor intervened in many labor organizations, and Ministry officials intimidated the remainder with the threat of intervention. Deprived of their most able representatives, workers lost the capacity to organize opposition or even to protest the official policies. To take the place of the radical, militant pre-1964 leaders and to head off renewed labor radicalism, the American Institute for Free Labor Development — an anti-nationalist and anti-Communist training institute which the U.S. government funds and which the AFL-CIO and U.S. big business direct — began an intensive program to train Brazilian labor leaders in U.S.-style business unionism. By 1973, nearly 30,000 union activists had attended its various courses in Brazil.[49] The Brazilian government, through a program established in 1970, also began training labor leaders in "the spirit of collaboration with the state in the execution of its social and economic development programs." It planned to train over 2,600 union officials between 1972 and 1974.[50] Thus, an anti-radical cadre of organizers came to the fore in many unions. And for those few radicals who did not get picked off by the police, the military, or the Labor Ministry, little opportunity for militant action remains. A study of unions in greater São Paulo in 1972 concludes: "Because of the threat of intervention and the bureaucratic imperatives of the unions, the behavior of radicals who are still in leadership positions is hardly distinguishable from that of bought-off *pelegos.*"[51]

Government repression, moreover, went far beyond intervening to replace union officers. Periodic arrests or interrogations and, by the late 1960's, the threat of torture served to intimidate many union officials. Amnesty International documented more than 1,000 cases of torture in 1972, and many workers figure on the list.[52]

At the mass level, too, threats of repression have curbed overt organizing activity. Workers who participate actively in strikes, job actions, or militant union activity are likely to run afoul of the police, and a police record can eliminate a worker's livelihood. This occurs because the termination of the job stability program in 1966 has forced most workers to live under the threat of

---

49. Kenneth Paul Erickson and Patrick V. Peppe, "Dependent Capitalist Development" (ch. 1 above, n. 22), p. 40. See also Hobart A. Spalding, Jr., "U.S. and Latin American Labor: The Dynamics of Imperialist Control," *Latin American Perspectives,* III (Winter 1976), 53-64.

50. Figueiredo, "Política governamental," p. 90; Mericle, "Conflict Regulation," pp. 110, 146.

51. Mericle, "Conflict Regulation," p. 143.

52. Amnesty International, *Report,* Annex 1.

dismissal; and to apply for a new job, if one is dismissed, one must present a certificate of good conduct from the police.[53]

Despite this repressive atmosphere, workers have resisted in several ways. No serious strikes occurred during the first few years after the coup, because the government had decapitated the former labor movement. In 1967, however, and in a manner that one might expect in this system where the state has traditionally controlled or strongly influenced organized labor, it was the state, through President Costa e Silva's labor minister, which created conditions for the first organized resistance. Labor Minister Jarbas Passarinho, seeking to build a mass power base, called for a change in the official wage policy and proclaimed his support for "trade-union renovation" (*renovação sindical*). Now, with a cabinet member opposing wage repression, union heads jumped on the bandwagon. By late 1967 many of them had formed organizations against the official wage policy, such as São Paulo's Interunion Movement Against the Wage Squeeze (MIA). These union officers, knowing full well that the Labor Ministry would tolerate MIA-type activities only so long as they did not challenge the government's authority, consciously sought to restrict participation to workers they could control. This was not an easy task, for the Costa e Silva government, by promising to "humanize" the post-1964 political system, raised hopes for an end to the authoritarian restrictions.

Students, church groups, left-wing organizations, and workers acting independently of their union heads all took advantage of the apparent political decompression to organize and protest, so the few demonstrations called by MIA leaders rapidly escaped their control. Since the MIA organizers did not wish to risk their union positions by defying the dictatorship, their activity declined while the other groups, most notably the students, stepped up their agitation. With the protests increasing in frequency and intensity, the government began to see them as a challenge.

In April 1968, against this backdrop of rising mobilization, a major wildcat metalworkers' strike in Contagem, Minas Gerais, confirmed the government's worst fears. Like the movements against the wage squeeze, this strike was stimulated in part by the initiatives of the new labor minister. Some union activists took him at his word when he called for a renovation of the sindicatos and, under the banner of "trade-union opposition" (*oposição sindical*), they contested the government-approved leaders in sindicato elections. These activists, in many cases drawn from a new generation and thus uncompromised by participation in the pelego- or populist-dominated pre-1964 unions, fought not only the official wage policy but also the very principle of government control of the sindicatos. The Contagem strike, led by the standardbearer of the local oposição sindical — a man who had been elected to the presidency of the sindicato in mid-1967, only to have the local office of the Ministry of Labor

---

53. Timothy Fox Harding, "Laboring Under the Dictatorship," *Brazilian Information Bulletin* (Berkeley), no. 10 (June 1973), 9.

disqualify him and give the position to another – lasted over a week. The 15,000 strikers openly attacked official wage policies and demanded an immediate raise. The minister of labor at first tried to settle the strike peacefully, but ultimately the military police occupied the city and crushed the strike with force.

Four months later, a major metalworkers' strike erupted in Osasco, São Paulo, and began to spread to other sectors. The metalworkers' sindicato, one of the few in which a victorious oposição sindical slate had been allowed to take office, called the strike for higher wages and thus confronted the authorities with another direct challenge. The government responded immediately: the São Paulo office of the Ministry of Labor declared the strike illegal, the Ministry intervened in the sindicato to remove the leadership, and the police broke up all workers' meetings and arrested many of the participants. The Contagem experience, the political atmosphere in the nation and especially in São Paulo (where students had occupied university buildings, causing political tensions to peak), and the links between the student movement and the sindicato, which were reinforced by the presence of many student-workers, led the government to crush the strike quickly and forcefully.[54]

The government thus showed its resolve to brook no further labor opposition. Moreover, in December 1968 the president decreed the Fifth Institutional Act and thus created a continuing legal basis to suppress any sort of opposition. He closed and purged the Congress, while military and police units arrested suspected "subversives" and began systematic, large-scale torture of prisoners.

These measures profoundly intimidated workers and for a while created a defeatist attitude among them. Based on their experiences of 1968, they first came to believe that one could do nothing against the dictatorship and that political organization and activity could only hurt them. By 1972, however, workers began to devise ways of defending their class interests without engendering massive repression from the government. In that year shipyard workers, bank employees, General Motors employees, São Paulo bus drivers, and subway construction workers won raises above the official guidelines by holding illegal, "spontaneous" strikes. And the labor shortage of 1973, with its attendant overtime, gave sindicatos a new lever to call legal strikes. Since Brazilian labor law sees overtime work as voluntary and, consequently, outside the normal contract, the wage guidelines do not cover it. Thus workers for Volkswagen, Mercedes-Benz, Chrysler, and Villares Elevators successfully refused to work overtime until they won 9 to 10 percent hikes over their contractual levels; a similar effort at Ford failed, because workers there lacked the requisite organizational experience and ability.[55]

These successes have led militant workers to create ad hoc factory committees in many plants. These bodies, which are roughly analogous to unofficial,

---

54. This description of the Contagem and Osasco strikes and their precipitants is drawn from Francisco C. Weffort's excellent case study, *Participação e conflito industrial: Contagem e Osasco, 1968* (São Paulo: Cebrap, 1972).

55. Almeida and Lowy, "Union Structure," p. 117.

legally unrecognized shop-steward units, have given workers new organizational experience. Even after the economic slowdown had begun in 1974, many of these committees obtained 10-percent raises midway through their contracts. Usually they achieved their goals by threatening or initiating a go-slow or work-to-rule action. The sindicatos, in order to avoid government intervention, did not involve themselves in these factory-level activities.[56]

During the boom years, workers in the modern sector of Brazil's industrial economy tried to shake the confining features of the CLT in order to rely solely on their own direct bargaining ability with their employers. Maria Hermínia de Almeida argues that the CLT's detailed, all-encompassing regulations and the industrywide union pattern were designed for the more uniform conditions of small and medium plants, the most typical factories prior to the late 1950's when the capital-goods and consumer-durables sectors expanded. Workers in the numerically expanding, largescale, capital-intensive factories find the CLT a burdensome anachronism, for it forces them to deal with their employers through the intermediary of the state, usually through unions which are controlled by members from the lower-paying traditional factories. Workers in the modern sector believe they would do better if they could transform the factory committees into legally recognized bargaining agents. In her case study of one of the few metalworkers' unions whose members come predominantly from the modern, largescale, and relatively well-paid sectors — in the plants where the seven elective officers of this union worked, wages averaged 3.6 to 4.1 times the minimum wage — Almeida found that the union heads sought to throw off the traces of the CLT because they confidently believed they could bargain from strength if not hindered from outside. Specifically, they demanded complete trade-union autonomy from the state; the right to bargain collectively and sign contracts with each enterprise, rather than with an entire sector; the right to set up a shop-steward system, with legal recognition for this position; and the right to establish relations with foreign unions whose members work for the same transnational enterprises. Almeida points out, however, that these demands fell upon deaf ears in government and employer circles.[57]

The international economic recession of 1974 and 1975 reduced foreign markets for Brazilian manufacturers at the same time that rising oil prices fed domestic inflation and caused economic dislocations. This has reduced employment and, therefore, the leverage of the workers' organizations. Moreover, the government of General Ernesto Geisel took office in March 1974 and immediately made it clear that it intended to keep labor under strict supervision. Officials in São Paulo began arresting and torturing "subversive" labor activists, including at least seven of those who participated in the Villares overtime strike.[58]

56. Heloisa Helena Teixeira de Souza Martins, "O sindicato e a burocratização dos conflitos de trabalho no Brasil" (master's thesis, University of São Paulo, 1975), pp. 143-144; Celso Frederico, "Amarrando a produção: notas sobre a inquietação operária," *Contexto*, no. 1 (November 1976), 33-42.

57. Maria Hermínia de Almeida, "O sindicato no Brasil" (ch. 3 above, n. 10), pp. 14-33.

58. Timothy Fox Harding, "Labor Challenge to Dictatorship," *Brazilian Information Bulletin*, no. 13 (Spring 1974), 3-4.

In February 1975, military and police authorities arrested dozens of São Paulo trade-union leaders, and many workers were swept up in a dragnet in October when General Ednardo D'Avila Melo, commander of the Second Army in São Paulo, moved to rid Brazil of subversive "red fascists." Because the Second Army's internal defense and intelligence department had distinguished itself by arresting union activists and preventing militant activity, many of São Paulo's large foreign firms bestowed gifts and honors upon General Ednardo. In January 1976, however, the Second Army went too far; one worker it arrested died under torture. The incident, coming only three months after an international and domestic stir caused by the similar torture death of a prominent São Paulo journalist, led President Geisel to sack Ednardo, but his replacement insisted that the fight against "subversives" would retain top priority.[59] The government has thus demonstrated that it will not allow any measure of autonomy to labor organizations and that workers should not expect economic rewards, despite the dramatic growth in output since 1967.

Conclusion

The civil-military coalition which took power in 1964 replaced the populist system with an authoritarian, technocratic polity. The new rulers, their political control bolstered by repression and their economic position strengthened by vast investment sums from foreign sources, applied technocratic measures to bring union militancy and strike activity under control. In addition to tightening the already existing corporative controls over labor leaders, they consciously transferred the wage-settlement process to the office of the president in order to deemphasize the sindicatos' most salient economic activity. At the same time, they directed union officers' energies into social-welfare endeavors, because these do not challenge the social and political status quo. The government, by thus bringing the unions back into conformity with the Estado Novo conception of workers' organizations and by creating a general atmosphere which equates sindicatos with subversion, has undoubtedly helped hold down union membership, even in the face of some material incentives to join. Militant labor activity now takes place outside the sindicatos, or at least behind the backs of the official leaders.

Some observers believe the late 1960's and early 1970's marked a turning point in the history of organized labor in Brazil.[60] Indicating the big metalworkers' strikes of 1968, the overtime strikes around 1973, and, particularly, the rise of factory committees in the 1970's as evidence that workers have begun organizing autonomously, they hope that labor may ultimately shake the bonds

---

59. *Latin America*, IX (Feb. 28, 1975), 72; IX (Nov. 14, 1975), 358; X (Jan. 23, 1976), 25; and X (Jan. 30, 1976), 36-37; and Robert M. Levine, "Brazil: The Aftermath of Decompression," *Current History*, LXX (February 1976), 55-56.

60. These observers are aware of the constraints upon labor in Brazil, so they do not let their hopes become predictions. See, for example, Almeida and Lowy, "Union Structure," pp. 108, 118; M. H. de Almeida, "O sindicato no Brasil," pp. 73-74; Harding, "Labor Challenge," p. 2.

of state control. These observers correctly point to new internal characteristics of the movement. The external context, however, has not changed. The government has responded as did earlier governments throughout most of this century. It repressed the strikes, jailed and harassed the leaders, and disrupted the movement. The Estado Novo legacy thus lives on.

PART V

Conclusion

Chapter 9

LABOR AND THE
POLITICAL PROCESS
IN BRAZIL

This study has addressed questions on three major levels. On the most specific level, it has documented the political power of Brazilian labor leaders and attempted to account for the sources of that power, as well as limitations upon it. At a higher level of generality, it has analyzed labor leaders' participation within the Brazilian political system, in order to shed light on the nature of that system. Finally, it has examined corporatism's effectiveness as a mechanism for accommodating the urban working class into the social and political system with minimal social disruption, enabling us to identify forces of change and of stability in the corporative type of political system.

The preceding chapters have not only produced information on these basic questions, but they have also used that information to test the applicability of a number of hypotheses on Latin American and Brazilian politics. The author hopes, therefore, that the conclusions and findings of this study will contribute to a growing body of literature on comparative political development reaching far beyond the borders of Brazil. Since relevant theoretical implications and conclusions appear in each of the preceding chapters, this concluding chapter briefly summarizes the study's findings and then speculates on the future.

Labor Leaders and Political Power in Brazil

Political power constitutes a critical requisite for effective participation in the political process. Our analysis, therefore, has indicated sources of power for labor leaders as well as the relative importance of such power in the Brazilian political process. During the populist period up to 1964, shrewd manipulation of the political strike and of the corporative state's patronage mechanisms provided the two principal sources of this power.

To understand the role of labor leaders in the political strike, we have distinguished two levels of power: power over the rank-and-file, and power in national politics. In the political strikes of the early 1960's, union heads possessed only tenuous control over the mass of workers, so strike success depended on variables not of the strike leaders' making. Firstly, successful political strikes owed their effectiveness to the rank-and-file's deeply felt economic grievances. Soaring inflation caused rapid, pronounced declines in real wages, so material deprivation predisposed workers to take to the streets. The term "political strike," therefore, carries misleading connotations, because for most workers these strikes were essentially economic in motivation and goals.

Secondly, the attitude and role of key military officers shaped strike outcomes. Most successful political strikes enjoyed at least tacit support from the military, and when key elements in the armed forces came openly to oppose strike movements, the success of such walkouts diminished visibly. Since 1964, the military government has tolerated no political strikes. It forcefully crushed the only two political strikes since the coup, those of Contagem and Osasco in 1968. By totally emasculating the official sindicatos, the government has caused workers to respond by setting up ad hoc factory committees. These committees have controlled most of the job actions, which have been narrowly economic rather than political in recent years. The military government in the seventies, ironically, seems to be stimulating something which the prominent labor leaders of the early sixties could not achieve: grassroots labor organizations which, because they are independent of state funds, seek autonomy from the state.

Thirdly, strike success before 1964 often depended upon the assistance of political notables. Representing "authority" in the picket lines, their presence could convince workers with deferential values to defy the lesser authority of the employer. With the purging of many politicians who had supported labor, and in light of the virtual destruction of populism since 1964, this variable is no longer relevant.

Mass participation in strikes before the coup, therefore, did not result from the organizational strength of the sindicatos. Most of those labor leaders who did not content themselves with self-aggrandizement sought to build union resources or services or to enhance their political influence *within* the corporative state apparatus. They did not seek to construct autonomous organizational links with the mass of workers. Although some labor leaders attempted to strengthen their control over the rank-and-file through membership campaigns and training programs, they had achieved little before the military intervened. Surely the failure of the general strike they called to prevent the coup is testimony to the ineffectiveness of such efforts.

As Chapter Six indicated, most workers believed they occupied a rather privileged position in the national economy, at least when compared to the rural masses and the urban unemployed and underemployed. This relative comfort significantly held down the level of active participation in the labor movement. In the strikes studied, only relative deprivation caused by a drop in real wages brought protest, and most workers directed this protest toward economic, not political, goals. This evidence supports Gláucio Soares' hypothesis on late industrialization:

" . . . if the theorists of the old industrialization saw the middle class as a cushioning element between the conflicting upper and working class, I see the steadily employed working class as a cushioning element between the middle class and the unemployed and underemployed sectors of the working class."[1]

We should therefore distinguish between the mass of workers, who desired economic benefits, and the radical labor leaders of the CGT, who sought fundamental changes in the political system.

Paradoxically, the radical CGT leaders, despite their organizational frailty and relative lack of power over their constituents, did in fact amass considerable power on the national political scene. The success of the strikes they called — particularly in 1962 — was taken as an indicator of the strength of their organizations, even though our findings demonstrate such strength to be illusory. President Goulart as well as the CGT leaders themselves assumed that union offices carried considerable political power.

Because Goulart saw the labor leaders as an essential part of his coalition, they were able to exploit the technique of dissensus politics to exact concessions from him, further enhancing their own power. Taking advantage of this leverage, they began to influence national policy. At the rally on Friday the Thirteenth, for example, as we noted earlier, Goulart incorporated Osvaldo Pacheco's whispered suggestions into the policy he was formulating.

The corporative state reserved certain important positions in the labor and welfare bureaucracies for sindicato officers, and these posts constituted the CGT leaders' second major source of power. As directors of the social security apparatus, for example, they shared control over a bureaucracy employing nearly 100,000 persons. Patronage appointments thus increased their power. Their posts also enabled them to indulge or deprive welfare clients of benefits which these clients legally deserved. Woefully underfunded, the system could not possibly serve more than a fraction of its potential beneficiaries. The necessary selection process therefore increased the directors' leverage. In return for their services, the labor leaders expected to control the participation of their political debtors in elections, demonstrations, or strikes. Thus they built their political clientele.

Especially during the brief ministry of Almino Afonso, radical nationalist leftists made a concerted effort to use the social security system to build a cohesive political machine. The ouster of Almino, however, eliminated their

1. Gláucio Ary Dillon Soares, "The New Industrialization and the Brazilian Political System," in James Petras and Maurice Zeitlin (eds.), *Latin America: Reform or Revolution* (Greenwich, Conn.: Fawcett, 1968), p. 196.

major patron within the system and thus frustrated the attempt. The removal of some of them from institute presidencies in December 1963 further eroded their power in the social security system, though it did not terminate it. Only with the coup of 1964 did they lose all of these positions.

To sum up, the labor leaders were able to marshal power in the political system, but they never institutionalized it in the form of *autonomous* organizations. At all times, their organizational base remained dependent upon the state. The corporative system, which coopted union heads with perquisites, opportunities for social ascent, and apparent political prominence, functioned as its founders had hoped. Labor leaders were drawn to the state as moths to a flame. Not even during their period of greatest activism did they desire or seek real autonomy from the state.

The Brazilian Political System

The leaders of the Revolution of 1930 were social conservatives as well as modernizing nation-builders. They sought to unify, strengthen, and industrialize Brazil, but they hoped to preserve as much of their country's traditional culture and social structure as possible. They believed that under conditions of rapid urbanization, industrialization, and social mobilization, liberal democratic political institutions would permit aggravated class conflict which would inevitably bring on radical revolution. To head off this specter, they replaced the liberal institutions of the Old Republic with corporative institutions designed to foster class harmony. They created sindicato organizations for both proletariat and bourgeoisie, and between these two parallel hierarchies they interposed the organizations of the administrative state. In theory, this state was merely to stand vigil and mediate, in the name of the general will of society, among its component social groups. In reality, it initiated a vast interventionist role in the economy and the society from which it has never since retired.

Liberal democracy ostensibly replaced corporatism when the military overthrew Vargas in 1945. Indeed, the Constitution of 1946 broadened suffrage and established direct elections for the legislature and executive at national, state, and local levels. On the other hand, however, the Constituent Assembly retained the corporative sindicato structures of the thirties as well as the state controls over them. The fundamental nature of the Brazilian polity, therefore, remained corporative right through the democratic period from 1946 to 1964.

Electoral democracy and its product, populism, worked at cross-purposes to the control function of the corporative framework. Laws passed by the popularly elected Congress provided radical labor leaders with participation not only in the trade unions but also in other corporative institutions such as the social security system. This statutory participation assured them the very leverage they needed to increase their power in the political process.

Many contemporary observers, witnessing the labor leaders' growing political presence, concluded that populism was paving the way for thoroughgoing social and political change. In the years immediately prior to Goulart's ouster, a euphoria reigned within the Brazilian left and many leftists believed that radical social revolution was imminent. Events proved this belief tragically ill-founded. Populism played as important a role in limiting the strength of the supposedly revolutionary forces as it did in building the euphoria.

The observers had confused populist political movements with revolutionary movements, because both mobilize the lower classes. Populist movements, it is true, mobilize working-class and peasant followings, but their organizations are not independent of their middle- or upper-class leaders whose ultimate interests diverge from those of the lower classes. For a revolution to succeed in the seventh decade of the twentieth century, autonomous working-class organization would have been essential. Yet it was conspicuously absent from the movement we have studied. In corporative Brazil, the institutions of the "revolutionaries" existed at the suffrance of the state and derived their funds largely from public coffers. Brazilian populism, therefore, was quite capable of generating euphoria, but it proved totally incapable of generating revolution.[2]

Foremost in making revolution an unrealistic expectation was the inability or unwillingness of radical politicians and labor leaders to restructure the populist movement, giving it organizational comprehensivensss and autonomy as well as a viable ideological or programmatic vision. Thus, populism should be distinguished from successful socialist movements. On only one occasion in the period covered in this study did such an attempt seem in the offing – the ministry of Almino Afonso – and even then, Almino used the state institutions rather than building independent organizations. Given more time, however, he might have taken the next step. The study of Almino's ministry also illuminates the relationship between patronage and system maintenance. Patronage, we find, is a two-edged sword. Both supporters and opponents of the status quo made effective use of it.

The corporative structures had begun to weaken by the early 1960's, so one might look to other sets of political institutions to impose a sense of direction on the nation. The principal ones, however, the party system and associational interest groups, were so organizationally deficient that they could not assert any effective power.[3] Goulart's political style, moreover, exacerbated their weaknesses. He vacillated between reliance on his Brazilian Labor Party (PTB) and on radical nationalist groups such as the CGT, giving neither a full commitment. He thus made himself all the more vulnerable to overthrow.

---

2. A critique of populism and an analysis of the misperceptions of the left during this period is presented in Caio Prado Júnior, *A revolução brasileira* (São Paulo: Brasiliense, 1966), pp. 21-24 and passim. Also see Erickson, "Populism and Political Control" (ch. 4 above, n. 1), pp. 117-144.

3. This weakness has been noted by many authors: e.g., see Octávio Ianni et al., *Política e revolução social no Brasil* (Rio de Janeiro: Civilização Brasileira, 1965), pp. 37-45; Hélio Jaguaribe, *Economic and Political Development* (Cambridge: Harvard University Press, 1968), p. 172. For an analysis of the Latin American party systems, see Douglas A. Chalmers, "Parties and Society in Latin America," *Studies in Comparative International Development,* VII (Summer 1972), 102-128.

This study of labor's political activity illustrates the utility of Charles Anderson's generalizations about the Latin American political process during the populist era.[4] Political actors, he claims, wielded a variety of "power capabilities." For Brazil's labor leaders, these included the strike and street demonstrations, control of state patronage in the social security system, and the leverage derived from their constituting a very valuable part of the president's coalition.

Anderson stresses that in Latin American politics, political power frequently originates from the mere demonstration of a power capability rather than from its actual use. We found in Chapter Seven that labor leaders relied almost exclusively on threat rather than on actual sanctions against the president. In a very real sense, their power had not been put to the test. In April 1964 when the challenge involved the actual exercise of force rather than its threat, their power capability proved far less formidable than they and others had believed.

In 1964 the rules of the game changed completely. The military purged the radical labor leaders and the populist politicians who supported them. Strict authoritarian controls, spelled out in the Institutional Acts, keep a tight rein on the remaining politicians. The sindicato system now serves less as a mechanism for integrating workers into the society and polity than as an instrument for controlling them while official wage and economic policies extract resources from them, to be invested in industrial development.

Change and Stability in a Corporative System

The purpose of Brazilian corporatism is a conservative one. The Estado Novo's architects designed the corporative institutions to protect as much of the social status quo as possible during a period of rapid economic change. These institutions incorporated emergent social forces into the body politic and structured their participation under the direction of the administrative state.

This Brazilian case study has shown that corporative institutions possess a good deal of vitality and may enjoy considerable longevity if they meet certain conditions. First, the political system must maintain sufficient economic growth to prevent deprivation from causing unrest; and second, it must provide an adequate system of communications so state authorities can learn of grievances and attend to them before they give rise to generalized protest.

Corporative institutions by themselves, of course, do not automatically assure longevity to a political system; they merely provide the context for effective policies which may prevent breakdown. While economic development in Brazil has remained high, repressive authoritarianism since 1964 has denied most citizens an effective role in national politics and has plugged the channels of communication. And the rulers have proved increasingly unwilling to distribute the increasing output in a way which would be perceived as just, or at least as not intolerably unjust. This situation could ultimately threaten the regime.

4. Charles W. Anderson, *Politics and Economic Change* (ch. 1 above, n. 21), pp. 87-114.

All polities seek to endow themselves with legitimacy, that is, with generalized acceptance in the eyes of their citizens. For at least two decades after the Second World War, American political scientists, when not ignoring political corporatism, lumped it in with fascism, which they considered so morally reprehensible as to be ipso facto illegitimate. The Brazilian case, however, suggests that corporative structures are not of themselves illegitimate. Indeed, when the constituents restored electoral democracy in 1946, they retained Vargas' corporative institutions. Authoritarianism, therefore, not corporatism, brought Vargas down.

Resolving a legitimacy crisis by combining corporative and democratic institutions, however, creates certain contradictions which may chip away at the control functions of the corporative institutions. Populist politicians seeking workers' votes may provide them with ways to escape the corporative controls. Brazilian legislators, for example, passed the social security reform of 1960. This law gave great power within the corporative institutions to labor leaders, who in turn mounted a frontal challenge to the status quo from their stronghold in these institutions.

Corporatism's control function has played an important role in Brazil's economic growth, because it has guaranteed autonomy for government policymakers. By preventing labor from acting freely to demand a greater share of output, it has allowed economic planners to divert a larger share of resources to capital accumulation in industry. In other words, the corporative system constitutes an instrument for exacting sacrifices from the working class in the name of the common good. Leff's case studies show that sacrifices have been made by the industrialists as well. Using Barrington Moore's terms, however, we would describe their sacrifice as "exchanging the right to rule for the right to make money."[5] That theirs is a "sacrifice" of a very different order from that of the workers should be obvious.

What is the relationship between corporatism and the representative system? In a very perceptive article on this subject, Eric Nordlinger notes that representation through the electoral system is of decreasing significance today, and he compares it with the state of the English monarchy at the beginning of the nineteenth century:

> Both are declining in the performance of their manifest functions in the decision-making process; both serve as a set of rituals, ceremonies, and symbols that tend to integrate the society in the form of a unified political system; both legitimize governmental authority through their continuation, even while the importance of their manifest roles is shrinking.[6]

5. Barrington Moore, Jr., *Social Origins of Dictatorship and Democracy: Lord and Peasant in the Making of the Modern World* (Boston: Beacon, 1966), p. 437.

6. Eric A. Nordlinger, "Representation, Governmental Stability, and Decisional Effectiveness," in J. Roland Pennock and John W. Chapman (eds.), *Representation* (New York: Atherton, 1968), p. 124.

Norway, as described by Stein Rokkan, provides an excellent example of a democratic country where

> ... the crucial decisions on economic policy are rarely taken in the parties or in Parliament: the central area is the bargaining table where the governmental authorties meet directly with the trade union leaders, the representatives of the farmers, the smallholders, and the fishermen, and the delegates of the Employers' Association.[7]

Corporative characteristics can also be seen in many other Western democracies. Samuel H. Beer has described the interaction between interest groups and the government in Britain as "quasi-corporatism."[8] France offers a more successful example of corporative practices. Despite the Fourth Republic's pronounced cabinet instability, economic recovery and expansion advanced remarkably. The French planning system, which involves a form of corporative representation, contributed greatly to this economic growth, particularly by removing the most important economic issues from parliamentary control.[9] West German economic representation is highly corporative.[10] In the Third World, Mexico's official party and its business and industrial associations are decidedly corporative in form and substance and, as in Brazil, technocrats make the major decision affecting Mexico's notable economic development.[11]

More often than is commonly realized, therefore, one finds corporative political institutions which reduce the power of elective legislatures and partisan politics while increasing that of the executive and public administration. Perhaps mental identification of corporatism with nazism and fascism led the postwar generation of American political scientists to ignore or sweep under the rug the corporative features of nations with which they sympathized. These institutions, by assuring the state administration a degree of autonomy, have enhanced governmental effectiveness, at least in the realm of economic development. The Brazilian corporative system has performed such a function through most of its

7. Stein Rokkan, "Norway: Numerical Democracy and Corporate Pluralism," in Robert A. Dahl (ed.), *Political Oppositions in Western Democracies* (New Haven: Yale, 1966), p. 107.

8. Samuel H. Beer, "Group Representation in Britain and the United States," in Roy C. Macridis and Bernard E. Brown (eds.), *Comparative Politics: Notes and Readings* (Homewood, Ill.: Dorsey, 1968), p. 244; see also Beer's *British Politics in the Collectivist Age* (New York: Knopf, 1965), pp. 318-351.

9. John and Anne-Marie Hackett, *Planning in France* (Cambridge: Harvard University Press, 1963), pp. 35-58.

10. Lewis J. Edinger, *Politics in Germany* (Boston: Little, Brown, 1968), pp. 205-235.

11. See Charles W. Anderson, "Bankers as Revolutionaries," in William P. Glade, Jr., and Charles W. Anderson, *The Political Economy of Mexico* (Madison: University of Wisconsin Press, 1963), pp. 105-185; Frank R. Brandenburg, *The Making of Modern Mexico* (Englewood Cliffs, N.J.: Prentice-Hall, 1964), pp. 141-165; Miguel S. Wionczek, "Electric Power: The Uneasy Partnership," in Raymond Vernon (ed.), *Public Policy and Private Enterprise in Mexico* (Cambridge: Harvard University Press, 1964), pp. 19-110; Robert Jones Shafer, *Mexican Business Organizations* (Syracuse, N.Y.: Syracuse University Press, 1973), pp. 30-63, 125-155.

existence. Brazilian corporatism, it should be emphasized, has generally provided control from the top down. It is not equivalent to a system of decision making by tripartite boards. The only major exception to this pattern occurred during Almino Afonso's ministry, when radical populists attempted to shift workers' political activity from distributive to redistributive issues. Through the years covered by this study, the sindicatos have not served the purpose of mass political mobilization. Rather, as in most authoritarian states, these institutions have functioned to prevent that mobilization.

The Future of the Brazilian Political System

We shall close by considering the future of the Brazilian political system. Contemporary writings on Brazil suggest three possible evolutionary paths: the system may remain an authoritarian corporative one, though of course it would continue to modify its structures to meet challenges as they appear; it might be democratized; or it might evolve into a totalitarian, fascist system. As a point of departure, let us take Barrington Moore's model of the pre-fascist stage on the fascist road to development. The origins of fascism lie in a modernizing revolution from above, in which elites attempt to modernize their nation's economy and improve its international power position while retaining as much as possible of its traditional social structure.[12]

In the pre-fascist stage of development, industrialization does not result from a bourgeois revolution in which industrial and commercial interests impose a new value structure upon the nation at the expense of the once-dominant traditional rural aristocracy. Rather, industrialization proceeds through "a rough working coalition between influential sectors of the landed upper classes and the emerging commercial and manufacturing interests."[13]

In Brazil, industrialization since the Depression has been characterized by a symbiotic relationship between landed and manufacturing interests. When the world coffee market collapsed after the crash, the government intensified the practice of buying up excess stocks. The planters received cruzeiros rather than foreign exchange, which forced them to support national industry by purchasing domestically produced consumer goods. As Celso Furtado put it, "Since the process of industrialization has not involved a conflict with the old vested interests in the sector of agricultural exports, the country did not give rise to an industrial ideology favoring effective political expression."[14]

Industrialists, in other words, did not threaten the position of the landed elite in the traditional social structure. Instead, they merely joined the landlords at the top of the pyramid. While industrialists and the politicians allied with them sought, through populist politics, to gain working-class support for their efforts

12. Moore, *Social Origins*, pp. 436-442.
13. *Ibid.*, p. 436.
14. Celso Furtado, "Political Obstacles to Economic Growth" (ch. 1 above, n. 21), pp. 146-153; quote, pp. 152-153.

to protect and expand the industrial sector, they did not mobilize the workers to break the old landed upper class and the seignorial society. Indeed, the dominant coalition, respecting its tacit alliance with the landlords, did not tamper with the rural social structure. The voluminous labor legislation developed after 1930, for example, specifically excluded rural areas from its regulations. Peasants and agricultural laborers could not form sindicatos until late in the radical populist period of the sixties.

This pattern of modernization has left its imprint upon the nation's value structure. Richard N. Adams has made especially clear the predominance of the traditional value structure throughout Latin American society, even among the middle sectors which were until recently thought to hold values favoring the expansion of real participation in the political system. Adams observes that ". . . the apparently new middle group is only an extension of the traditional upper class, both in terms of economic position and of basic values." This traditionalism on the part of the "middle sectors" is one of the major obstacles to fundamental reform in Latin American politics.[15] In the Brazilian context, Charles Wagley has shown that traditional values have persisted despite the growth of a group which can be designated as middle-class in terms of occupation and income.[16]

Why have these traditional values persisted so tenaciously? The Moore framework offers an explanation: these values have endured because the bourgeoisie exchanged the right to rule for the right to make money. The symbiosis between the rural elites and the industrial bourgeoisie perpetuated the socioeconomic system which generated these values in the first place. Its key component is what Moore calls "labor-repressive agriculture" — that is, a productive system which places greater reliance upon political mechanisms than upon the labor market to ensure an adequate labor supply and to create an agricultural surplus for consumption by other classes.[17] Such a system is documented in innumerable accounts of rural Brazil.[18] To a lesser degree, this pattern also underlies the urban labor market, where the corporative system has served to control organized labor. And at moments when this system seemed incapable of channeling workers' energies into acceptable activities, Brazilian conservative forces employed other, more repressive mechanisms to restore control over labor. Since

15. Richard N. Adams, "Political Power and Social Structures," in Veliz (ed.), *The Politics of Conformity* (ch. 6 above, n. 72), p. 16; see also the other excellent essays in that collection. The view that the middle sectors represent a progressive force in Latin America is presented in John J. Johnson, *Political Change in Latin America: The Emergence of the Middle Sectors* (Stanford, Calif.: Stanford University Press, 1958), p. 1.

16. Charles Wagley, "The Brazilian Revolution: Social Change Since 1930," in *Social Change in Latin America Today* (New York: Vintage, 1960), pp. 220-221.

17. Moore, *Social Origins*, p. 434.

18. For example, Celso Furtado, *Dialética* (ch. 4 above, n. 5), pp. 143-146; Daniel R. Gross, "Sisal Agriculture and Social Stagnation in Northeastern Brazil" (paper read at November 1969 meeting of the American Anthropological Association).

1964, in consequence, the working class has been paying an increasingly high price to sustain the industrialization process as well as the traditional value structures.

Moore notes that once the tacit coalition between the landed and manufacturing elites has been established and competent state bureaucrats maintain it, there may follow "a prolonged period of conservative and even authoritarian government, which, however, falls far short of fascism."[19] Speaking of Germany, Japan, and Italy in the decades prior to the 1930's, he observes: "These authoritarian governments acquired some democratic features: notably a parliament with limited powers. Their history may be punctuated with attempts to extend democracy which, toward the end, succeeded in establishing unstable democracies. . . ."[20] This description fits Brazil since 1930 as well.

These pre-fascist regimes achieved significant economic development due to the applied expertise of government planners. Leff's work attests to the presence of such developmental technocrats in Brazil.[21] Moore's pre-fascist examples succeeded in transforming a series of limited labor and capital markets into nationwide systems by centralizing the polities and breaking down barriers between regional units. The ceremony at which Vargas burned the state flags in 1937 graphically symbolizes the same process in Brazil. These pre-fascist polities also succeeded in taming the labor force. As this was the central issue of our study, no more need be said here.

This type of system must hold together the agro-industrial coalition, for some of the more reactionary elements will surely wish to turn the clock back and preserve the old system absolutely unchanged. Outstanding political leadership is therefore necessary. Vargas and Kubitschek possessed this talent. Furthermore, fear of communism lent cohesion to the elite coalition, as has recent leftist guerrilla activity.

Thus far, Moore's model deals with an evolutionary pattern that is pre-fascist, and this term implies that it must ultimately mature into fascism. In view of Brazil's historical pattern of development, however, that eventuality seems to be only one, and not the most likely one, of several possible outcomes. First, authoritarian corporatism may be relatively stable and does not necessarily need to transform itself into totalitarian fascism. One student of Latin American politics stresses that authoritarian, patrimonialist corporatism is the form of political organization most consonant with the legal, cultural, institutional, and political evolution of Iberian societies and their offspring:

> Corporatism, thus, is not a mere throwback to an earlier and conservative model of society and polity, nor can it be lumped together with the fascist

19. Moore, *Social Origins,* p. 437.
20. *Ibid.,* pp. 437-438.
21. Nathaniel H. Leff, *Economic Policy-Making* (ch. 1 above, n. 11), pp. 143-153 and passim.

and nazi regimes in a blanket condemnation. Rather, what we are looking at in the corporatist model is a complex and varied form, distinct from both liberalism and totalitarianism. . . .[22]

Modernizing corporatism in the Brazilian context has manifested considerable vitality and adaptability since its establishment in the 1930's. Given the imperatives of social and political coordination in Brazil's rapidly growing economy, there is every reason to believe the spirit and general outline of these institutions will continue to set the parameters of political action for economic groups. This held true for the liberal democratic phase from 1946 through 1964, and it probably will hold true for any future relaxation in the present authoritarian military rule.

A second evolutionary path, preferred by many observers, is democratization of the authoritarian corporative system. Fernando Henrique Cardoso, one of Brazil's most prominent political sociologists, argues that over the long run, generalized repression and continual tightening of authoritarian controls will cost his nation dearly, both economically and politically. As a possible way out of this impasse, he proposes "substantive democratization" — that is, a series of measures to work changes on the political culture and the behavior of individuals so as to increase their right to participation, criticism, and control at all levels of society. In the present age of bigness and bureaucratization in government, in enterprises, and in all walks of life, substantive democratization would begin by forcing these governmental, administrative, and economic units to disclose their books and the data and criteria on which they base their decisions. While no easy task, this, if achieved, would put employees, customers, or clients in greater contact with the decisions which affect their daily lives. It would be a first important step toward creating a genuinely participatory political culture.[23]

Cardoso thus seeks, within the constraints of an authoritarian regime, to direct attention away from the commanding heights of the state and back to civil society. To avoid the continuance of the status quo or, at best, some new bureaucratic state in place of the present one, Cardoso notes that a new movement must develop an anti-bureaucratic ideology based on the responsibility of the individual. This, over time, will allow labor, cultural, religious, political, and civic organizations to foster a participatory political culture. He notes that to achieve this, it will be necessary to reorganize the parties and to create associations which can express the authentic interests of most Brazilians.

This plan for democratization has a major snag: it depends upon members of the present ruling groups to create the conditions or rules for mass participation. Cardoso argues that, by tightening the system, Brazil's military politicians have

22. Howard J. Wiarda, "Corporatism and Development in the Iberic-Latin World: Persistent Strains and New Variations," *Review of Politics*, XXVI (January 1974), p. 11.
23. This discussion of Cardoso's views is based on his *O modelo político brasileiro e outros ensaios* (São Paulo: Difusão Européia do Livro, 1973), pp. 3, 29, 82, and passim; and on his *Autoritarismo e democratização* (Rio de Janeiro: Paz e Terra, 1975), pp. 20-22, 160-163, 177, 184-186, 231-240, and passim.

restricted political and administrative communication to official channels which are every day more backed up and blocked. The inefficiency of such a situation will not only create potentially disruptive political tensions. It will also ultimately hold back economic development. Cardoso therefore hopes that enlightened members of the ruling groups will realize that it would serve their own self-interest to create participatory avenues.[24] Indeed, during the several years after 1974, the government has relaxed some of its most arbitrary controls over the press and political communication and expression. This relaxation of tensions has perceptibly increased the "political space" within which many Brazilian academics and journalists act. Over the long run, such measures may facilitate the "substantive democratization" desired by Cardoso.

At least over the short and medium term, however, three major processes are likely to inhibit Brazil's rulers from meaningfully democratizing their nation. The first is political. Expanding mass participation at any level, in this highly centralized and strictly supervised nation, carries threatening implications for the national political elite. Neither the civilian nor the military elite — the latter bent on achieving great power status for their nation and counting on rapid economic growth as the means to this end — shows any willingness to risk the policy goals they seek. Whenever a serious threat presents itself, the president protects the elites and the very system itself by exercising the arbitrary powers of the Fifth Institutional Act.

The current presidency of General Ernesto Geisel illustrates this point. Although he relaxed some aspects of press censorship and allowed invigorated party competition in his first few years in office, he has kept close tabs on the nation's political life and has annulled the mandates of a number of politicians who appeared to threaten the system. In 1974, he supervised personally, in consultation with state party officials, the selection of the indirectly-elected governors, including the one in the state with an MDB majority. In this way, the post-1964 presidents have controlled recruitment into the upper echelons of both parties. Indeed, the socioeconomic status and political pronouncements of the MDB leaders have indicated that, even if their party became the majority party, they would not oppose the main policy lines of the post-1964 system,

24. Cardoso, *Autoritarismo,* pp. 231-240. In its appeal to the self-interests of Brazil's ruling groups, Cardoso's work reminds one of a similar appeal a decade earlier by Pablo González Casanova, a Mexican political sociologist, to the ruling politicians of his country. Mexico, despite the window-dressing of regular elections, was another corporatively organized authoritarian state, and it had a regressive income distribution pattern similar to Brazil's. After González Casanova's *Democracy in Mexico* (New York: Oxford, 1970; first published in Mexico, 1965) opened public discussion on these topics, some politicians made efforts to increase political participation and to improve income distribution. Their efforts were not welcomed by most members of Mexico's dominant political and economic elite — and, a decade later, political participation there remains as elite-dominated as ever and income distribution has continued to move against the bottom 70 percent of the employed population. See L. Vincent Padgett, *The Mexican Political System,* 2nd ed. (Boston: Houghton-Mifflin, 1976), pp. 82-90; Stephen R. Niblo, "Progress and the Standard of Living in Contemporary Mexico," *Latin American Perspectives,* II (Summer 1975), pp. 109-124.

even though they might pursue those policies with more compassion than ARENA politicians.[25]

In legislative elections in late 1974, the MDB took many seats in the Chamber and Senate from ARENA and carried a majority in four additional state assemblies. The opposition party thus appeared assured of four more governorships in the 1978 indirect elections, while it also expected to further expand its position in Congress. Nonetheless, it appeared at that time that gradual opposition gains would not prevent the president from maintaining control over the polity.

By early 1977, however, the situation had changed. The austerities and economic dislocations caused by the oil-price rise and world recession were now felt by all strata, leading to widespread discontent and boosting the fortunes of the MDB. With increasing calls from many quarters for an end to the dictatorship, the MDB began to appear as a potential threat to the system. In April 1977, therefore, President Geisel briefly closed Congress and, using the decree powers of the Fifth Institutional Act, changed a number of rules of the political game.

The new rules perpetuate the minority status of the MDB. Now, indirect elections will select one-third of the senators as well as the state governors. These officials will be chosen in each state by a newly constituted electoral college, to be composed of the state deputies *and* councillors from all the state's municípios. The ARENA, safely in control of a majority of the local councils, will dominate the electoral colleges. In this manner, Geisel not only limited potential opposition gains in the Senate, but he snatched away the governorships as well.

One American analyst notes, like Cardoso, that authoritarian state corporatism is becoming increasingly costly to maintain, and he states that the obvious answer is an institutional shift from the state-imposed to the consensual, voluntary type of corporatism. (The Norwegian case cited above would be an example of the latter.) The sticking point here lies in the transition, for the writer suggests that in the process, ". . . the state-corporatist system must first degenerate into openly conflictful, multifaceted, uncontrolled interest politics — pluralism in other words — as appears to be happening in contemporary Spain." [26] Normatively, such a transition may be appealing — but, empirically, no precedent exists in modernizing nations like Brazil. Such an institutional breakdown in Brazil in the early 1960's, for example, provoked the strengthening of corporative, authoritarian controls. It did not permit the development of a consensual form of corporatism. It is likely, therefore, that if the present relaxa-

25. *OESP,* Sept. 5, 1976, p. 5; on the 1974 elections, see Fernando Henrique Cardoso and Bolívar Lamounier (eds.), *Os partidos e as eleições no Brasil* (Rio de Janeiro: Paz e Terra, 1975). The entire issue of *Revista Brasileira de Estudos Políticos,* no. 43 (July 1976), is devoted to analyses of the 1974 elections.

26. Philippe C. Schmitter, "Still the Century of Corporatism? " in *Review of Politics,* XXVI (January 1974), p. 127.

tion of controls over the press, political expression, and party competition permits another apparent institutional breakdown, some faction of the military will forcefully reimpose the controls.

A second major impediment to democratization lies in Brazil's pattern of economic development. Brazil has chosen the import-substitution approach to industrialization, an approach which is extremely susceptible to boom-and-bust cyclical fluctuations. The booms come while new industries produce to satisfy demand for previously imported products along with formerly repressed demand. Once this demand has been met, expansion slumps until investment moves into another field of former imports. The downturn of the early 1960's was one such slump. The decline in the economic growth rate to 4 percent in 1974, after seven years averaging above 10 percent, is another.[27] Generalized dissatisfaction during the downturns creates stresses which a tentative democratization would be unlikely to survive.

Finally, demographic pressure poses another impediment to democratization. Brazil's rulers have encouraged rapid population growth in order to hasten their nation's arrival at great-power status. Brazil, which counted 50 million inhabitants in 1949, reached 100 million in 1972, giving its population a doubling time of 23 years. While population growth has slowed slightly in recent years, let us project Brazil's population into the future with a doubling time of 23 years. In 1995, there would be 200 million Brazilians; in 2018, 400 million; in 2041, 800 million; and in 2064, 1.6 billion. The implications are staggering, particularly in a nation where runaway urbanization has already strained public services to the breaking point. By 1976, some top Brazilian officials had begun advocating population control, but it has not yet become policy, and, even when it does, dramatic reduction in population growth will not be achieved overnight.[28]

The tensions inherent in these political, economic, and demographic processes are likely to inhibit any tendency of the nation's rulers to experiment with participatory political forms. And the less they feel free to experiment, the more they will rely on the nonparticipatory, authoritarian corporative controls of Brazil's Iberian heritage and of their own personal experience. Brazil's authoritarian sustem does not appear likely to admit real democratization in the near future.

Is it possible, on the other hand, that the authoritarian corporative model may evolve into a fascist system, following the path which Moore describes? While such a transition is unlikely, a number of preconditions for fascism exist. First, anti-liberalism has roots deep in Brazil's past, and President Emílio Garrastazu Médici demonstrated its continued vitality in 1970. He claimed that

27. On the slump of the early 1960's, see Albert Fishlow, "Some Reflections on Post-1964 Brazilian Economic Policy," in Alfred Stepan (ed.), *Authoritarian Brazil* (ch. 2 above, n. 20), pp. 104-107. On the slump beginning in 1974, see Fernando Henrique Cardoso, "Estatização e autoritarismo esclarecido: tendências e limites," *Estudos Cebrap*, 15 (January 1976), 21.

28. *Latin America*, X (June 18, 1976), 190-191.

under military tutelage, Brazil had "buried a political liberalism incompatible with violent changes in socioeconomic structures."[29]

Second, industrialization has not destroyed the anti-egalitarian pre-industrial social and value structures. Further economic development therefore merely reinforces the existing system. Attempts to improve agricultural production in the traditional northeastern sugar zone, for example, have relied on converting traditional landlords into efficient capitalists rather than making landless peasants into smallholders through a distributive agrarian reform. Success here will merely strengthen institutions which bolster the anti-egalitarian value structure.

Third, corporative institutions make for strong central control, and Médici's call for "integrally active" sindicatos, on Labor Day in 1970, illustrated the government's commitment to corporatism:

> It is our objective to encourage and revitalize sindicato life.... We not only envision the sindicato as doctor's office, medical laboratory, and clinic, but we also seek the sindicato-school, the sindicato-civic center for recreation, sports, and culture, as well as the sindicato-consumers' cooperative, to which we will provide the means to stock food, clothing, medicine, and tools.[30]

Fourth, the difficulties inherent in industrialization will not be resolved overnight, so national frustration may result in a search for a panacea.

Fifth, foreign, and particularly American, capital occupies a very visible place in the national economy, and the burden of the foreign debt is evident to many. Thus, the panacea may assume extreme nationalist lines.

Sixth, nationalism has been on the rise in Brazil since the economic boom of the late 1960's. While its popular expression includes bumper stickers with the flag and legend, "Brazil: Love It or Leave It," on the policy level it has been pragmatic and oriented particularly toward further economic growth, with an eye on achieving great-power status by the end of this century.[31] It is not yet, however, jingoistic.

The missing ingredients are an appeal to the peasants, the rhetoric of anti-capitalism, and mass mobilization. It is possible that a focus on the peasants will emerge when the younger officers reach dominant positions in the government. Unlike the now-dominant artillery officers, these younger officers are mostly Army engineers who have spent much of their careers in the interior. This career pattern has exposed them to the misery of the Brazilian countryside, and they have expressed a desire to attack that misery and its causes. Promotion at the upper ranks of the Brazilian armed services takes place very slowly, however, so by the time younger officers reach top positions, they have undergone a long

29. Text of speech to Superior War College in *JB,* March 11, 1970, p. 5.
30. Text in *JB,* May 1, 1970, p. 4.
31. Ronald M. Schneider, in *Brazil: Foreign Policy* (ch. 8 above, n. 5), clearly shows how economic performance is crucial to the great-power vision of Brazil's military rulers.

period of socialization in staff agencies.[32] Only under the most unusual of circumstances, perhaps involving frustration of the dream for great-power status, could one expect them to choose extreme measures to deal with social injustice and economic backwardness in the rural areas.

Increasing opposition to foreign capital could also be extended to capitalism in general, at least on the level of rhetoric. If rising petroleum prices, foreign barriers to Brazilian exports, a world economic crash, or some combination of similar external factors seriously disrupts Brazil's spectacular economic growth, foreign capital could easily become the target of mobilized mass wrath. One must, however, keep this caveat in mind: the anti-capitalist rhetoric of the European fascists did not by any means spell the demise of capitalism in their countries.

Although this alternative appears much less likely than the one first sketched — that of continued authoritarian corporatism — it is impossible to ignore the possibility that the above elements could be woven into the rhetoric of a Brazilian version of fascism. Excellently outfitted with corporative mechanisms for social control, the government could shift from the present authoritarian regime to a totalitarian one which would mobilize the populace on a war footing to do battle with underdevelopment.

32. On the political importance of military promotion processes and structures, see Schneider, *Brazil: Foreign Policy,* chs. 3 and 8.

BIBLIOGRAPHY

I. Books, Articles, Dissertations, and Manuscripts

A. General

Adams, Richard N. "Political Power and Social Structures," in *The Politics of Conformity in Latin America,* ed. Claudio Veliz. New York: Oxford University Press, 1967, pp. 15-42.

Alba, Victor. *Historia del movimiento obrero en América Latina.* Mexico: Libreros Mexicanos Unidos, 1964.

Alexander, Robert J. *Communism in Latin America.* New Brunswick, N. J.: Rutgers University Press, 1960.

———. *Organized Labor in Latin America.* New York: Free Press, 1965.

Almond, Gabriel A., and G. Bingham Powell. *Comparative Politics: A Developmental Approach.* Boston: Little, Brown, 1966.

Anderson, Charles W. "Bankers as Revolutionaries," in *The Political Economy of Mexico*, by William P. Glade, Jr., and Charles W. Anderson. Madison: University of Wisconsin Press, 1963, pp. 103-185.

———. *Politics and Economic Change in Latin America.* Princeton, N.J.: Van Nostrand, 1967.

Apter, David. *The Politics of Modernization.* Chicago: University of Chicago Press, 1965.

Beer, Samuel H. *British Politics in the Collectivist Age.* New York: Knopf, 1965.

———. "Group Representation in Britain and the United States," in *Comparative Politics: Notes and Readings*, ed. Roy C. Macridis and Bernard E. Brown. Homewood, Ill.: Dorsey, 1968, pp. 240-248.

Bendix, Reinhard. *Max Weber: An Intellectual Portrait.* Garden City, N.Y.: Doubleday, 1962.

Bonilla, Frank. "The Urban Worker," in *Continuity and Change in Latin America*, ed. John J. Johnson. Stanford, Calif.: Stanford University Press, 1964, pp. 186-205.

Brandenburg, Frank R. *The Making of Modern Mexico.* Englewood Cliffs, N.J.: Prentice-Hall, 1964.

Camp, Richard L. *The Papal Ideology of Social Reform: A Study in Historical Development, 1878-1967.* Leyden, Holland: E. J. Brill, 1969.

Chalmers, Douglas A. "Parties and Society in Latin America," *Studies in Comparative International Development,* VII (Summer 1972), 102-128.

Chaplin, David (ed.). *Peruvian Nationalism: A Corporatist Revolution.* New Brunswick, N.J.: Transaction Books, 1976.

Crozier, Michel. *The Bureaucratic Phenomenon.* Chicago: University of Chicago Press, 1964.

Dahl, Robert A. *Modern Political Analysis.* Englewood Cliffs, N.J.: Prentice-Hall, 1963.

"Dependency Theory: A Reassessment," special issue of *Latin American Perspectives,* I (Spring 1974).

Di Tella, Torcuato. "Populism and Reform in Latin America," in *Obstacles to Change in Latin America,* ed. Claudio Veliz. London: Oxford University Press, 1965, pp. 47-74.

Edinger, Lewis J. *Politics in Germany.* Boston: Little, Brown, 1968.

Field, G. Lowell. "Comparative Aspects of Fascism," *Southwestern Social Science Quarterly,* XX (March 1940), 349-360.

Frank, Andre Gunder. *Capitalism and Underdevelopment in Latin America: Historical Studies of Chile and Brazil,* rev. ed. New York: Monthly Review Press, 1969.

Glade, William P., and Charles W. Anderson. *The Political Economy of Mexico.* Madison: University of Wisconsin Press, 1963.

González Casanova, Pablo. *Democracy in Mexico.* New York: Oxford University Press, 1970.

Hackett, John, and Anne-Marie Hackett. *Planning in France.* Cambridge: Harvard University Press, 1963.

Hamon, Léo. *Les Nouveaux comportements politiques de la classe ouvrière.* Paris: Presses Universitaires de France, 1962.

Heidenheimer, Arnold J. "Trade Unions, Benefit Systems, and Party Mobilization Styles: 'Horizontal' Influences on the British Labour and German Social Democratic Parties," *Comparative Politics,* I (April 1969), 313-342.

Hobsbawm, E. J. *Labouring Men.* Garden City, N.Y.: Doubleday Anchor, 1967.

Huntington, Samuel P. "Political Development and Political Decay," in *Political Modernization: A Reader in Comparative Political Change,* ed. Claude E. Welch, Jr. Belmont, Calif.: Wadsworth, 1967, pp. 207-246.

_____ . *Political Order in Changing Societies.* New Haven: Yale University Press, 1968.

Johnson, John J. *Political Change in Latin America: The Emergence of the Middle Sectors.* Stanford, Calif.: Stanford University Press, 1958.

Kenny, Michael. "Patterns of Patronage in Spain," *Anthropological Quarterly,* XXXIII (January 1960), 14-23.

Kornhauser, William. *The Politics of Mass Society.* Glencoe, Ill.: Free Press, 1959.

Landsberger, Henry A. "The Labor Elite: Is It Revolutionary?" in *Elites in Latin America,* ed. Seymour Martin Lipset and Aldo Solari. New York: Oxford University Press, 1967, pp. 256-300.

LaPalombara, Joseph. "The Utility and Limitations of Interest Group Theory to Non-American Field Situations," *Journal of Politics,* XXII (February 1960), 29-49.

Linz, Juan J. "An Authoritarian Regime: Spain," in *Cleavages, Ideologies, and Party Systems: Contributions to Comparative Political Sociology,* ed. E. Allardt and Y. Littunen. Helsinki, Finland: Transactions of the Westermarck Society, 1964, pp. 291-341.

Lipset, Seymour Martin, Martin Trow, and James Coleman. *Union Democracy: The Internal Politics of the International Typographical Union.* Garden City, N.Y.: Doubleday Anchor, 1962.

Lorwin, Val. *The French Labor Movement.* Cambridge: Harvard University Press, 1954.

Lowi, Theodore J. "American Business, Public Policy, Case Studies, and Political Theory," *World Politics,* XVI (July 1964), 677-715.

Mallet, Serge. *La Nouvelle classe ouvrière.* Paris: Editions du Seuil, 1963.

Malloy, James M. (ed.). *Authoritarianism and Corporatism in Latin America.* Pittsburgh, Pa.: University of Pittsburgh Press, 1977.

Menges, Constantine C. "Public Policy and Organized Business in Chile: A Preliminary Analysis," *Journal of International Affairs,* XX (1966), 343-365.

Mills, C. Wright. *The Power Elite.* New York: Oxford University Press, 1956.

Moore, Barrington, Jr. *Social Origins of Dictatorship and Democracy: Lord and Peasant in the Making of the Modern World.* Boston: Beacon, 1966.

————. *Soviet Politics – The Dilemma of Power.* New York: Harper and Row, 1965.

Morris, James O. *Elites, Intellectuals, and Consensus: A Study of the Social Question and the Industrial Relations System in Chile.* Ithaca: Cornell University Press, 1966.

Newton, Ronald C. "On 'Functional Groups,' 'Fragmentation,' and 'Pluralism' in Spanish American Political Society," in *Politics and Social Change in Latin America: The Distinct Tradition,* ed. Howard J. Wiarda. Amherst: University of Massachusetts Press, 1974, pp. 129-156.

Niblo, Stephen R. "Progress and the Standard of Living in Contemporary Mexico," *Latin American Perspectives,* II (Summer 1975), 109-124.

Nisbet, Robert A. *Community and Power.* New York: Oxford University Press, 1962.

Nordlinger, Eric A. "Representation, Governmental Stability, and Decisional Effectiveness," in *Representation,* ed. J. Roland Pennock and John W. Chapman. New York: Atherton, 1968, pp. 108-127.

Nun, José. "The Middle-Class Military Coup," in *The Politics of Conformity in Latin America,* ed. Claudio Veliz. New York: Oxford University Press, 1967, pp. 66-118.

O'Donnell, Guillermo A. *Modernization and Bureaucratic Authoritarianism: Studies in South American Politics.* Berkeley: Institute of International Studies, University of California, 1973.

Padgett, L. Vincent. *The Mexican Political System,* 2nd ed. Boston: Houghton-Mifflin, 1976.

Payne, James L. *Labor and Politics in Peru: The System of Political Bargaining.* New Haven: Yale University Press, 1965.

Peppe, Patrick V. "Corporatism and Dependent Capitalist Modernization: The Frei Government Experience," *Proceedings of the Pacific Coast Council on Latin American Studies,* IV (1975), 145-170.

Pike, Frederick B., and Thomas Stritch (eds.). *The New Corporatism: Social-Political Structures in the Iberian World.* Notre Dame, Ind.: University of Notre Dame Press, 1974.

Piven, Frances Fox, and Richard A. Cloward. "Dissensus Politics," *New Republic,* 158, no. 16 (April 20, 1968), 20-24.

Poppino, Rollie E. *International Communism in Latin America.* New York: Free Press, 1964.

Purcell, Susan Kaufman. *The Mexican Profit-Sharing Decision: Politics in an Authoritarian Regime.* Berkeley and Los Angeles: University of California Press, 1976.

Rokkan, Stein. "Norway: Numerical Democracy and Corporate Pluralism," in *Political Oppositions in Western Democracies,* ed. Robert A. Dahl. New Haven: Yale University Press, 1966, pp. 70-115.

Romualdi, Serafino. *Presidents and Peons: Recollections of a Labor Ambassador in Latin America.* New York: Funk and Wagnalls, 1967.

Schattschneider, E. E. *Politics, Pressures, and the Tariff.* New York: Prentice-Hall 1935.

_____. *The Semi-Sovereign People.* New York: Holt, Rinehart and Winston, 1960.

Schmitter, Philippe C. "Still the Century of Corporatism?" In *Review of Politics,* XXVI (January 1974), 85-131.

Shafer, Robert Jones. *Mexican Business Organizations.* Syracuse, N.Y.: Syracuse University Press, 1973.

Spalding, Hobart A., Jr. "U.S. and Latin American Labor: The Dynamics of Imperialist Control," *Latin American Perspectives,* III (Winter 1976), 45-69.

Stepan, Alfred. *The State and Society: Peru in Comparative Perspective.* Princeton, N.J.: Princeton University Press, forthcoming.

Veliz, Claudio (ed.). *Obstacles to Change in Latin America.* London: Oxford University Press, 1965.

————. (ed.). *The Politics of Conformity in Latin America.* New York: Oxford University Press, 1967.

Ward, Robert E. "Political Modernization and Political Culture in Japan," in *Political Modernization: A Reader in Comparative Political Change,* ed. Claude E. Welch, Jr. Belmont, Calif.: Wadsworth, 1967, pp. 88-104.

Weinstein, Martin. *Uruguay: The Politics of Failure.* Westport, Conn.: Greenwood Press, 1975.

Welch, Claude E., Jr. (ed.). *Political Modernization: A Reader in Comparative Political Change.* Belmont, Calif.: Wadsworth, 1967.

Wiarda, Howard J. "Corporatism and Development in the Iberic-Latin World: Persistent Strains and New Variations," *Review of Politics,* XXVI (January 1974), 3-33.

————. *Corporatism and Development: The Portuguese Experience.* Amherst: University of Massachusetts Press, 1977.

————. *The Corporative Origins of the Iberian and Latin American Labor Relations Systems.* Amherst: Labor Relations and Research Center, University of Massachusetts, 1976.

————(ed.). *Politics and Social Change in Latin America: The Distinct Tradition.* Amherst: University of Massachusetts Press, 1974.

Wionczek, Miguel S. "Electric Power: The Uneasy Partnership," in *Public Policy and Private Enterprise in Mexico,* ed. Raymond Vernon. Cambridge: Harvard University Press, 1964, pp. 19-110.

World Bank. *Health Sector Policy Paper.* Washington, D.C., October 1975.

B. Brazil: Politics and History

Alves, Márcio Moreira. *A Grain of Mustard Seed.* Garden City, N.Y.: Doubleday Anchor, 1973.

Alves, Mário, and Paul Singer. *Análise do Plano Trienal.* Rio de Janeiro: Editôra Universitária, 1963.

Amaral, Antônio José Azevedo. *O estado autoritário e a realidade nacional.* Rio de Janeiro: José Olympio, 1938.

Amaral, Carlos Veríssimo do. "As controvertidas nomeações para a Previdência Social em 1963: estudo de um caso," in *Política e administração de pessoal: estudo de dois casos,* by Carlos Veríssimo do Amaral and Kleber Tatinge do Nascimento. Rio de Janeiro: Fundação Getúlio Vargas, 1966, pp. 3-36.

Ames, Barry. "Rhetoric and Reality in a Militarized Regime: Brazil Since 1964," in *Sage Professional Papers in Comparative Politics,* IV (1973), 1-55.

Amnesty International. *Report on Allegations of Torture in Brazil.* London, 1972.

Baer, Werner. *Industrialization and Economic Development in Brazil.* Homewood, Ill.: Irwin, 1965.

Bastos, J. Justino Alves. *Encontro com o tempo.* Porto Alegre: Globo, 1965.

Bell, Peter D. "Brazilian-American Relations," in *Brazil in the Sixties,* ed. Riordan Roett. Nashville, Tenn.: Vanderbilt University Press, 1972, pp. 77-102.

Brazil. *Coleção das leis do Brasil.* Rio de Janeiro: Departamento de Imprensa Nacional, 1900-1976.

Brazil. *Diário Oficial da União.*

Brazil, Departamento Administrativo do Serviço Público and Instituto Brasileiro de Geografia e Estatística, Serviço Nacional de Recenseamento. *Censo dos servidores públicos civis federais, 31 de maio de 1966, resultados preliminares.* Rio de Janeiro: IBGE, n.d. (mimeo.).

Brazil, Instituto Brasileiro de Geográfia e Estatística. *Anuário Estatístico do Brasil,* 1939-40 through 1975, vols. 5-36. Rio de Janeiro, 1940-1975.

Brazil, Ministério da Fazenda, Contadoria Geral da República. *Balanços Gerais da República,* Exercício de 1930 through Exercício de 1965. Rio de Janeiro: Imprensa Nacional, 1931-1967.

Brazil, Tribunal Superior Eleitoral. *Dados estatísticos: eleições federais, estaduais, realizadas no Brasil em 1960.* Rio de Janeiro: Departamento de Imprensa Nacional, 1963.

British Chamber of Commerce of São Paulo and Southern Brazil. *Personalidades no Brasil – Men of Affairs in Brazil.* São Paulo, 1933.

Bruneau, Thomas Charles. *The Political Transformation of the Brazilian Catholic Church.* London: Cambridge University Press, 1974.

Café Filho, João. *Do sindicato ao Catete.* Rio de Janeiro: José Olympio, 1966.

Campos, Francisco. *O estado nacional: sua estructura, seu conteudo ideologico.* Rio de Janeiro: José Olympio, 1940.

Cardoso, Fernando Henrique. *Autoritarismo e democratização.* Rio de Janeiro: Paz e Terra, 1975.

———. "Estatização e autoritarismo esclarecido: tendências e limites," *Estudos Cebrap,* no. 15 (January 1976), 5-24.

———. *Ideologías de la burguesía industrial en sociedades dependientes (Argentina y Brasil).* Mexico: Siglo XXI, 1971.

———. *O modelo político brasileiro e outros ensaios.* São Paulo: Difusão Européia do Livro, 1973.

Cardoso, Fernando Henrique, and Bolívar Lamounier (eds.). *Os partidos e as eleições no Brasil.* Rio de Janeiro: Paz e Terra, 1975.

Carneiro, Levi. *Pela nova Constituição.* Rio de Janeiro: A. Coelho Branco Filho, 1936.

Carvalho, Ary R. "Medidas legais de promoção e contrôle," in *Impacto da ação do Govêrno sôbre as emprêsas brasileiras,* ed. Raimar Richers et al. Rio de Janeiro: Fundação Getúlio Vargas, 1963.

Carvalho, Manuel Cavalcanti de. *Evolução do Estado brasileiro: estrutura política, ordenação jurídica, organização corporativa, e política legislativa de trabalho.* Rio de Janeiro: A. Coelho Branco Filho, 1941.

Castello Branco, Humberto de Alencar. *Discursos,* 1964, 1965, and 1966. Rio de Janeiro: Departamento de Imprensa Nacional.

Cerqueira, Eli Diniz, and Maria Regina Soares de Lima. "O modêlo político de Oliveira Vianna," *Revista Brasileira de Estudos Políticos,* no. 30 (January 1971), 85-109.

César, Afonso. *Política, cifrão e sangue.* Rio de Janeiro: Editorial Andes, 1955.

Cohn, Gabriel. "Perspectivas da Esquerda," in *Política e revolução social no Brasil,* ed. Octávio Ianni et al. Rio de Janeiro: Civilização Brasileira, 1965, pp. 129-157.

Cortes, Antônio Maria Cardozo. *Homens e instituições no Rio.* Rio de Janeiro: IBGE, 1957.

Cortés, Carlos E. "The Role of Rio Grande do Sul in Brazilian Politics, 1930-1967." Doctoral dissertation, University of New Mexico, 1969.

"A Crisis for Democracy — Brazil," *Review of the International Commission of Jurists,* no. 4 (December 1969), 16-17.

Daland, Robert T. *Brazilian Planning: Development Politics and Administration.* Chapel Hill: University of North Carolina Press, 1967.

Dean, Warren. *The Industralization of São Paulo, 1880-1945.* Austin: University of Texas Press, 1969.

Dias, Everardo. *História das lutas sociais no Brasil.* São Paulo: Editora Edaglit, 1962.

Dines, Alberto, et al. *Os idos de março e a queda em abril.* Rio de Janeiro: José Alvaro, 1964.

Duarte, Nestor. *A ordem privada e a organização política nacional.* São Paulo: Editora Nacional, 1939.

Dulles, John W. F. *Unrest in Brazil: Political-Military Crises, 1955-1964.* Austin: University of Texas Press, 1970.

————. *Vargas of Brazil: A Political Biography.* Austin: University of Texas Press, 1967.

Ellis Júnior, Alfredo. *A evolução da economia paulista e suas causas.* São Paulo: Editôra Nacional, 1937.

Faoro, Raymundo. *Os donos do poder: formação do patronato político brasileiro.* Porto Alegre: Globo, 1958.

Faria, Antônio Bento de. *Annotações theórico-practicas ao Código Penal do Brasil,* 4th ed. Rio de Janeiro: Jacintho Ribeiro dos Santos, 1929.

Fernandes, Florestan. *A revolução burguesa no Brasil.* Rio de Janeiro: Zahar, 1975.

Ferreira, Oliveiros S. "Comportamento eleitoral em S. Paulo," *Revista Brasileira de Estudos Políticos,* no. 8 (April 1960), 162-228.

_____. "A crise do 'sistema' e as eleições paulistas de 1963," *Revista Brasileira de Estudos Políticos*, no. 16 (January 1964), 179-226.

_____. *As fôrças armadas e o desafio da revolução.* Rio de Janeiro: GRD, 1964.

Figueiredo, Wilson. "Goulart e a renovação dos dispositivos," *Jornal do Brasil* (September 7, 1963), Caderno Especial, p. 4.

Fishlow, Albert. "Some Reflections on Post-1964 Brazilian Economic Policy," in *Authoritarian Brazil: Origins, Policies, and Future,* ed. Alfred Stepan. New Haven: Yale University Press, 1973, pp. 69-118.

Franco, Afonso Arinos de Melo. *Curso de direito constitucional brasileiro: formação constitucional do Brasil,* vol. II. Rio de Janeiro: Forense, 1960.

Franco, Virgílio A. de Mello. *A campanha da U.D.N. (1944-45).* Rio de Janeiro: Zélio Valverde, 1947.

_____. *Sob o signo de resistência.* Rio de Janeiro: Zélio Valverde, 1947.

Furtado, Celso. *Dialética do desenvolvimento.* Rio de Janeiro: Fundo de Cultura, 1964.

_____. "Political Obstacles to Economic Growth in Brazil," in *Obstacles to Change in Latin America,* ed. Claudio Veliz. London: Oxford University Press, 1965, pp. 145-161.

Gomes, Major-Brigadeiro Eduardo. *Campanha de libertação.* São Paulo: Martins, 1946.

Graham, Lawrence S. *Civil Service Reform in Brazil: Principles Versus Practice.* Austin: University of Texas Press, 1968.

Gross, Daniel R. "Sisal Agriculture and Social Stagnation in Northeastern Brazil." Paper presented at November 1969 meeting of the American Anthropological Association, New Orleans, La.

Harding, Timothy F. "Revolution Tomorrow: The Failure of the Left in Brazil," *Studies on the Left,* IV (Fall 1964), 30-54.

Havighurst, Robert J., and J. Roberto Moreira. *Society and Education in Brazil.* Pittsburgh, Pa.: University of Pittsburgh Press, 1965.

Horowitz, Irving Louis. *Revolution in Brazil.* New York: Dutton, 1964.

Ianni, Octávio, *Estado e capitalismo.* Rio de Janeiro: Civilização Brasileira, 1965.

_____. *Industrialização e desenvolvimento social no Brasil.* Rio de Janeiro: Civilização Brasileira, 1963.

Ianni, Octávio, et al. *Política e revolução social no Brasil.* Rio de Janeiro: Civilização Brasileira, 1965.

Jaguaribe, Hélio. *Desenvolvimento econômico e desenvolvimento político.* Rio de Janeiro: Fundo de Cultura, 1962.

_____. "The Dynamics of Brazilian Nationalism," in *Obstacles to Change in Latin America,* ed. Claudio Veliz. London: Oxford University Press, 1965, pp. 162-187.

————. *Economic and Political Development: A Theoretical Approach and a Brazilian Case Study.* Cambridge: Harvard University Press, 1968.

————. *O nacionalismo na atualidade brasileira.* Rio de Janeiro: Instituto Superior de Estudos Brasileiros, 1958.

————. "Political Strategies of National Development in Brazil," in *Latin American Radicalism,* ed. Irving Louis Horowitz, Josué de Castro, and John Gerassi. New York: Random House, 1969, pp. 390-439.

Jurema, Abelardo. *Sexta-feira, 13.* Rio de Janeiro: O Cruzeiro, 1964.

Kubitschek de Oliveira, Juscelino. *Discursos,* 1956, 1958, and 1959. Rio de Janeiro: Departamento de Imprensa Nacional.

Lambert, Jacques. *Le Brésil.* Paris: Armand Colin, 1953.

Leal, Victor Nunes. *Coronelismo, enxada e voto: o município e o regime representativo no Brasil.* Rio de Janeiro: n.p., 1948.

Leeds, Anthony. "Brazil and the Myth of Francisco Julião," in *Politics of Change in Latin America,* ed. Joseph Maier and Richard W. Weatherhead. New York: Praeger, 1964, pp. 190-204.

————. "Brazilian Careers and Social Structures: A Case History and Model," in *Contemporary Cultures and Societies of Latin America,* ed. Dwight B. Heath and Richard N. Adams. New York: Random House, 1965, pp. 379-404.

Leff, Nathaniel H. *Economic Policy-Making and Development in Brazil, 1947-1964.* New York: Wiley, 1968.

————. "Long-Term Brazilian Economic Development," *Journal of Economic History,* XX (September 1969), 473-493.

Levine, Robert M. "Brazil: The Aftermath of Decompression," *Current History,* LXX (February 1976), 55-57.

Levy, Herbert V. *O Brasil e os novos tempos: considerações sôbre o problema de reestruturação política, econômica e social do Brasil.* São Paulo: Martins, 1946.

Lima, Alceu Amoroso. *Indicações políticas: da revolução à Constituição.* Rio de Janeiro: Civilização Brasileira, 1936.

Lima Sobrinho, Barbosa. *Presença de Alberto Tôrres.* Rio de Janeiro: Civilização Brasileira, 1968.

Linz, Juan. "The Future of an Authoritarian Situation or the Institutionalization of an Authoritarian Regime: The Case of Brazil," in *Authoritarian Brazil: Origins, Policies, and Future,* ed. Alfred Stepan. New Haven: Yale University Press, 1973, pp. 233-254.

Loeb, Gustaaf Frits. *Industrialization and Balanced Growth, with Special Reference to Brazil.* Groningen, Holland: J. B. Wolters, 1957.

Lopes, Juárez Rubens Brandão. "Relations industrielles dans deux communautés brésiliennes," *Sociologie du Travail,* III (December 1961), 330-344.

————. *Sociedade industrial no Brasil.* São Paulo: Difusão Européia do Livro, 1964.

_____. "Some Basic Developments in Brazilian Politics and Society," in *New Perspectives of Brazil,* ed. Eric N. Baklanoff. Nashville, Tenn.: Vanderbilt University press, 1966, pp. 59-77.

Love, Joseph L. *Rio Grande do Sul and Brazilian Regionalism, 1882-1930.* Stanford, Calif.: Stanford University Press, 1971.

Lowenstein, Karl. *Brazil Under Vargas.* New York: Macmillan, 1942.

Martínez Pita, Nilda Águeda, and José Maria de Arruda. "Composição sociológica da Assembléia Legislativa do Estado da Guanabara," *Revista de Direito Público e Ciência Política,* IX (July 1966), 120-144.

Martins, Luciano, *Industrialização, burguesia nacional e desenvolvimento.* Rio de Janeiro: Editora Saga, 1968.

Melo, Luiz Correia de. *Dicionário de autores paulistas.* São Paulo: Irmãos Andrioli, 1954.

Mendes, Cândido. "O govêrno Castelo Branco: paradigma e prognose," *Dados,* no. 2/3 (1967), 63-111.

_____. "Sistema político e modêlos de poder no Brasil," *Dados,* no. 1 (1966), 7-41.

Morel, Edmar. *O golpe começou em Washington.* Rio de Janeiro: Civilização Brasileira, 1965.

Nabuco, Joaquim. *O abolicionismo.* São Paulo: Progresso, 1940.

Nascimento, Kleber Tatinge do. "O aumento de vencimentos do funcionalismo federal em 1963: estudo de um caso," in *Política e administração de pessoal; estudo de dois casos,* by Carlos Veríssimo do Amaral and Kleber Tatinge do Nascimento. Rio de Janeiro: Fundação Getúlio Vargas, 1966, pp. 37-87.

Nogueira Filho, Paulo. *Idéias e lutas de um burguês progressista: o Partido Democrático e a Revolução de 1930,* 2 vols. São Paulo: Editora Anhambi, 1958.

Oliveira, Francisco de. "A economia brasileira: crítica à razão dualista," *Estudos Cebrap,* no. 2 (October 1972), 3-82.

Palha, Américo. *Lindolfo Collor, um estadista da revolução.* Rio de Janeiro: MTIC, 1956.

Pasqualini, Alberto. *Bases e sugestões para uma política social.* Porto Alegre: Editora Globo, 1948.

_____. *Diretrizes fundamentais do trabalhismo brasileiro.* Porto Alegre: Thurmann, 1951.

Pedreira, Fernando. *Brasil política, 1964-1975.* São Paulo: Difusão Européia do Livro, 1975.

Peterson, Phyllis Jane. "Brazilian Political Parties: Formation, Organization, and Leadership, 1945-1959." Doctoral dissertation, University of Michigan, 1962.

Prado Júnior, Caio. *A revolução brasileira.* São Paulo: Brasiliense, 1966.

Quem é quem no Brasil: biografias contemporâneas. São Paulo: Sociedade Brasileira de Expansão Comercial, 1948.

Richers, Raimar, et al. (eds.). *Impacto da ação do Govêrno sôbre as emprêsas brasileiras.* Rio de Janeiro: Fundação Getúlio Vargas, 1963.

Rodrigues, Waldemar. *Rumos do trabalhismo no Brasil.* Rio de Janeiro: Tupy, 1957.

Roett, Riordan (ed.). *Brazil in the Sixties.* Nashville, Tenn.: Vanderbilt University Press, 1972.

Schmitter, Philippe C. *Interest Conflict and Political Change in Brazil.* Stanford, Calif.: Stanford University Press, 1971.

————. "The 'Portugalization' of Brazil? " in *Authoritarian Brazil: Origins, Policies, and Future,* ed. Alfred Stepan. New Haven: Yale University Press, 1973, pp. 179-232.

Schneider, Ronald M. *Brazil: Foreign Policy of a Future World Power.* Boulder, Colo.: Westview Press, 1976.

————. *The Political System of Brazil: Emergence of a "Modernizing" Authoritarian Regime, 1964-1970.* New York: Columbia University Press, 1971.

Serra, José. "The Brazilian 'Economic Miracle,'" in *Latin America: From Dependence to Revolution,* ed. James Petras. New York: Wiley, 1973, pp. 100-140.

Silveira, Tasso da. *Estado corporativo.* Rio de Janeiro: José Olympio, 1937.

Singer, Paul. "A política das classes dominantes," in *Política e revolução social no Brasil,* ed. Octávio Ianni et al. Rio de Janeiro: Civilização Brasileira, 1965.

Skidmore, Thomas E. "Politics and Economic Policy Making in Authoritarian Brazil, 1937-71," in *Authoritarian Brazil: Origins, Policies, and Future,* ed. Alfred Stepan. New Haven: Yale University Press, 1973, pp. 3-46.

————. *Politics in Brazil, 1930-1964: An Experiment in Democracy.* New York: Oxford University Press, 1967.

Stepan, Alfred (ed.). *Authoritarian Brazil: Origins, Policies, and Future.* New Haven: Yale University Press, 1973.

————. *The Military in Politics: Changing Patterns in Brazil.* Princeton, N.J.: Princeton University Press, 1971.

Tejo, Aurélio de Limeira. *Jango: debate sôbre a crise dos nossos tempos.* Rio de Janeiro: Andes, 1957.

Todaro, Margaret Patrice. "Pastors, Prophets, and Politicians: A Study of the Brazilian Catholic Church, 1916-1945." Doctoral dissertation, Columbia University, 1971.

Tôrres, João Camillo de Oliveira. *A democracia coroada.* Rio de Janeiro: José Olympio, 1957.

Trinidade, Hélgio Henrique C. "Plínio Salgado e a Revolução de 30: antecedentes da A. I. B.," *Revista Brasileira de Estudos Políticos,* no. 38 (January 1974), 9-33.

United States Senate. *Foreign Assistance and Related Programs Appropriations for Fiscal Year 1972; Hearings Before a Subcommittee of the Committee on Appropriations.* Washington, D.C., 1971.

Vianna, Francisco José de Oliveira. *Direito do trabalho e democracia social (o problema da incorporação do trabalhador no estado).* Rio de Janeiro: José Olympio, 1951.

_____. *O idealismo da Constituição,* 2nd ed. rev. São Paulo: Editora Nacional, 1939.

_____. *Instituições políticas brasileiras,* 2nd ed. rev.; 2 vols. Rio de Janeiro: José Olympio, 1955.

_____. *Pequenos estudos de psychologia social.* São Paulo: Revista do Brasil, 1921.

_____. *Problemas de direito corporativo.* Rio de Janeiro: José Olympio, 1938.

_____. *Problemas de organização e problemas de direção (o povo e o govêrno).* Rio de Janeiro: José Olympio, 1952.

_____. *Problemas de política objetiva,* 2nd ed. rev. São Paulo: Editora Nacional, 1947.

Wagley, Charles. "The Brazilian Revolution: Social Change Since 1930," in *Social Change in Latin America Today,* ed. Richard N. Adams et al. New York: Vintage, 1961, pp. 177-230.

_____. *An Introduction to Brazil,* rev. ed. New York: Columbia University Press, 1971.

Weffort, Francisco C. "Estado y masas en el Brasil," *Revista Latinoamericana de Sociología,* I (March 1965), 53-71.

_____. "Política de Massas," in *Política e Revolução Social no Brasil,* ed. Octávio Ianni et al. Rio de Janeiro: Civilização Brasileira, 1965, pp. 159-198.

_____. "Raízes sociais do populismo em São Paulo," *Revista Civilização Brasileira,* I (May 1965), 39-60.

Xausa, Leônidas, and Francisco Ferraz. "As eleições de 1966 no Rio Grande do Sul," *Revista Brasileira de Estudos Políticos,* no. 23/24 (July 1967/January 1968), 229-274.

C. Brazil: Labor Law, Organization, and Politics

Aguiar, Néuma Figueiredo de. "O Sindicato dos Trabalhadores na Indústria Gráfica do Estado da Guanabara," *Revista de Direito Público e Ciência Política,* V (January 1962), 62-80.

Alexander, Robert J. *Labor Relations in Argentina, Brazil, and Chile.* New York: McGraw-Hill, 1962.

Almeida, Ângela Mendes de, and Michael Lowy. "Union Structure and Labor Organization in the Recent History of Brazil," *Latin American Perspectives,* III (Winter 1976), 98-119.

Almeida, Maria Hermínia Tavares de. "O sindicato no Brasil: novos problemas, velhas estruturas," *Debate e Crítica,* no. 6 (June 1975), 49-74.

Amazonas, João. *O direito de greve: discurso.* Rio de Janeiro: Horizonte, 1946.

————. *Pelo fortalecimento e unidade sindical.* Rio de Janeiro: Horizonte, 1945.

American Federation of Labor–Congress of Industrial Organizations. "Report on Brazil," May 4, 1964 (mimeo.).

Aranha, Oswaldo. *O syndicalismo no Rio Grande do Sul.* Porto Alegre: Globo, 1929.

Barreto, Derli. "Falta de liberdade sindical no Brasil existe até hoje," *Jornal do Brasil,* May 1, 1962, p. 10.

Barros, Alexandre de Souza Costa, and Argelina Maria Cheibub Figueiredo. *The Creation of Two Social Programs, the FGTS and the PIS: A Brazilian Case Study on the Dissemination and Use of Social Sciences Research for Governmental Policy Making* (preliminary version). Rio de Janeiro: Escola Brasileira de Administração Pública, 1975.

Barros Filho, Teotônio Monteiro de. "O impôsto sindical," *Legislação do Trabalho* (São Paulo), February 1951.

Bastos, Tocary Assis. "Anotações sôbre a greve dos bancários em Minas," *Revista Brasileira de Estudos Políticos,* no. 14 (July 1962), 111-128.

Batalha, Wilson de Souza Campos. "Aspectos do Sindicalismo Brasileiro," *Arquivos do Instituto de Direito Social,* XIV (December 1962), 119-132.

————. *Relações coletivas do trabalho (conflitos abertos do trabalho e sua solução jurisdicional).* São Paulo: Federação e Centro das Indústrias, 1958.

————. *Tratado elementar de direito processual do trabalho.* Rio de Janeiro: Konfino, 1960.

Brandão, Alonso Caldas (ed.). *Legislação trabalhista não consolidada.* Rio de Janeiro: Coelho Branco Filho, 1957.

Brandão Filho, Francisco de Moura. *Teoria e prática da organização sindical do Brasil.* Rio de Janeiro: Borsói, 1961.

Brant, Vinícius Caldeira, et al. *São Paulo 1975: crescimento e pobreza.* São Paulo: Edições Loyola, 1976.

Brasil, Ely. "O programa do partido e a atividade dos comunistas na luta pela unidade e a organização da classe operária," *Problemas,* no. 64, 226-234.

Brazil, Agência Nacional. *O nume tutelar das massas trabalhadoras do Brasil (benefícios e direitos assegurados pelo Presidente Getúlio Vargas ao proletariado nacional).* Rio de Janeiro: Imprensa Nacional, 1942.

Brazil, Comissão Técnica de Orientação Sindical. *Curso de orientação sindical.* Rio de Janeiro, 1944.

Brazil, Ministério do Trabalho, Indústria e Comércio. *Assuntos Trabalhistas.* Rio de Janeiro, 1958.

————. Serviço de Documentação. "Documentário fóto-biográfico dos ex-ministros que ocuparam a pasta do Trabalho, Indústria e Comércio (Edição comemorativa do XXV aniversário do MTIC)." Rio de Janeiro, 1955.

————. Serviço de Documentação. *Guia prático para tratar de assuntos no MTIC.* Rio de Janeiro, 1956.

————. Serviço de Estatística da Previdência do Trabalho. *Estatística de salários (Lei de nacionalização do trabalho).* Rio de Janeiro, September 1947.

————. Serviço de Estatística da Previdência do Trabalho. *Alguns aspectos da política do salário mínimo.* Rio de Janeiro: Vitória, 1946.

Brito, Armando de. "Relatório do Delegado Governamental, Procurador da Justiça do Trabalho, Armando de Brito, no Processo da CNTI-CGT." Rio de Janeiro: MTPS, May 5, 1964 (mimeo.).

Calógeras, João Pandiá. *Conceito christão do trabalho.* São Paulo: Editôra Nacional, 1932.

"Características sócio-econômicas dos delegados ao III Congresso Nacional dos Metalúrgicos," *Boletim do DIEESE,* II (August 1961), 3-8.

Cardoso, Fernando Henrique. "Proletariado no Brasil: situação e comportamento social," *Revista Brasiliense,* no. 41 (May–June 1962), pp. 98-122.

Centro Industrial do Brasil, Rio de Janeiro. *Regulamentação do direito de greve.* Rio de Janeiro: n.p., 1959.

Cesarino Júnior, Antônio Ferreira. *Consolidação das Leis do Trabalho anotada,* 2nd ed. rev.; 2 vols. Rio de Janeiro: Freitas Bastos, 1945.

————. *Direito corporativo e direito do trabalho.* São Paulo: Martins, 1940.

————. *Estabilidade e fundo de garantia.* Rio de Janeiro: Forense, 1968.

Chamorro, Antônio. "O III Congresso Nacional dos Trabalhadores," *Revista Brasiliense,* no. 31 (September–October 1960), 72-84.

Chaves, Pires. *Da ação trabalhista.* Rio de Janeiro: Forense, 1956.

————. *Da execução trabalhista.* Rio de Janeiro: Forense, 1955.

Conferência Nacional de Dirigentes Sindicais, Rio de Janeiro, June, 1964.

Conferência Nacional dos Trabalhadores nas Indústrias Metalúrgicas, Mecânicas e de Material Elétrico do Brasil. *Primeira Conferência Nacional, Volta Redonda, 1956.* Rio de Janeiro: Sylvio Romano, 1956.

Congresso Sindical dos Trabalhadores Brasileiros, Rio de Janeiro, 1946. *Resoluções.* Rio de Janeiro: Jornal do Commercio, 1946.

Congresso dos Trabalhadores do Estado de Minas Gerais. *Anais do sexto congresso, Juiz de Fora, 1951.* Belo Horizonte: Imprensa Oficial, 1952.

Consolidation of the Brazilian Labor Laws, English trans. Rio de Janeiro: American Chambers of Commerce in Brazil, 1960.

Costa Neto, Carlos Renato. "O que é o Movimento de Renovação Sindical," *Revista Brasiliense,* no. 32 (November–December 1960), 59-87.

Departamento Intersindical de Estatística e Estudos Sócio-Econômicos. "Salário mínimo 1/74," April 25, 1974 (mimeo.).

"Desenvolvimento recente do sindicalismo no Brasil," *Boletim do DIEESE,* I (February 1961), 7-15.

Devisate, Antônio. *Salário mínimo e investimentos estrangeiros.* São Paulo: Federação e Centro das Indústrias, Serviço de Publicações, 1956.

Dias, Everardo. *História das lutas sociais no Brasil.* São Paulo: Edaglit, 1962.

"Encargos sociais e Fundo de Garantia," *Conjuntura Econômica,* XXI (January 1967), 57-64.

Erickson, Kenneth Paul. "Labor in the Political Process in Brazil: Corporatism in a Modernizing Nation." Doctoral dissertation, Columbia University, 1970.

————. "Populism and Political Control of the Working Class in Brazil," *Proceedings of the Pacific Coast Council on Latin American Studies,* IV (1975), 117-144.

Erickson, Kenneth Paul and Patrick V. Peppe. "Dependent Capitalist Development, U.S. Foreign Policy, and Repression of the Working Class in Chile and Brazil," *Latin American Perspectives,* III (Winter 1976), 19-44.

Erickson, Kenneth Paul, Patrick V. Peppe, and Hobart A. Spalding, Jr. "Research on the Urban Working Class and Organized Labor in Argentina, Brazil, and Chile: What Is Left To Be Done? " in *Latin American Research Review,* IX (Summer 1974), 115-142.

"Família assalariada: padrão e custo de vida," *Estudos Sócio-Econômicos,* no. 2 (January 1974), 1-76.

Faria, Otávio. "Sindicalismo Nôvo," *Síntese Política Econômico Social* (April 1964), 23-28.

Fausto, Bóris. *Trabalho urbano e conflito social, 1890-1920.* São Paulo: Difusão Européia do Livro, 1976.

Ferrari, Fernando. *Mensagem renovadora.* Rio de Janeiro: Globo, 1960.

————. *Minha campanha.* Rio de Janeiro: Globo, 1961.

————. *Trabalhismo: nova armadura para novos rumos (Discurso parlamentar e documentos políticos).* Rio de Janeiro: Departamento de Imprensa Nacional, 1959.

Figueiredo, Argelina Maria Cheibub. "Política governamental e funções sindicais," Master's thesis, University of São Paulo, 1975.

Fischlowitz, Estanislau. *Problemas cruciais da previdência social brasileira em 1964.* Rio de Janeiro: Fundação Getúlio Vargas, 1964.

Frederico, Celso. "Amarrando a produção: notas sobre a inquietação operária," *Contexto,* no. 1 (November 1976), 33-42.

"Os 'Generais' da Derrota," *O Cruzeiro,* May 2, 1964.

Góis Filho, Joaquim Faria. *Produtividade: aspecto educacional.* Rio de Janeiro: Instituto de Ciências Sociais, 1960.

Grande, Humberto. *A política do trabalho: educação, direito e filosofia do trabalho.* Porto Alegre: A Nação, 1944.

Groehs, Ronaldo Waldemiro. *A lei orgânica da Previdência Social,* 4th ed. rev. Porto Alegre: Sulina, 1967.

Harding, Timothy Fox. "Implications of Brazil's Third Labor Congress," *Hispanic American Report,* XIII (October 1960), 567-572.

————. "Labor Challenge to Dictatorship," *Brazilian Information Bulletin* (Berkeley), no. 13 (Spring 1974), 2-5.

————. "Laboring Under the Dictatorship," *Brazilian Information Bulletin* (Berkeley), no. 10 (June 1973), 8-10.

————. "The Political History of Organized Labor in Brazil." Doctoral dissertation, Stanford University, 1973.

Huguenin, Orlando Carlomagno. *O que é a justiça do trabalho.* Rio de Janeiro: MTIC, 1957.

Hutchinson, Bertram (ed.). *Mobilidade e trabalho: um estudo na cidade de São Paulo.* Rio de Janeiro: Centro Brasileiro de Pesquisas Educacionais, 1960.

"Impôsto sindical e assistência social," *Boletim do DIEESE,* I, no. 11 (March 1961), 7-11.

Iório, Oswaldo. "Previdência Social: o problema da quota da União," *Mensário Estatístico Atuarial,* no. 85 (January 1960), 1-2.

Júnior, Theotônio. "O movimento operário no Brasil," *Revista Brasiliense,* no. 39 (January–February 1962), 100-118.

Lacerda, Maurício de. *Evolução legislativa do direito social brasileiro.* Rio de Janeiro: MTIC, 1960.

Leite, Celso Barroso, and Luiz Paranhos Velloso. *Previdência social.* Rio de Janeiro: Zahar, 1963.

Lima, Admastor. *Trabalhismo: estudo.* Rio de Janeiro: A. Coelho Branco Filho, 1951.

Lima, Alceu Amoroso. *O problema do trabalho (ensaio de filosofia econômica).* Rio de Janeiro: Agir, 1947.

Lowy, Michael, and Sarah Chucid. "Opiniões e atitudes de líderes sindicais metalúrgicos," *Revista Brasileira de Estudos Políticos,* no. 13 (January 1962), 132-169.

Loyola, Andrea Rios. "Les ouvriers et le populisme: les attitudes ouvrières à Juiz de Fora." Doctoral dissertation, École Pratique des Hautes Études, Paris, 1973.

Malloy, James M. "Authoritarianism and the Extension of Social Security Protection to the Rural Sector in Brazil." Unpublished manuscript, University of Pittsburgh, 1976.

————. "The Evolution of Social Security Policy in Brazil: Policy Making and Income Distribution." Paper presented at the 1975 Annual Meeting of the American Political Science Association, San Francisco.

————. "Participation in the Formation of Public Policy in Brazil: The Case of Social Security Policy." Unpublished manuscript, University of Pittsburgh, 1976.

————. "Social Insurance Policy in Brazil: A Study in the Politics of Inequality." Unpublished manuscript, University of Pittsburgh, 1976.

————. "Social Security Policy and the Working Class in Twentieth-Century Brazil," *Journal of Inter-American Studies and World Affairs,* in press.

Maram, Sheldon Leslie. "Anarchists, Immigrants, and the Brazilian Labor Movement, 1890-1920." Doctoral dissertation, University of California, Santa Barbara, 1972.

Marcondes, J. V. Freitas. *First Brazilian Legislation Relating to Rural Labor Unions: A Sociological Study.* Gainesville: University of Florida Press, 1962.

————. *Radiografia da liderança sindical paulista.* São Paulo: Instituto Cultural do Trabalho, 1964.

————. "Social Legislation in Brazil," in *Brazil: Portrait of Half a Continent,* ed. T. Lynn Smith and Alexander Marchant. New York: Dryden Press, 1951, pp. 382-400.

Martins, Heloisa Helena Teixeira de Souza. "O sindicato e a burocratização dos conflitos de trabalho no Brasil." Master's thesis, University of São Paulo, 1975.

Martins, Ibiapaba. "Notas sôbre o II Congresso Sindical dos Trabalhadores," *Revista Brasiliense,* no. 29 (May-June 1960), 103-106.

Mericle, Kenneth Scott. "Conflict Regulation in the Brazilian Industrial Relations System." Doctoral dissertation, University of Wisconsin, 1974.

"Os metalúrgicos e a industrialização," *Revista Brasiliense,* no. 29 (May-June 1960), 79-93.

Moraes Filho, Evaristo de. *Direito do trabalho e mundança social.* Rio de Janeiro: MTIC, 1958.

————. *O problema do sindicato único no Brasil (seus fundamentos sociológicos).* Rio de Janeiro: A Noite, 1952.

Motta, Omar Gonçalves. *O syndicato e a realidade brasileira.* Curitiba: n.p., 1936.

Movimento Sindical Democrático. *A República sindicalista do Brasil.* São Paulo, 1963.

"Nível alimentar da população trabalhadora da cidade de São Paulo," *Estudos Sócio-Econômicos,* no. 1 (July 1973), 1-32.

"O operário e a questão agrária," *Boletim do DIEESE,* I (July 1960), 1 and 11.

"A organização sindical dos trabalhadores textís no Estado de São Paulo," *Boletim do DIEESE,* I (January 1961), 2-8 and 15-20.

Passarinho, Jarbas. *O Ministério do Trabalho e Previdência Social e o Plano Estratégico do Govêrno.* Rio de Janeiro: Ministério do Trabalho, 1968.

Peralva, Osvaldo. "A esquerda positiva nos sindicatos," *Jornal do Brasil,* August 18, 1963, Caderno Especial, p. 6.

Pereira, Luiz. *Trabalho e desenvolvimento no Brasil.* São Paulo: Difusão Européia do Livro, 1965.

Pimentel, Marcelo, Hélio C. Ribeiro, and Moacyr Pessoa. *A previdência social interpretada.* Rio de Janeiro: Forense, 1969.

Pires, Wilberto. *Os bancários – suas lutas, seus problemas.* Recife: Correio Bancário, 1955.

Processo no. 3130, Tombo 10, 1964, in archives of Juizo de Direito da 15ª Vara Criminal, Estado da Guanabara.

Puech, Luiz Roberto de R. "Evolução do sindicalismo no Brasil," *Revista de Estudos Sócio-Econômicos,* I (March–April 1962), 3-12.

Rabello, Ophelina. *A rêde sindical paulista: tentativa de caracterização.* São Paulo: Instituto Cultural do Trabalho, 1965.

Rêgo, Alcides Marinho. *A vitória do direito operário no govêrno Getúlio Vargas.* Rio de Janeiro: Departamento de Imprensa e Propaganda, 1941.

Reis, Nélio. *Novas conquistas do direito do trabalho.* Rio de Janeiro: MTIC, 1955.

————. *Problemas sociológicos do trabalho.* Rio de Janeiro: Freitas Bastos, 1964.

Reis, Wilson. *Notas de um dirigente sindical: conquistas dos trabalhadores telegráficos.* Rio de Janeiro: São Francisco, 1965.

Ribeiro, A. Varela. *O problema da greve.* Rio de Janeiro: Litotipo Guanabara, 1959.

Rodrigues, José Albertino. "II Congresso Sindical dos Trabalhadores do Estado de São Paulo," *Revista Brasiliense,* no. 29 (May-June 1960), 73-78.

————. "Movimento sindical e situação da classe operária," *Debate e Crítica,* no. 2 (January 1974), 98-111.

————. *Sindicato e desenvolvimento no Brasil.* São Paulo: Difusão Européia do Livro, 1968.

Rodrigues, Leôncio Martins. *Conflito industrial e sindicalismo no Brasil.* São Paulo: Difusão Européia do Livro, 1966.

————. *Industrialização e atitudes operárias: estudo de um grupo de trabalhadores.* São Paulo: Brasiliense, 1970.

————. *Trabalhadores, sindicatos e industrialização.* São Paulo: Brasiliense, 1974.

Rowland, Robert. "Classe operária e estado de compromisso," *Estudos Cebrap,* no. 8 (April 1974), 5-40.

Russomano, Mozart Víctor. *Comentários à Consolidação das Leis do Trabalho,* 3 vols. Rio de Janeiro: José Konfino, 1955.

Sarti, Ingrid A. "Estiva e política: estudo de caso no porto de Santos." Master's thesis, University of São Paulo, 1973.

Simão, Aziz. "Funções do sindicato na sociedade moderna brasileira," *Revista de Estudos Sócio-Econômicos,* I (September 1961), 5-14.

————. "Industrialização e sindicalismo no Brasil," *Revista Brasileira de Estudos Políticos,* no. 13 (January 1962), 87-101.

————. *Sindicato e estado.* São Paulo: Dominus, 1966.

————. "O voto operário em São Paulo," *Revista Brasileira de Estudos Políticos,* no. 1 (December 1956), 130-141.

Soares, Gláucio Ary Dillon. "The New Industrialization and the Brazilian Political System," in *Latin America: Reform or Revolution,* ed. James Petras and Maurice Zeitlin. Greenwich, Conn.: Fawcett, 1968, pp. 186-201.

Souza, Amaury de. "The Nature of Corporative Representation: Leaders and Membership of Organized Labor in Brazil; Dissertation Prospectus." Unpublished manuscript, Massachusetts Institute of Technology, 1975.

Stern, Ivonne. "Estatísticas sôbre as pessoas econômicamente ativas no Brasil." Unpublished manuscript, n.d.

"Suspención de la afiliación extraordinaria de la Confederación Nacional de Círculos Operarios a la Confederación Latino-Americana de Sindicalistas Cristianos." Supplement to *Noticiario Obrero Latino-Americano,* Santiago, Chile, July 7, 1964.

Sussekind, Arnaldo, Délio Maranhão, and José de Segadas Viana. *Instituições de Direito do Trabalho,* 4th ed.; 3 vols. São Paulo: Freitas Bastos, 1967.

Telles, Jover. *O movimento sindical no Brasil.* Rio de Janeiro: Vitória, 1962.

Touraine, Alain. "Industrialisation et conscience ouvrière à São Paulo," *Sociologie du Travail,* III (December 1961), 389-407.

Viana, José de Segadas. *Brasil trabalhista.* Rio de Janeiro: Departamento de Imprensa e Propaganda, 1944.

————. *Greve: direito ou violência?* Rio de Janeiro: Freitas Bastos, 1959.

————. *Organização sindical brasileira, contendo os dispositivos da CLT e outras leis referentes as entidades sindicais.* Rio de Janeiro: O Cruzeiro, 1943.

————. *O sindicato no Brasil.* Rio de Janeiro: Olímpica, 1953.

Vianna, Francisco José de Oliveira. *Problemas de direito sindical.* Rio de Janeiro: Editora Max Limonad, 1943.

Vianna, Luiz Werneck. *Liberalismo e sindicato no Brasil.* Rio de Janeiro: Paz e Terra, 1976.

Vieira, Oldegar Franco. *Bibliografia brasileira de direito de trabalho.* Salvador: University of Bahia, 1958.

Walker, Neuma Aguiar. "The Mobilization and Bureaucratization of the Brazilian Working Class, 1930-1964." Doctoral dissertation, Washington University, 1969.

————. "The organization and ideology of Brazilian Labor," in *Revolution in Brazil,* ed. Irving Louis Horowitz. New York: Dutton, 1964, pp. 242-256.

Weffort, Francisco C. "Origens do sindicalismo populista no Brasil: a conjuntura do após-guerra," *Estudos Cebrap,* no. 4 (April 1973), 65-105.

————. *Participação e conflito industrial: Contagem e Osasco, 1968.* São Paulo: Cebrap, 1972.

————. "Sindicatos e política." Thesis presented for the *livre docência,* University of São Paulo, 1972.

Wiarda, Howard J. *The Brazilian Catholic Labor Movement: The Dilemmas of National Development.* Amherst: University of Massachusetts, Labor Relations and Research Center, 1969.

II. News Media and Serial Publications

A. Newspapers and Magazines

Correio da Manhã.   *Latin America* (London).   *O Globo.*
Diário Carioca.   *Los Angeles Times.*   *O Semanário.*
Diário de Notícias.   *New York Times.*   *Última Hora.*
Jornal do Brasil.   *Novos Rumos.*   *Veja.*
Jornal do Commercio.   *O Estado de S. Paulo.*   *Visão.*

B. Bulletins and Journals

Brazil, Ministério do Trabalho, Indústria e Comércio. *Boletim do Ministério do Trabalho, Indústria e Comércio.* (Title changed to *Boletim do Ministério do Trabalho e Previdência Social* in 1961.)

Brazil, Ministério do Trabalho e Previdência Social, Serviço de Estatística da Previdência e Trabalho. *Boletim Técnico do SEPT.*

Confederação Nacional dos Trabalhadores no Comércio. *Confederação Nacional dos Trabalhadores no Comércio.*

Conjuntura Econômica.

Desenvolvimento e Conjuntura.

Hispanic American Report.

Instituto de Aposentadoria e Pensões dos Industriários. *Industriários.*

————. *Mensário Estatístico-Atuarial.*

Organización Regional Interamericana de Trabajadores. *Bulletin.*

Partido Comunista Brasileiro. *Problemas.*

III. Interviews

Almino Monteiro Álvares Afonso. Former Labor Minister. Santiago, Chile, May 30, 1967.

Herbert Baker. Labor Attaché, United States Embassy in Brazil. Rio de Janeiro, June 23, 1966.

Nelson Ferreira de Bastos. Officer of Guanabara Petroleum Workers' Sindicato. Rio de Janeiro, Aug. 2, 1966.

Armando de Brito. Ministry of Labor official, interventor in CNTI, journalist. Rio de Janeiro, Sept. 19, 1967.

Ari Campista. Officer of CNTI and IAPI. Rio de Janeiro, Oct. 16, 1966.

Pires Chaves. First Regional Labor Court Judge. Rio de Janeiro, Dec. 7, 1966.

Gilberto Crockatt de Sá. Former labor adviser to João Goulart. Rio de Janeiro, Oct. 12, 1966.

João Belchior Marques Goulart. Former President of Brazil. Montevideo, Uruguay, May 18, 1967.

Richard Guinnold. Assistant Labor Attaché, United States Embassy in Brazil. Rio de Janeiro, Nov. 10, 1966.

Jack Liebof. Labor Attaché, United States Consulate in São Paulo. São Paulo, May 9, 1967.

Francisco Machado. Labor Court Judge. Rio de Janeiro, Dec. 9, 1966.

Antônio Pereira Magaldi. President of Movimento Sindical Democrático and former president of CNTC. São Paulo, ca. May 10, 1967.

Mário Martins. Brazilian Senator. New York, Dec. 2, 1967.

José Nunes Pires. Labor reporter and former Ministry of Labor employee. Rio de Janeiro, Sept. 14 and 18, 1967.

Darci Ribeiro. Head of President Goulart's civilian cabinet (*chefe da casa civil*). Montevideo, Uruguay, May 20, 1967.

Waltrudes Santos. Former employee of Chemical Workers' Sindicato in Guanabara. Rio de Janeiro, Oct. 7, 1966.

Amaury Silva. Former Labor Minister. Montevideo, Uruguay, May 21, 1967.

Arnaldo Lopes Sussekind. Former Labor Minister, Judge on Superior Labor Tribunal. Rio de Janeiro, July 7, 1967.

José Gomes Talarico. Former PTB State Deputy in Guanabara. Rio de Janeiro, ca. Sept. 15, 1967.

Osvaldo Vilhana. Prosecutor of First Regional Labor Court. Rio de Janeiro, Dec. 7, 1966.

Emmanoel Waismann. Former Federal Deputy for Rio de Janeiro State. Rio de Janeiro, May 8, 1967.

INDEX